S0-BJN-306

Library
Brevard Junior College
Cocoa, Florida

ALFRED KROEBER

A Personal Configuration

A. L. Kroeber

ALFRED KROEBER

A Personal Configuration

by THEODORA KROEBER

UNIVERSITY OF CALIFORNIA PRESS
BERKELEY · LOS ANGELES · LONDON · 1970

UNIVERSITY OF CALIFORNIA PRESS, BERKELEY AND LOS ANGELES, CALIFORNIA
UNIVERSITY OF CALIFORNIA PRESS, LTD., LONDON, ENGLAND

© COPYRIGHT 1970 BY THEODORA KROEBER

LIBRARY OF CONGRESS CATALOG CARD NUMBER: 71-94983
STANDARD BOOK NUMBER: 520-01598-3

DESIGNED BY DAVID COMSTOCK

PRINTED IN THE UNITED STATES OF AMERICA

"There is nothing I find pleasanter than to visit with old friends in an unvisited place and to meet a new group of students."

Alfred Kroeber

This book about Alfred Kroeber is dedicated to those students of anthropology who were his friends and to the new students of anthropology whom he would have so much enjoyed knowing.

Theodora Kroeber

PREFACE

This biography of Alfred Louis Kroeber was begun under the title "Biographical Notes" and was to be an account of certain events and consequences in Kroeber's life, as they occurred to me and about which I had some conviction that my knowledge or my understanding was beyond that of others now living: a miscellany in other words, an *aide mémoire* to some ultimate biographer. I resigned the original title with reluctance. It so perfectly defined, I believed, the actuality and the limits of my scope. Nor did my purpose and range enlarge with the change of title except, Kroeber being Kroeber, there was, I began to discover, no unpatterned miscellaneous way of writing meaningfully of him. To tell anything of him is to become aware of the pattern and the configuration which are at the heart of the person and the personality. This is true, I am sure, of any achieved adult personality: it is just that Kroeber was more of a piece than are many of us, his life pattern deeply cut, cleanly outlined.

To begin a biography, in my experience, is to catch the earliest evanescent wraiths of pattern when they first emerge from the dust of one's stirring and puddling about among the raw materials. Once I had done this, once I had begun to trace the shape of the Kroeber configuration I knew I could no longer evoke the noncommitting *aide* title in extenuation of my inadequacy. I must accept the responsibility of my presumption.

As to what I have done and what I have not attempted: I am neither an anthropologist nor other scientist, hence I must leave it to the professionally competent to take the measure of Kroeber the anthropologist, the scientist. Within the year after Kroeber's death, Julian Steward's article on him appeared in an issue of the *American Anthropologist* which contained also a bibliography of his writings compiled by John Howland Rowe, to be followed by other articles in the several journals and scientific publications in linguistics, archaeology, physical anthropology, and other fields of his interests and specializations, each written by a distinguished person in the field and each assessing an aspect of Kroeber's anthropological *oeuvre*. Between them I should judge as fair a measure to have been taken as can be by his contemporaries. There will be, eventually, ultimate judgments which must wait upon a later time.

I have given, as I knew and understood it, whatever background I could to Kroeber's separate activities, books, teaching, interests—to what he did and what he did not do, to what he was and what he was not. The account I make is personal. Personal, but not intimate in any sense which would betray Kroeber's lifetime preference for keeping his intimately personal life intimately personal in his own lifetime and after. These are not family chronicles: his wife and his children have not been welcomed in freely, but only where they helped or were needed to elucidate the man and the event.

The ordering of the materials is chronological, with some departures. These departures are deliberate and the reason for them is stated.

About the matter of names: in the section on Kroeber's childhood I use the first name, Alfred, as being most suited to his age and activities. I use the first name again only at the end, in a brief statement, my own most personal statement, where it seemed to fit. Throughout the rest of the book I refer to him as "Kroeber" as the reader will already have seen. This name comes naturally enough to the writing, giving me the needed distancing from my subject. And this is so because I never so addressed him or so spoke of him, nor did any of his children; on the other hand, his graduate students and his colleagues except those of them who were his close friends, customarily addressed him and spoke of him as "Kroeber." His children called him Alfred. Kroeber called me Krakie (a nickname derived from my maiden name, "Kracaw") when speaking to me, Theodora when speaking of me. I use the first person pronoun for myself, finding it in fact less obtrusive than the third person which I tried to use at first.

I make no claim to exhaustiveness. I have not written of matters of which I knew little or less than someone else. There was in any case so much from which to choose. I shunned the anecdotal, except when it shed fresh light, and the colorful unless it intensified or added to the colors already on the loom. Kroeber himself was not much given to the anecdotal, either in conversation or in writing. In answer to a request for reminiscences, he once wrote: "There is a great demand for reminiscences as I get older, but I am resistive. People's real appetite for them is very much shorter than they think—Also I have lots of unfinished business that I think is more important."

I can recall no single statement of my own throughout the book which I would point to as "definitive" or "important"—portentous adjectives when used against a biographer. It is my hope rather that what I have written will give some pleasure to those who knew Kroeber well, explain some matters which they never understood; and that for those young anthropologists who never knew him, may suggest some flicker of what he was, of how he got that way, of how deep and vital was his interst in their future. For Kroeber said, "Anthropology is my religion," and I would like the "new horizon anthropologists" to know he wished them so very, very well; that he would have so liked to know them and their work.

Because all I say remains the most personal of statements, I have gone sparingly to Kroeber's colleagues—only to confirm a given anthropological or archaeological or operative fact. It appeared to me incorrect to put upon them the onus of judging what I wrote.

As for me, writing of Kroeber is its own reward: it has been a way sometimes to relieve the burden of memory; it is always for the pleasure of his company. As for my readers, I invoke Henry James' excuse for writing of Venice. "I hold any writer sufficiently justified who is himself in love with his theme."

CONTENTS

PROLOGUE

The Handbook of The Indians of California, written by Alfred Kroeber in 1916-1917, is the single piece of writing from among more than five hundred titles in his bibliography by which most people, Indians and other Americans, foreigners, laymen and scholars know and identify him. Anthropology, 1923, by him, is known well only within the profession. Kroeber was content to have this primary identification with the Handbook. He said the first fruits of his work were in it. He also said the wide-flung historical and theoretical interests of his later years were rooted in his field work with living Indians.

Until his first field trips, undertaken in the two years before he got his doctorate and which took him into Wyoming and Oklahoma, Kroeber had not been as far west as western New York State. In 1900 he went to California. From that time, with the exception of some months of the same year, his home was in San Francisco or later in Berkeley across the bay from San Francisco. He returned to the East Coast every year or two to see his family and old friends, to teach for a term as a guest professor, to give a talk or attend a meeting and otherwise to keep in touch, but he went always as a visitor. The move west was final.

Within weeks of coming to the West Coast he was in the field where he became part of the rural scene, going by stage, surrey, buckboard or on horseback or afoot up and down and inland over the dusty roads and trails to the rancherias and villages of Indians who usually became his friends. Soon word of him preceded his arrival: he was the serious young man with the black beard, the pockets of whose khaki coat bulged with an assortment of pipes, a well-filled tobacco pouch, an all-purpose jackknife, notebooks and pencils, and a bag of hard candies for the grandmothers and children of the households he visited.

During all the California years he looked out from the museum or from his study and garden to the Pacific Ocean. It was not by chance but by deep preference that the two Indian peoples who most engaged his imagination were riverine tribes who looked also to the west downriver to the sea: the Yurok Indians of the Klamath River in northern California and the Mohave Indians of the Colorado River in southern California. It was not the grandeur of mountains which drew him but the lakes those mountains might encircle, and better than lakes were creeks and rivers, bays, inlets, lagoons, and the shore of the sea.

The West held him but the West had not to do with the years which formed the man. Those years were passed within the encircling river, estuary, and inner-harbor waters which surround Manhattan Island, at home with parents, brothers and sisters, grandparents, and cousins; at school with friends whom he found early and whose friendship was a continuing relation throughout their lives however far apart they were and for however long a time.

Let us look at those years.

MANHATTAN

FAMILY

Alfred Louis Kroeber was born June 11, 1876. His birth registry is Hoboken, New Jersey, where his parents "went across the river for a year or two," as Kroeber once explained in an interview, their home being in New York City on Manhattan Island. There is a village, Kroebern, near Leipzig, from which the immediate ancestral family, a Bavarian branch, is supposed to have come. Alfred was the first child of Florence Martin Kroeber and Johanna Muller Kroeber. His father, Florence, was born in Cologne, Germany, in 1840, coming with his parents when he was ten years old to New York City where they made their home. Only a tatter of anecdote remains among the lost memories concerning Florence's parents: his father, Louis, volunteered and served in the Army of the United States during the Civil War. In view of the role in this country of immigrant Germans of the nineteenth century, patriotism for the new land would appear a sufficient reason for such action. His grandchildren were to insist, however, that the real motive was a preference for adventure over the monotony of family life. They were perhaps recalling a dour and severe grandmother of later years.

(Whatever the motive, the circumstance was invoked by Kroeber ninety years later. He was arranging by long-distance telephone from California to rent a house on Brattle Street in Cambridge, Massachusetts, for the coming year. The owner hesitated to rent the house to a German. Kroeber reassured her by mentioning his Civil War grandfather; with no further parley she consented to his having her house.)

This grandfather allowed his eldest son, Florence, to take jobs at an early age which helped support his younger brothers and sisters, and Florence did not go to school after age sixteen or thereabouts. His beginnings in the adult business world may indeed have been grim for him. However, by the time he married, he was an established independent importer of *objets d'art*, specializing in European clocks, much in demand in those days. The swinging pendulums of tall floor clocks, the monotonous repetitions of cuckoo clocks, and the silent motion of the delicate French mantel clocks whose intricate works were visible inside protecting glass domes composed one of young Alfred's earliest sound-sight memories. It was among the bric-a-brac, the mantel and pedestal marbles and the silver bronze and wood pieces of small sculpture destined for the formal entrance halls and parlors of New Yorkers that the small boy first learned to distinguish Doric, Ionian, and Corinthian columns. His first Greek temple housed not a god but clockworks. In the shop were elaborate boxes carved after the designs of Egyptian and Roman sarcophagi; there were bronze and gold putti, Apollos, Pallas Athenas, Aphrodites.

When he was older he sometimes delivered one of these pieces to a customer. He once took a French clock to an uptown address, probably to the Waldorf-Astoria. The new clock owner came to the door of her suite and invited him to come inside while she unpacked the clock. "She was a very beautiful lady, dressed all in black silk, a great beauty she was." The lady was Mrs. Jefferson Davis; the year, 1889 or 1890.

Florence's principal shop was on Broadway at Franklin Street, with a branch shop on Union Square. This did not happen overnight. He was nearly thirty years old when he married, and there had been, on his part, an intervening marriage, or was it only an engagement? Florence's and Johanna's imaginative children were vague as to the relevant facts but were much intrigued by this earlier attachment of which they could make little since it came to them from the gossip of aunties and nursemaids. Mimi, as they called their mother, was embarrassed when they queried her about it; they settled among themselves to regard it as a disgrace that she should have been accorded second choice. Kroeber's retrospective picture of his father during the years of Florence's success was of a man who, without playing it up or temperamentally too much wanting it, accepted the authoritative and authoritarian role of father and family arbiter. Florence was serious—life was serious to him—but he enjoyed the opportunity provided by congenial guests to take part in good conversation, to open an extra bottle of wine after dinner, to have a game of billiards with particular friends; and he liked to go to the Thalia theatre or to Symphony Hall. His children's passion for all forms of theater was surely stimulated by their father's appreciation of music and drama.

Johanna Muller was born of Rhinelander German parents in New York City on Vesey Street, which she spoke of as being in Greenwich Village, but which is perhaps below the presently understood boundaries of the Village. She went to private elementary and finishing schools on Manhattan, married, lived, and died there. The Muller family burial plot is in Trinity Church Cemetery, which was moved uptown many years ago to Broadway and 156th Street. Next to Manhattan, she knew most familiarly the other boroughs of New York City, Long Island, and the Adirondack Mountains; and she knew western continental Europe where she went with Florence: buying trips for him and occasions for sight seeing and visiting with relatives in France and Germany for both of them. During the last years of her long life—she lived to be eighty-four—she visited San Francisco and Berkeley and the Napa Valley in California: the places where her son lived. She looked then much as she looks in the picture taken when Alfred was perhaps four years old, except for the inevitable age lines. She was small, not more than five feet one, with dark hair, large grey eyes, regular features, a large mouth and an over-all expression of sensitiveness. She dressed with quiet elegance; a dressmaker fashioned her clothes to fit her and her style; her dresses were lined and boned. In later years she was never without a black velvet band around her throat if the dress she was wearing lacked a high fitted collar. She was an entirely gentle person, but not soft gentle. The generous mouth was a readily smiling one; she had as strongly marked tastes in people, music, books, and food as did her elder son; she ran an economical competent pleasant house almost to the end of her life; she knew what reasonably to expect of children and of servants and of anyone under her direction or responsibility. She was a serious-minded, a truly and deeply ethical person; she sponsored and worked for many good causes in her quiet way

Alfred, age seven.

Mimi, 1881.

Florence, 1881.

but she was without aggressiveness or any wish to impose her own strict code on others. Her daughters are sure their father dominated her. Probably he did. He did not, however, dampen the sparkle of fun and the gaiety with which she participated in family jokes and teasing or the give and take of the many-generationed occasions with family and family friends. And her children's saltiness of speech and thought would appear to have stemmed from Mimi's own.

Younger than Alfred were one brother, Edward, who died

when he was nineteen years old, and two sisters: Johanna, whom Alfred called Yanchi, and Elsbeth, both of whom died in 1969.

There were two successively owned homes during the years when the children were growing up, one on the corner of Madison Avenue and 78th Street and a later one at 316 West 89th Street. The 78th Street house had the unusual feature of a wrought iron fence to enclose the garden from the street. The house was demolished to make way for the American Automobile Association building at that address, which is built on the old house foundations.

The houses, brick with brownstone trim, were built on the customary New York lot, twenty feet wide by one hundred feet deep, and were four stories above ground with basement and cellar below street level. This was the old house pattern for the city, the humanely generous rear garden being a regular feature, the glowing red brick houses of Washington Square and the sculptured granite and marble ones of midtown, exquisite architectural flowerings of the style. I mention the style because it was distinctive and because it was in such houses the Kroebers and their friends lived, as did in great part the middle-class of New York. Above them were the Fifth Avenue mansions of the very wealthy and, increasingly as the years passed, the elaborate Park Avenue apartments; below were the tenements, the walk-ups. The wrecker's ball, making rubble of these houses, which are replaced with giant tenements both lower and upper class, is a perfect metaphor of the flight of the middle-class from the city and the destruction of precisely the sort of life and values Alfred knew as a child and a young man and which were the common experience of middle-class New Yorkers of the period.

CHILDHOOD

A cook, a second or "upstairs" girl, and a nursemaid lived in, and a seamstress came each Thursday for the day. All these people were German immigrants who spoke little or broken English. Florence and Mimi spoke German to them. German was Florence's first language and was as familiar to Mimi as English, she having grown up bilingual, so it came about that German was Alfred's first language. All the children learned German, but as the eldest, his exposure to it was the longest and most saturated. Elsbeth said, "We all read German before English and until Mimi's death we often used German in speaking of household things. Lots of family jokes almost have to stay untranslated, but it is a long time since I tried to carry on an intellectual conversation in German." Speaking German at home was natural enough, but it was also deliberate. The elder Kroebers, like their relatives and friends, wanted their children to be bilingual. They particularly wanted them to know their Goethe, Heine, and Schiller and to read Shakespeare first in German translation. (One wonders when and how shame of the ancestral tongue crept into American mores? Perhaps it came from steerage beginnings and slum and ghetto living in the new country. It was not in any case part of the thinking or practice of German-American upper-middle class New Yorkers.)

Kroeber insisted he had an accent when he first went to school; that he knew only a few words of English when he was five years old. Mimi denied this, reminding him that he was beginning to read by the age of five and that some of what he read was in English. But the earliest books, she admitted, were in German: *Der Struwelpeter*, a book of doggerel verse, and an alphabet book. The first book Alfred read through alone was an abridged *Robinson Crusoe* in German.

The baby Alfred was well tended. There were willing and affectionate people to sing him songs, teach him proverbs, tell him stories, play with him in house and garden. The pram was never set on the front stoop nor did the runabout boy play on sidewalk or street. Twice each day in all except the most inclement weather he was taken by pram, later on foot, by Nurse to Central Park; his childhood was passed within a block of the park. No non-New Yorker can easily appreciate what Central Park means to a person whose first and permanent playground it was. To Alfred, the little park zoo was the Animal Kingdom of the World; the Shakespeare Garden, a hilly, stream-crossed Land of Mystery; the park's many caves, well hidden and large enough to hold two or three small people, were pirates' dens and robbers' hideaways; the ponds, the seven seas; the craggy rock outcroppings, the Himalayas; and the Belvedere, a medieval castle to be stormed by brave knights armed with bows and slings. Under an old pedestrian bridge supported by sandstone pillars whose bases are lions' paws, there is today as there was so long ago, a rounded depression in one of the paws. There the runabout Alfred mixed together the earth and water mortar for the walls and castles he was building.

Long enough for Alfred to remember but not for Elsbeth, there stood across 78th Street from the Kroeber house and facing Madison Avenue a farm which went back to pre-Revolutionary days. On the way to the park, Alfred and Nurse passed it daily and stopped to peer through the fence at the cow, the barn, and the barnyard with chickens in it. It must have been one of the last "uptown" farms on Manhattan.

Looking from their upper bedroom windows, the Kroebers had a view across the park, and to the north in the park they saw a modest red brick building at 81st Street and Fifth Avenue—the Metropolitan Museum of Art.

Alfred was five years old; in the nursery with him was his three-year-old brother. At the end of summer Alfred was graduated from the nursery to a small room of his own and from Nurse to a tutor. This was one of those natural age shifts, the first step in a new direction, which forever colored and determined in some measure the interests and choices of the years ahead.

The Tutor, Dr. Hans Bamberger, a young man, German-born, was principal of the Workingmen's School on West 54th Street, which would become the nucleus of the Ethical Culture School. It was a progressive school of its day whose theory of education was that the child should learn first to observe and recognize the objects and aspects of the phenomenal world about him and to become a user of tools. Only then should he be taught the symbolic and abstract and necessarily verbal extensions from this experimental world with which he had already made conscious sensory contact. It was an education theory which stemmed innocently and naturally from the first impact of Darwinism on the followers of Carl Schurz.

School was over at one o'clock, after which Dr. Bamberger came to the Kroeber home for an hour or two, two days a week, which schedule was extended to include occasional Saturday mornings or afternoons. The strictly tool-using part of the program remained somewhat perfunctory; there was some carpentering, sketching, and modeling; Dr. Bamberger's heart was not in the manual arts except as they served to illuminate nature. He rigged up a homemade planetarium by which a small blue moon and proportionately sized planets could be made to orbit, somewhat jerkily, around a larger, yellow sun. Under his direction, thick mud pies were smoothed carefully on the window sill and left to fold and split and form miniature mountains which gradually eroded under the action of sun and rain. Soon there was a microscope; the shelves of the little room began to fill with rocks, plants, and the varieties of fungi that grow in Central Park. Through the next years many hours went into careful preparation of slides; there were beetle and butterfly collections, rock collections, cages for living creatures, aquaria, terraria, test tubes, Bunsen burners and other chemical equipment as well as dissecting knives and pincers. (Mimi once found an old list Alfred had made of articles he needed from town, the summer of 1889: "A pair of dumbells. A book about moths. A book about geology and rocks. Addison's essays. A sharp knife for dissecting. Circles or squares of thin glass. Brunswick Black, a small bottle. Turpentine, a little. Glycerine, a little. Solution of caustic potash. Canada Balsam. A pack of cards.") Mimi tolerated it all, hating the mess, disapproving the acid burns on furniture and carpets, fearing the sometimes bizarre results of experiments, but enduring it, forbidding the upstairs girl to remove any of the paraphenalia of science, convinced that this way lay enlightenment.

Dr. Bamberger liked to read aloud and to tell the stories of history, his favorite time being from the siege of Troy through the Iliad and Odyssey to the fall of Rome: campaigns, forced marches, migrations and battles were vivid to him and to his telling. Alfred learned his first Greek with him as he was by this time learning his first French with Mimi.

CARL ALSBERG

Dr. Bamberger was tutoring another boy, Carl Alsberg, whose parents the Kroebers knew slightly and who lived at Lexington Avenue and 74th Street, six blocks away. Carl's father, Meinhard Alsberg, was German-born and educated, a chemist. He later became the chief chemist for New York City's first Board of Health and founder of the American Chemical Society. Carl's mother, Berthe, was, like Mimi, American-born of German parents; the Alsbergs like the Kroebers spoke both German and English.

Dr. Bamberger suggested he take the boys together to the park and on other expeditions. This was agreed to and thus Carl, a year younger and considerably larger than Alfred, became Alfred's first and closest friend. It was not long before Carl and Alfred were together almost daily as the families came to know each other better. Carl once told me, "I learned to read sitting on a park bench. On one side of me was Dr. Bamberger, a big man with a bristling red beard and gold-rimmed spectacles; on the other side Alfred, of whom I stood a little in awe. He could already read and he was tidy and contained—not like me." Carl wrote a chapter of personal reminiscences for a volume of essays in honor of Alfred's sixtieth birthday, in which he tells of their first geography lesson: "[Dr. Bamberger] took us to the center of the span of Brooklyn Bridge, then only a few years completed; our teacher took a compass and a map of New York harbor out of his pocket, spread the map out and explained north and south, east and west to us, and how to read a map. For most children—and adults, too, for that matter—north is up and south is down because that is the way maps are hung on walls—but not for us."

Carl and Alfred began piano lessons at about the same time and under the same teacher who, according to their later descriptions, was a severe German drill master. He succeeded in giving Alfred a lifelong prejudice against the piano, whose "generality" and "impurity" he found annoying. But he did learn the Western musical scale and notation which would be useful to the later linguist and listener to music in other modes, and he and Carl were once stimulated to figure out the structure of a symphony about which Carl's younger brother, Henry, asked a logical if deflating question, "Then why can't you write a symphony?"

Carl and Alfred each loved dearly to go to the other's home. Carl found the quiet voices, the cool effortless order in the Kroeber house attractive, and he and Alfred enjoyed a privacy there not to be had on 74th Street. On the other hand, Alfred and the younger Kroebers were enchanted with the liberty allowed children in the Alsberg home. In a chapter he wrote, "The Making of the Man," for the book, *Carl Alsberg, Scientist at Large*, Kroeber says, "A visit to the Alsbergs meant a roughhouse such as was never permitted at our home, with or without visitors; battles with brooms up and down the stairs, water fights in the attic, and a general piling on top of one another of the eight of us wherever we chose. Father Alsberg only smiled indulgently and Mother Alsberg rejoiced. The furniture was as shabby as comfortable, with no heirlooms or valuables to be broken. . . . Food was bountiful, and if it was a party, charlotte russes were pressed on us."

The August Zinnsers were other friends of the Kroebers and the Alsbergs. Edward Kroeber and Hans Zinnser, two years younger than Alfred, were firm friends. Florence Kroeber and August Zinnser bought adjacent pieces of land at Sheepshead Bay on Long Island. There they built summer houses, and there for the next fifteen years the mothers, children and servants removed for the whole of the summer vacation, the fathers spending their briefer vacations there and their weekends, which meant departing for the city early Monday morning. The trip to Sheepshead Bay was made by ferry across the East River, then by train to the bay station from which one walked unless there were baggage and babies, in which case a carriage took one to the house.

The deep verandahs and French windows of the ample wooden chalet of the Kroebers looked out over the bay and up to Coney Island. A formal driveway circled the front garden, and clamshell paths led from the house to a small private pier. The water of the bay was uncontaminated; the children swam and fished and boated in it. They were forbidden to take the sailboat into open water without an adult, but the canoe and rowboat which were tied up at the pier were used freely by them within the sheltered bay. The Alsbergs meanwhile had built a summer place on the Sound which meant that Carl and Alfred were together at one place or the other several times during each summer. In his reminiscences, Carl recalls one fortnight spent at Sheepshead Bay. There he and his brother played with the Kroeber and Zinnser children, fighting for the roles of Hector and Achilles, those heroes being favored over Agamemnon and Odysseus. Says Carl, "We built in the sand what we called the City of Troy—for us quite an elaborate structure with a moat and walls and attempts at gates and a drawbridge. Then we fought the siege of Troy over again. Our lances were the spent rockets from Paine's pyrotechnic displays across the bay at Brighton Beach. Our missiles were the pop and beer-bottle corks from Coney Island washed up in the windrows at every tide. Evenings we watched the fireworks at Brighton Beach across the bay and on one never-to-be-forgotten occasion we were taken over to sit in the audience and see the fireworks from near by. This was even more memorable than the occasion when we were taken for an all-day fishing trip for sheepshead, though I don't remember that we caught anything but a few sea robins and butterfish."

For Mimi, life at Sheepshead Bay was not too different from that at 78th Street: meals and the endless housekeeping routines were observed and executed with the same correctness and care as in the city, the plantings and paths were equally formal and well-tended; and the numbers of guests were greater. There was decorous bathing for the grown-ups in the ample navy-blue bathing suits of the time, there was lawn tennis, and there were afternoon "coffees" served out-of-doors at one house or another along the bay, with pitchers of lemonade for the children.

To the children it was a heaven which it remained in memory, a heaven never wholly displaced by the later, more exciting, lakes of the Adirondacks, or, for Kroeber, by the swift streams of the West and the pounding surf of the Pacific Ocean.

SCHOOL

Lessons, walks, park-bench reading and storytelling continued with Dr. Bamberger until June 1883 when Alfred became nine years old. That fall he went to school for the first time. It did not occur to him at the time to question why he was not sent to school earlier; one did not usually question parental decisions, to be sure, but in this case, life was full and happy with Carl, his own and Carl's brothers and sisters, and the Zinnser boys. Carl Alsberg once told me how Alfred was dressed in those days: black shoes well shined, black stockings which unlike Carl's did not wrinkle, short blue pants, a white shirt whose collar was worn outside an Eton jacket, and a "spring" topcoat reaching to just above his knees. From Mimi's and Kroeber's own characterization of himself at age nine there emerges a picture of a boy who was rather small for his age, light-boned, with a somewhat finicky stomach, easily excited and tired, all of which may have led to a lengthening of the period of tutoring. However, Carl, a robust and well-grown boy, was eight years old before he went to school full-time.

One result of the long tutoring was that Alfred and Carl found themselves in classes with boys as much as three years their seniors. This age disparity in the classroom was regarded with greater equanimity then than it now would be, but Alfred was uncomfortably aware of being the smallest boy in his class. He was saved much of the agony of such status, since his was not a boarding school and did not have a playing field. The school was Dr. Sachs's Collegiate Institute, considered to be one of the best college preparatory schools in the city and modeled on the pattern of the German *gymnasium* or the French *lycée* as closely as was possible in America. The school hours were from nine to two without intermissions except one brief recess to eat the sandwich lunch each pupil brought with him. There were no study, physical-education, or play periods. "Supervised" study was something no one at Dr. Sachs's school had heard of; studying was done at home and it was expected that the preparation would be careful and complete, which it usually was.

Unlike Dr. Bamberger, with his passion for history and his untiring curiosity, there was no teacher at Dr. Sachs's who was world-enlarging, who made an effort to understand the unfolding young minds of his pupils. It was a school of pedants, but competent pedants. The studies offered were Latin, Greek, and French; mathematics; grammar, rhetoric, and composition; literature and history; physics and chemistry. The pedants were humorless and unlovable, but fair. There was neither physical punishment nor undue holding up to ridicule nor other devices of the sadistic teacher. Dr. Sachs drew his pupils from a clientele who knew precisely the quality and style of learning they were paying for; he provided the teachers, books, and minimal other equipment to supply this learning. Four-fifths of his pupils were Jewish—the sons of rabbis and of intellectually oriented German-Jewish immigrants—who were more motivated toward learning than were most of the Anglo-Saxon, Dutch, and other ethnic groups of the city.

Alfred looked back on his years at Dr. Sachs's school without affection or rancor. There was the five-hour routine; then you were free, except for the studying. If you had already learned to study, as he had, there were some hours of each day that were one's own. These were the hours—walking to and from school and playing with an enlarged circle of friends—when the transition from predominantly German speech to predominantly English was made; when the trace of accent, if it was there as Kroeber believed, was erased; when the small boy learned his sidewalks of New York. There were for Alfred the historic encounters with the "other" gang; there were some fights; some bloody noses, and some elaborately planned retaliations and escapes, but there were none of the terrifying confrontations potential in a large city and now seemingly inescapable in New York. The rule of territoriality prevailed; you invaded the other's ground at your peril, but the tough Eastside gangs were also disadvantaged off home ground; the neighborhood policeman knew the boys who belonged to a particular street and neighborhood and those who were out of bounds. It was in these years also that Kroeber's interest in "sports" as such—American sports—first added itself to an earlier love of games, two interests which he never lost.

Neither the friendship with Carl nor the old interests with Dr. Bamberger were lost among the new interests and excitements. Carl and Alfred met after school and on weekends and they pursued an investigation of the world which was a continuation from the younger days. They organized the "Humboldt Scientific Society" whose nucleus was their friends and their own younger brothers. Meetings were on Saturdays, Sundays, and holidays. Carl says of these meetings, "We went into the Bronx Park region which was then largely open country to collect beetles and butterflies, to an iron-smelting furnace where we collected fossils from the limestone used in smelting, to the Franklin zinc smelter where we collected minerals, to Staten Island where we collected serpentine and related minerals, to the Palisades, to Snake Hill in the Jersey marshes, to such factories as would let us in; and when we were older we had winter evening meetings at which we read papers and had heated discussions on many subjects we really knew very little about. These meetings lasted well into our sophomore year at college. First and last about fifteen boys were involved." Two titles of papers from those later years are: "The Object of Life" and "Resolved that Realism Conveys a Greater Moral Lesson than Idealism."

HOME

At about the time Alfred became a school boy he participated in some adult activities. There were afternoon concerts with his mother and an occasional matinee at the theater with his father. And there were the Sunday family dinners, at one o'clock after a morning walk in the park *en famille*. The meal was formal, with the courses tryingly long for a child. It was nonetheless gratifying to be admitted to the Sunday dinner table; it meant you were very grown-up; that you were served wine in the precious stemmed glasses which Florence and Mimi had brought home from the last trip abroad. The wine was good Rhine wine whose taste was merely a sour one to the tyro imbiber; but it was the ritual drink of first adulthood and was downed with distaste and deep respect.

The household was father-dominated as were most households of the time in America. It was not the noisy, ego dominance of Clarence Day's "Life with Father." There was no flailing of arms or raising of voices in the Kroeber home. Mimi sufficiently conveyed to the children her own sense of awe and respect for the paterfamilias to keep them fairly in line, and disobedience to her so distressed the gentle Mimi that it seems to have occurred rarely indeed. Kroeber had no complaints concerning his parents or his childhood. It was a strictly disciplined and ordered life, but there was nothing stifling or mean about it, its rigidity confined to rules about hours and manners and physical routines. It did not reach out to encompass and repress the intellectual and aesthetic growth of the enlarging personalities of the children. All Kroebers whom I have known smile readily; an amiable and often ironic humor is never far below the surface; they are spontaneously creative.

DEUTSCHAMERIKANISCH

Clarence Day, whom Kroeber knew in later years, describes and satirizes the bourgeois New York of the same period as Alfred's and Carl's, but his New York was Anglo-Saxon, not German. Both the similarities and the differences are interesting. The Kroebers and the Days lived in almost identical houses, bought clothes and furnishings in the same shops, dressed alike, followed similar summer vacation patterns, attended the same concerts and some of the same theaters, took politics equally seriously, sent their children to private although different schools—in short, shared a current New York-American bourgeois way of life, and for the most part conducted themselves and reacted to their world similarly. There were, however, real differences. In his chapter in the book, *Carl Alsberg, Scientist at Large,* Kroeber suggests these differences in describing the intellectual and social climate within which he, Carl, Hans Zinnser, and the others came to adulthood. He says, "[Our parents'] way of life . . . was called German American, or more often *deutsch-amerikanisch,* and was in no sense felt as hyphenated. As regards all public affairs we were wholly American. I came nearer falling out with Carl than at any other time that I can remember when at the age of seven and eight we walked up Madison Avenue from 54th to 74th Street arguing the Blaine-Cleveland campaign. Carl's father held that virtue resided in the only patriotic party, whereas mine put character of the candidate first though I suspect this Mugwumpery was a bit tainted by previous Democratic predilections. And we were all intensely anti-Tammany. On the other hand, none of us seemed ever to have personal or familial relations with Americans of Anglo-Saxon origin until we were well along in school. Our fathers dealt with them as customers and our mothers bought groceries and milk from them; but somehow we scarcely got to associating with them. Not that there was a barrier; but life was full and preoccupied without them."

Behind the particularity of this description is to be comprehended the relative slowness of mingling between the Anglo-Saxon and German strains of the city at a time when the lines between German-Gentile and German-Jew had not been drawn. New Yorkers and non-New Yorkers alike today, and this includes most sociologists and social historians, either do not know or fail to appreciate the potency of this brief, earlier period when German Gentile and German Jew felt a mutual and single identification as German American. Of this, Kroeber says:

> [As to] the relation of Gentile and Jew of German extraction . . . one knew the difference, but assumed it did not matter. There was a solid ghetto in Manhattan and an incipient one in the Bronx; and Avenue A was a "Little Germany" which supported the Thalia, the Irving Palace, and for a while another German theater. In the upper economic levels, Jewish brokers and bankers evidently maintained a somewhat separatist social segment of their

own. But the bourgeoisie that had crossed the ocean neither from direct need nor trouble nor from desire for increase of wealth, but for new or better opportunity, came ingrainedly and almost fanatically liberal. The roots of their conviction lay in the French Revolution, though their Germanic provincialism rendered them unaware of this fact; and they were instinctively both anti-Jacobin and anti-Napoleonic. But creed and race were to be wiped out, or at least ignored.

None of the German families I knew were church members. None of the Jewish families went to synagogue—a few perhaps on the Day of Atonement, in satisfaction of their elders or the memory of them. But they took for granted that one did not believe in religion. Ex-Catholic and ex-Protestant Germans, being in nearly equal numbers, probably contributed to the disintegration of barriers.

In one minor way the varying antecedents did show. In Carl's home, two subjects were not discussed: sex and religion. In mine, only one was taboo: sex. Carl's ebullient mother [she was Gentile] was religiously indifferent and uninterested. But his father, raised under a mother who ate only kosher foods and made him learn the Torah, was still in revolt, and his agnosticism was aggressive. His children should live completely free and know nothing of trammels. If there was a God, or if they wanted one, let them find Him for themselves when they had grown up. With us, it was my extrovert and self-made father whom religion bored. One of my mother's parents was Protestant, the other Catholic: on both sides there were apostasies from one faith to the other for generations back. She was baptized a Catholic: therefore I was baptized Lutheran—and my younger brother and sisters were left unbaptized, as befitted enlightenment. But the religious heritage was not so easily abolished: my mother joined Ethical Culture,

> a society founded in 1876 by Felix Adler, an agnostic rabbi (and a family friend), who came to lead a part-Gentile congregation; and Mimi instigated me to sample Sunday services there, and in Unitarian and liberal Congregational churches. Carl escaped these vacillations. He was encouraged to read Huxley's scientific essays: I, his controversies with the Bishop of Peterborough. Of course, I sided with Huxley, but had a sneaking feeling that the manners were with the Bishop.

Later in the same chapter, Kroeber says:

> One other factor was of permanent influence: the unalloyed respect which this environment had for learning and the arts, and the premium which it put upon their cultivation. They were not something compartmented, a segregated specialty of the few, but things of daily experience, of constant contact. Not everyone became a scholar, an artist, a practitioner of a learned profession; but everyone lived in an atmosphere of association with them. The most gifted slid easily into the status of such a career; the others maintained the association and attitude. This value for enlightenment may have been slightly reinforced in some Jews by a transmuted carry-over of the fetish of rabbinical learning. Essentially, however, it was the carry-over of the Europe of Voltaire, which the founders of America of necessity largely escaped, in spite of the genius exception of Franklin. The form which molded Carl Alsberg [and Alfred Kroeber] was its mid-nineteenth-century German facies: the mellow golden sunset of the German civilization of Kant and Goethe, translated to a late afterglow among congenial and harmonious American institutions, while the shadows of rigour were imperceptibly creeping up in the homeland.

THE GUNNERY

When Alfred was nearly eleven, the family physician noted that he was growing tall without adding weight, that the "nervous stomach" symptoms, small appetite, and tautness remained part of the psychosomatic profile. The doctor recommended a full year in the country away from the demanding school program and his role as eldest of four children in a household whose routines and rules, if not excessive, were unremitting. Alfred was taken out of school for a few weeks to board with a family in the country across the line in Connecticut. A late series of snowstorms prevented Mimi's coming to get him as soon as she had planned to, but to his own and his family's surprise, he was never homesick. He accompanied the mother when she milked the two cows, and was allowed to feed the chickens and ducks; he watched the father at work in his blacksmith shop; he shared an attic room with the slow-moving, slow-speaking almost-grown son. And although this was not part of the plan, he went with him to the one-room school, a mile or more away, where a single schoolmaster taught all eight grades and coped through a direct-action discipline with the largest and most reluctant of his pupils, who overtopped him in height though not in wits.

Alfred was charmed with it all, but Mimi and Florence thought this was not quite the answer to the problem of a change. He came home and finished the term at Sachs's; Mimi and the children and Berthe Alsberg and her children went for a long month to the Adirondacks in the summer; and in the fall, Alfred went to the Gunnery, a boarding school for boys in Washington, Connecticut.

The doctor had been right; it was a good year, from which

Alfred returned home taller than when he left, heavier, sturdier, browner, and more independent. Nor did he ever again lapse into the earlier semifragility. The scholastic requirements of the Gunnery were modest after Dr. Sachs; there was a gymnasium and a playing field; and Alfred was now in association with Anglo-Saxon New Englanders. Washington is one of New England's loveliest villages; the Shepaug River, its falls and oxbow, and the woods and rocky hills are of a size to be comprehended, explored, and exploited by an eleven-year-old boy. With the other boys, Alfred fished in the brooks, swam naked in the swimming hole deep in the woods, climbed the overhanging cliff above the oxbow, coasted and tobogganed down the steep snow-covered slopes, and skated on the frozen pond. For the first time he experienced, close-up and in its daily progression, the descent of the flaming northeastern autumn over trees and shrubs. Even then, he felt the death behind the brilliantly disguising colors; autumn would never be his favorite season. It was the magical multiple awakenings of his first New England spring which made him realize that this was his season—he was born in early June—the days of rebirth when the sun, day by day, shines a little longer on the earth. Years later he would understand at once the frenetic joy, the ritual song and dance, with which Indians of interior northern California greeted the Big Winds, the First Green Clover, and the New Salmon of their spring.

JAMES ROSENBERG

At the Gunnery Alfred met James Rosenberg. Jim, two years Alfred's senior, is living today; he has been my source for some of the materials of this book. He and Alfred were the "strange" boys in the school, the only ones from outside New England and the only non-Anglo-Saxons. As such they were objects of some interest and curiosity, and for the first time in their lives they were made aware of American anti-Semitism, a prejudice springing in this case from such ignorance as to be almost innocent. Alfred came from Dr. Sachs's school, whose repute had reached the Gunnery: it was "a noted Jewish New York private school"; therefore Alfred was a Jew. Jim on the other hand came from the Ethical Culture School, a school which would easily suggest Thoreau and Emerson to a New Englander. Even with his name, most Gunnery boys did not realize that Jim was a Jew. Jim says there were some strong efforts to ostracize Alfred who, with him, found the mistaken racial identification very funny. They were careful not to enlighten the enemy, and a semi-ostracism was short-lived. But even while they saw the episode as a joke, they knew it was more than that. Jim never forgot the epithets cast at Alfred which were meant for him had their authors but known; nor did Alfred forget: as anthropologist and as a political and social member of society, he fought all his life any act or belief which denied the equality of races.

From Jim I have some few further recollections of the Gunnery year which forecast in odd ways the later man. One is political, Jim writes of it as follows:

> It was a Presidential election year. Benjamin Harrison was the Republican candidate, Cleveland I think was the Democratic candidate. The Gunnery was all for Harrison. We school boys had a Republican Club, paraded and had torchlight processions. Alfred paraded alone, carrying a banner for the Democratic Party and its candidate.

Perhaps he had one supporter—not me. I had inherited staunch Republicanism from my father (a heritage long since abandoned). Unmoved by jeers of the pack and occasional rotten tomatoes Alfred marched alone. Did he ever tell you that story?

(He did, after his son's teacher reported to him the results of a second-grade standing vote election held in the autumn of the Hoover-Smith presidential campaign. When Hoover's name was called, twenty-nine little Republicans stood up; five Democrats came to their feet for Smith; and one lone hold-out stood when Norman Thomas' name was called, to cast his Socialist vote—the seven-year-old Kroeber boy, Ted. Ted's choice remained somewhat gnomic to his family which was for Smith except for one pro-Hoover grandmother. . . . When Kroeber found himself for the first time voting for a winning presidential candidate—it must have been the Franklin Roosevelt years—his comment was that he really disliked being with the majority—"it is more natural to be with a minority of my own choosing.")

Jim also tells of the putting down of the school bully, Big John, age sixteen. Says Jim:

> He was a thorough-going sadist. He used to catch us little fellows, bend our wrists back, make us kneel before him while he applied the newest torture he had learned. In defense Alfred, three other boys, and I organized the Scugee Club whose sole purpose was to avenge ourselves on Big John. [Jim says "Scugee!" was Alfred's invention, probably of the moment, although Alfred seems to have insisted it was the key word of a powerful magical incantation.] The other three boys were bigger than Alfred and me but we practiced until we could tie quick knots which were not

Edward, 1889, *age eleven.*

Yanchi, 1889, *age nine.*

easy to untie and Alfred studied Big John's every move. He learned that for reasons we never knew he would go to the brook below the football field alone after practice. This was a fairly remote spot and there was no one else around. We got our ropes ready, hid them in the brush, and finally hid ourselves earlier in the afternoon. Sure enough, after practice, along came Big John. We surprised him, were on him and had him tied up, ankles and arms, before he could get into action. We carried him to the pond and laid him in the water while we held a trial over him

Elsbeth, 1889, *age seven.*

Alfred, 1889, *age thirteen.*

which found him guilty. We decided to give him one chance to live. If he reported us, we would leave him to drown the next time. From that evening, if Big John so much as looked at any of us, we said, "Scugee!" He never bothered us again.

There was the trapping episode: the boys were making twitch-up traps in which they caught rabbits. Alfred's trap one day held a dead skunk. This was the opportunity he had been waiting for—to dissect a skunk to understand its spray mechanism. The members of the Scugee Club were required to take an extra bath and put on a complete change of clothing before they were allowed to come in to dinner that evening.

The country year came to an end; Alfred returned to the city and Dr. Sachs. Three years passed. More and more, Alfred was the grownup one of the four children. For two seasons he had gone with Mimi and Florence to the symphony and the opera, the latter a formal-dress and carriage affair with the younger children excitedly watching the departure, Mimi grand in rustling taffetas with feather fan and a lorgnette.

It was the summer following Alfred's fifteenth birthday—1891. Because he was to take the preliminary examinations for entrance to Columbia College, he stayed in the hot city while Mimi and the younger children went to Sheepshead Bay. Still in short pants, Alfred studied alone, going with his father on weekends to the Bay and returning with him again on Monday mornings. The examinations over, there were a few weeks in the Adirondacks with Carl and Jim, and then a last year with Dr. Sachs. He entered Columbia College in the fall of 1892 at the age of sixteen.

Florence and Mimi had expected to send their sons to Harvard and their daughters to Bryn Mawr, but business reverses and death intervened to change these orderly expectations.

Florence, who had so well understood the earlier city, became unattuned to its changing face. The pattern of New York City's growth was to spread north and east up the island from its Dutch beginnings at the Battery and behind

Wall Street. Every few years a new center saw a clustering of smart shops and homes which in turn were left behind to become shabby and passé; small and modest businesses came in to occupy the former smart shops, and the single-family houses became tenements or were replaced with lofts and warehouses as the west-side development began. So had it been with Union and Stuyvesant Squares and 14th Street; Madison Square became a bit far downtown; a business address in the thirties and forties on Fifth Avenue was now smart. But Florence could not imagine Union Square as other than a good location, and instead of moving with the flow uptown he stayed behind, enlarging and making more elegant his shops on the Square and on Broadway. Close to Wall Street was where the money would remain, said Florence. In a manner of speaking he was right, but close to Wall Street and on Union Square would become less and less the places where money would be spent in Florence's sort of shop. There were probably many reasons for his disastrous misreading of the dynamics of the city's growth. Always inclined to be "dyspeptic," Florence had been seriously unwell and would in the succeeding ten years suffer a late flare-up of tuberculosis from which he would die in 1916. Nowadays we are much given to wondering which end of the stick is up when bodily illness and worldly reverses come hand in hand. Whatever the causes, the financial crisis was real as was the illness and there was never total or even satisfactory recovery either of business success or of health.

Yanchi, the older of Alfred's sisters, was the only one of the four children for whom the original college plans were realized. She was graduated from Bryn Mawr in 1900, a biology major. She taught in a private school in the city and worked in the American Museum of Natural History as assistant to Henry Fairfield Osborn until her marriage to Herman Mosenthal, one of the musical Damrosch family. Yanchi's life was a full and rewarding one: she had four children and a harvest of grandchildren; a home in the east sixties, its four stories and garden reminiscent of the 78th Street house of her childhood; close identification with her husband's career as physician specializing in the treatment of diabetes, helping him in the establishment of a hospital for the early treatment of diabetic children; one of the founders and principal supports in time, imagination, and money of the Crippled Children's Hospital; whenever she could manage it, a return to the museum to work with Osborn.

Elsbeth, the younger sister, went to Barnard College, family finances having worsened; she lived at home; like Yanchi, she majored in biology. She taught in the city's public schools until her retirement in 1953: first, biology to high-school classes; then she was assistant principal in virtual charge of biology teaching. She wrote and continued to bring up to date a high-school textbook which is lively reading and sound biology. Doctors and men and women in one or another of the biological sciences still introduce themselves to me, recalling that it was in Elsbeth's laboratory they first committed themselves to scientific study and research.

Edward, the curly-haired gay and beloved second Kroeber brother, was a worry to Mimi and an exasperation to the unhappy father. Because a classical education was not what he wanted, he left school to work with his father. The shop offered opportunity for him to do the exquisite cabinet work at which he had been skilled since childhood. Otherwise the shop was not a good place for him; he and his father rubbed against each other. His irregularities were innocent enough—he neglected all tasks except woodworking, in order to have time for easel painting for which he showed real flair; and his taste was for rather gayer and "faster" companions than were usual to the other children. He was beginning to grow up, to convince his parents that about his painting at least he was serious and should be taken seriously. Then he died quickly, shockingly, of meningitis. A lifetime after, brother and sisters edged away from talking of that time. Edward was the only one to have come in for more than passing parental disapproval; his was the first meaningful death in their experience. The children were unusually close; the breaking of the foursome was not readily mended. And they would never forget the father's grief or Mimi's need for his sake to hide her own.

JOSEPH PROSKAUER

James Rosenberg whom Alfred knew at the Gunnery entered Columbia College as a freshman in 1891; Alfred and Carl Alsberg in 1892. Another '92 freshman was Joseph Proskauer, and with him, the quadrumvirate—Alfred, Carl, Jim, and Joe—was complete. Unlike a club whose members identify by a common name, insignia, and purpose, the closeness of these four rested on intangibles powerful enough to survive time, distance, economic and personal unlikenesses. Alfred, Carl, Jim, and Joe grew up together during their undergraduate and graduate years, playing, studying, writing poetry, listening to music, talking endlessly. Together, in the summer vacations, they learned the Adirondacks, looking forward there to the inevitable days of rain when with the help of a large campfire and the shelter of a cave and their upside-down canoe, they read and talked and dreamed.

19TH CENTURY HUMANISM

Each of these four young men would leave his mark on his own and future times as an inseminating original in his profession and as an unusual human being. So would Kroeber's older cousin on his father's side, Fritz Lauber, the craftsman who designed and fashioned stained glass windows of antique beauty for churches in New York City and in Philadelphia—the Church of the Ascension, Fifth Avenue at Tenth Street, had some of his best windows. So would Kroeber's cousin on his mother's side—Herman Muller—fourteen years his junior, one of the most original geneticists, a Nobel Prize winner, best known for placing the study of mutations on an experimental and quantitative basis. So would his boyhood playmate Hans Zinnser who broke the secret of typhus and who wrote *Rats, Lice and History* and other books which made science vivid to the layman; Carl Alsberg's brother Henry, author and playwright; and the sons and daughters and nieces and nephews of Alfred's and Carl's and Jim's and Joe's friends and neighbors from the subcommunity of bourgeois German-Gentile-Jewish immigrants and first-generation or second-generation Americans. They distinguished themselves in the arts and sciences in numbers and proportions beyond the statistically expectable and are to be understood individually and severally only within this phenomenon of brief bright clustering of realized talent and genius. Why, for a generation or two, their homes and environment should have been the center for so full a stream of exuberant creativity is a question for the social historian.

The parents of these children expected them to do well, it is true, but it was not yet part of the elders' thinking or teaching that their children should do better than their neighbors'. Such dog-eat-dog competitive motivation would exacerbate and accelerate later and less advantaged generations of New York children, establishing itself as obsession and habit only after the serener German identity was lost and all subcommunities in the city had become—whatever else—separately Gentile, separately Jew. It would seem that, willy-nilly, the elder Alsbergs and Zinnsers and Kroebers and Rosenbergs left their children freer, better equipped than other contemporary young Americans to enter and to begin joyous cultivation in the territories which Darwin and the rush of the new science and a new humanistic vision were opening up. Unlike their peers in the rest of America, even in Brahmin-intellectual New England, these young New Yorkers were relatively unfettered by fundamentalism whether Catholic, Protestant, or Judaic. And they were free of the unconscious aggressive anti-intellectualism which opposed itself to the new science and the new humanism even as it continues to oppose itself to today's science and today's humanism over so much of America—obscuring enlightenment and honest intellectualism.

I quote Kroeber on this childhood view which he and Carl Alsberg shared. He is writing of Carl, but what he says applies to himself and to their friends as well:

> I speak with a certain nostalgia, because, with all its naïve idealism, this way of living, impossible as it would

> be to resuscitate it, does represent a solution, however transient and provincial, of a problem that is still agitating the world. And being born into this set of habits and ideals —racial and religious and intellectual tolerance—profoundly affected all Carl Alsberg's career. It gave him for life the rare and valuable attitude of being every man's equal and no one's superior; a genuine ease and warmth in relations with people; an ability to subordinate himself to the majority, to authority, to circumstances, without suspending his independence of private judgment; and an even more outstanding faculty of directing others with their full loyalty and approval. He succeeded in making the world take him as its full citizen because he unwaveringly felt himself such a citizen.

James Rosenberg and Joseph Proskauer are to this day distinguished liberal members of the Bar of New York State. Both have traveled far up the economic and social scale; both fight, differently but with equal passion, for social betterment in many areas of life. Jim it was who first spelled out the need for power within the United Nations to prevent and punish the practice of genocide, and he was instrumental in having the Metropolitan Museum hang in its galleries the paintings of contemporary American artists. He is today (1969), at the age of ninety-five still a productive painter. His paintings hang in the galleries of the Metropolitan, Fogg, Fine Arts (of Boston), in museums and in some twenty other galleries. Jim is a warm accessible man under his keenness and drive, a universal man who has written stories, poetry, and plays—this alongside his assault on crooked bankruptcy practices whose laws he was prominent in rewriting. Like his paintings, he is romantic, dedicated, humorous.

Joseph Proskauer is handsome, urbane, witty, with something austere which colors and darkens the temperament. He it was who, as speech writer for Franklin Roosevelt, first called Al Smith "The Happy Warrior." He refused in 1926 to issue an injunction against 2200 A.F.L. dress-workers who threatened to tie up the whole garment industry. Instead he held a prolonged closed session in which he persuaded both sides to sign an agreement to submit their differences, present and future, to arbitration. The strike was averted and the arbitration system then set up is still in use. Joe was at the heart of the inception of the United Nations. In San Francisco he pressed hard for inclusion in the U. N. charter of an international bill of rights. Its wording is his own; he was principally responsible for the minority-protection clauses added at the Paris Conference a year later, and was much disappointed that the enforcing machinery was not stronger. He wrote, and continues to write, poetry; he thought of some day being a conductor of a symphony orchestra.

Carl Alsberg and Alfred, destined for research and teaching careers, never achieved or made an effort to reach the economic and social distinction of the other two. Carl went from Columbia to Harvard Medical and from his M. D. to medical research. As Director of the Food and Drug Administration, he clarified and put teeth and meaning into the then young and ineffectual Food and Drug Act. His final research positions were in the Food Institute at Stanford and as Director of the Giannini Research Foundation at the University of California at Berkeley. I think of Carl as the friend to whom one turned for wise advice and for patient help and as the best conversationalist I have known. His voice was a low rumble, a cello obbligato to other voices. He could talk on all sorts of subjects—politics, art, books, faraway places—but his was no monologue: he picked up the trail of interest or competence of his companions and somehow, without effort on his part or self-consciousness on theirs, drew their best from them. He and Alfred were much together after he came West. Alfred was with him when he died—the first of them to go—at the age of sixty-four—the last crisis of the many they had shared, seeking each other out all their lives in emotional and financial need, in times of decision about a change of job, on some matter of business, to criticize a piece of work done, to share in the special occasions of public acclaim and private celebration.

Throughout the later years and with wives and children, the four men were together when they could be—any combination which offered—warmly, familiarly, joyously. What were the binding threads which held them together and close? I do not know. Kroeber and I were once speaking of the tensions, the heightened sensibilities, the meshing and accommodations of personalities which go into making a true string quartet of two violinists, one cellist and one violist playing together. I said, "It is like you and Carl and Jim and Joe."

COLUMBIA COLLEGE

Kroeber began his Columbia College career living at home as usual and with some sense of letdown: Columbia was much like a continuation of Dr. Sachs's school. The courses for the freshman year were prescribed: Latin, Greek, modern languages, mathematics, history. Only chemistry and physics might be elected in the lower division. Most of the freshmen were less well prepared than Kroeber; the work was easy and not interesting.

He said of himself at this time that he was shy and solemn. His friends are in agreement that he was shy, but the solemnity seems to have been partly diffidence with strangers, partly simply a following of his own thoughts; outside a small circle he was neither much aware of nor much interested in the college community. James Rosenberg, in his autobiography, speaks of Kroeber as "an imp of mischief." Carl Alsberg says that Kroeber was the least hampered of the four by convention or fear of consequences; that the escapades which occupied them were more frequently than not of Kroeber's invention, the glory and trials of leadership being left to the others.

One escapade he carried through himself—painting the statuary in Central Park in the blue and white of Columbia with flourishes of red moustaches and hair, as a protest against the ugliness of the sculpture. It led to considerable expense to his father, the source of the paint being traced to the store from which Kroeber bought it, and was the occasion of some worry to Mimi. He regretted these unforeseen consequences, but maintained that as for the pompous Victorian bronzes and marbles, they deserved a stronger and more effective protest.

(The statue-painting is worth recalling, not because Kroeber thought much of it later, nor because it was either particularly funny or particularly serious, but because this sort of protest, this sort of absurdity, was an ingredient of his humor as of his philosophy. Nearly sixty years later, on a sunny Sunday morning, Kroeber, his wife, and two of his grown children were strolling down 116th Street from Columbia University. Long streamers of colored crepe paper lay over the sidewalks and filled the gutters, leftovers from some Saturday night neighborhood party. Kroeber began festooning the paper from son to wife to daughter, the space between them gradually distancing, so that they formed a sort of decorated procession, and in this formation they arrived at Claremont Avenue. With a little help from them, he put a streamer across Claremont where the street widens and debouches into 116th. Tying the streamer to signposts on either side of the street, he achieved a pink paper barrier at a height of about five feet from the ground. Then for the next half hour, he watched in total delight as car after car was driven up, brakes were applied, the cars were turned around and driven back to 119th, to reach Broadway or Riverside Drive by a longer route. No driver questioned the authority, the officialness of the fragile, fluttering and many-times tied barrier which was ultimately torn apart by the wind. These episodes, many years apart, were social protest within the absurd, a weapon for which he had a lifetime preference.)

In Kroeber's sophomore year, the quadrumvirate found itself in a class given by George E. Woodberry, poet, critic, and teacher, who soon became a friend with whom the four young people entered a world of literary magic. Great poetry and literature of whatever time and place and language were Woodberry's world, and there they explored with him to their hearts' content; whole afternoons and evenings passed in poetry reading and writing and criticism, in the exchange of manuscripts and ideas. For the remainder of his undergraduate days, Kroeber would be turned toward literature as a profession.

It was in their sophomore year also that Alfred, Carl, Jim, Joe, and a few others of the Woodberry group brought out the first numbers of a new literary magazine, *The Morningside,* the name forecasting the early removal of Columbia from East 49th Street to Morningside Heights on Upper Manhattan. The magazine was born of dissatisfaction with the current college undergraduate publications and survived for some years after its initiators were graduated. It was expectably unorthodox and lively, attacking any aspects of student and university life with which its editors and contributors disagreed. Carl Alsberg said that a strong plea in *The Morningside* for the teaching of culture history as opposed to political history, of which Kroeber was the author, was widely discussed and quoted and was in part responsible for Columbia's appointment of James Henry Robinson to a chair of history there in 1896.

Woodberry was professor in the Department of Literature at Columbia; there was a separate Department of Rhetoric and Composition but no Department of English. This seeming quaintness was perhaps good sense; the continuance of such division of labors and interests in Columbia and its adoption in other universities might well have saved many an English Department headache. Kroeber's B.A. was in literature. He took a fifth year, earning a Master's degree for which he wrote on the Romantic Closet Drama. He was by then an assistant half-time in literature, teaching a course in eighteenth-century literature, and half-time in rhetoric teaching freshman English composition.

FRANZ BOAS

In 1896, the year Kroeber was teaching his first composition classes, Franz Boas was appointed Lecturer in

Anthropology at Columbia. Kroeber met Boas there for the first time, a meeting which was also his introduction to anthropology and which determined his professional life. It was also the beginning of close friendships between him and Boas, Mimi and Mrs. Boas, and Elsbeth and Helena Boas, youngest of the four Boas children.

That year Boas offered a course in American Indian languages. Kroeber and two other young men enrolled. Boas was a curator in anthropology at the American Museum of Natural History; he had his students come each Tuesday evening to his home on 82nd Street, close to the museum, where, at the dining table lighted by a fringe-shaded lamp, he held his class.

Boas had opened a door into a world about which Kroeber knew almost nothing except that it should become his own. It was an odd beginning to carry such conviction and illumination, but Kroeber himself once explained in a letter to the linguist Dell Hymes his early beginnings of linguistic interest:

> I think it was in my first year of school, in my tenth year of age, in studying English grammar that I learned of "irregular" or "strong" verbs, and that most of these were contained in several "classes" of forms, like sing-sang-sung, write-wrote-written, break-broke-broken. I was intensely excited by this set of phenomena, and proceeded to think up all possible additional strong verbs and corroborating German forms in the hope of discovering new classes or patterns. This episode may illustrate a strong bent, a satisfaction in recognizing patterns, which seems to be at the root of my linguistic interests. It was because of this proclivity that the first course I took with Boas, an inductive analysis of several American Indian languages, largely steered me into becoming an anthropologist.

Of this first course, Kroeber wrote many years later, "We spent about two months each on Chinook, Eskimo, Klamath, and Salish, analyzing texts and finding the grammar (with help and some straight-out presentation by Boas). I was enormously stimulated. Grammatical structure was interesting as presented; but to discover it was fascinating. Boas' method was very similar to that of the zoologist who starts a student with an etherized frog or worm and a dissecting table." Later in the year Boas brought to the class a Labrador half-breed Eskimo woman, Esther, the wife of a mechanic at the museum. With her, Kroeber worked for the first time with a living informant: she spoke her dialect of Eskimo and he wrote it down phonetically.

Continuing the American Indian Language course the next semester, Kroeber took also the two other courses Boas was offering: Statistical Theory and Method, and Physical Anthropology, the latter course held in the museum where there were necessary instruments for making anthropometric measurements and skulls and skeletons and various other specimens.

By 1897 Kroeber, assistant in literature and in rhetoric, had made his choice of a profession: the next year he was Assistant in Anthropology at Columbia. Lieutenant Robert Peary returned to New York City from Smith Sound in Greenland bringing with him four Eskimo men, one woman, and a ten-year-old boy. On the trip down all six caught cold—their first colds. They arrived sick and were taken to Bellevue Hospital where they contracted tuberculosis. From Bellevue they were taken to a private home to convalesce. For about two months the disease was thought to be controlled, and during that time Kroeber went to see and talk to them two or three afternoons a week. With Esther as interpreter, he took down vocabularies, myths, and legends from them, the publication of which materials commemorates this time and constitutes Kroeber's first publications in the Museum *Bulletin* and in the *Journal of American Folklore*. Before the year was out, four of the Eskimo were dead. A fifth, a young man, still sick, returned or started the return trip home with Peary—whether he arrived safely home or not, Kroeber never knew. Only the boy recovered and stayed in the city, where he ultimately became a taxi driver.

In 1898 Kroeber received a fellowship in anthropology from Columbia, and Boas sent him the next summer to do field work with the Arapaho Indians in Wyoming. The New York years, the years of growing up, of preparation, were drawing to a close. The academic semesters of 1899-1900 were Kroeber's last of graduate work and were followed by a second summer in the field, this time back with the Arapaho, then on to brief visits with adjoining Plains Indians, the Ute, Shoshone and the Bannock. On his way east once more he stopped in Montana for several weeks with the Atsina Indians. Home again, the spring of 1901 was spent in writing up his Atsina (Gros Ventre) material and in writing his doctoral dissertation, later published in the *American Anthropologist* under the title "Decorative Symbolism of the Arapaho." The doctoral examination took place in Low Library at Columbia, the examining committee being Franz Boas, Livingston Farrand (anthropology-psychology, later head of Red Cross, president of Cornell University); James Cattell (psychology, owner and editor of *Science* which became the organ of the A.A.A.S.); and Nicholas Murray Butler (philosophy, later president of Columbia University). The examination was conducted formally as to the wearing of academic cap and gown but

Alfred in his twenties.

informally as to question, answer, and discussion. Each of the examiners had had the candidate in classes and knew him well otherwise. They kept him only an hour and then adjourned, satisfied that the quality of his preparation and competence was superior and need not be further probed. Kroeber said it was not an ordeal, indeed, scarcely a challenge: that it had left him feeling a little let down.

Franz Boas was the directing influence on Kroeber the last years at Columbia and in New York. German-born and educated, Boas took a doctorate in physics under Theobold Fischer in Berlin, then followed him when Fischer shifted his focus of research to geography. It was as docent in geography that Boas went on his first expedition, an Arctic physico-geographic exploration of Baffinland. There he met living Eskimo and was linguist enough to take down phonetically their previously unrecorded language. With this experience, ethnolinguistics and ethnology replaced his earlier interests, and in 1889 he resigned the position he then held at the Ethnological Museum in Berlin to come to the United States and to Clark University. In 1896 he went as curator to the American Museum of Natural History and as lecturer in anthropology to Columbia. New York was his future home. In 1899 he was made a professor at Columbia where he served for forty years, a term shorter by only five years than Kroeber's at the University of California. He returned to the Arctic and the sub-Arctic Eskimo, and he went to the Northwest Coast—to many places, always to the ethnographic field, to the end of his life.

Boas was strong physically and psychically, dominant, daemonic, a proper culture hero who passed along to his students the peculiarly slanted romantic humanistic-scientific vision which continues, even with today's powerful and more mundane competing influences, to motivate and inspire New World anthropologists. Kroeber stood on Parnassus with Boas, who pointed out to him the land below, its shadowed parts and its sunny places alike virgin to the ethnologist. Virgin but fleeting—this was the urgency and the poetry of Boas' message. Everywhere over the land were virgin languages, brought to their polished and idiosyncratic perfection of grammar and syntax without benefit of a single recording scratch of stylus on papyrus or stone; living languages orally learned and transmitted and about to die with their last speakers. Everywhere there were to be discovered Ways of Life, many many ways. There were gods and created worlds unlike other gods and worlds, with extended relationships and values and ideals and dreams unlike anything known or imagined elsewhere, all soon to be forever lost—part of the human condition, part of the beautiful heartbreaking history of man. The time was late; the dark forces of invasion had almost done their ignorant work of annihilation. To the field then! With notebook and pencil, record, record, record. Rescue from historylessness all languages still living, all cultures. Each is precious, unique, irreplaceable, a people's ultimate expression and identity, which, being lost, the world is made poorer as surely as it was when a Praxitelean marble was broken and turned to dust.

Such the vision; and to Kroeber, overridingly and finally committing. Beyond the vision, Boas brought to humanistic studies a severe objectivity, a mathematical exactitude, a wariness of the subjective, the intuitive, the empathetic. He called Kroeber epicurean, meaning to reproach him, but

Kroeber accepted the adjective with equanimity. It was proper and inevitable that he, temperamentally very different from Boas, should come to have his own world view, with intuition and empathy allowed to infuse it, once the objective data—all those to be had—were in hand and digested. But the propulsive, idealistic vision had been as well Boas' vision.

SAN FRANCISCO

ACADEMY OF SCIENCES

In 1900 Kroeber did not yet have his Ph.D., but on his two field trips he had purchased specimens for the American Museum which he had catalogued and documented and in some cases installed for the museum, and for two years he had spent much time in its laboratories and preparators' quarters as student and informal assistant.

In 1853 the Academy of Sciences was organized in San Francisco. By 1900 it had accumulated collections of local natural history and California Indian artifacts. A curator was needed. David Starr Jordan, President of Stanford University and head of the Board of Directors of the Academy, consulted Boas who recommended Kroeber.

Thus it was Jordan who first brought Kroeber to San Francisco. He came in August of 1900 with the title of Curator, at a salary of eighty dollars a month. He took a room in an inexpensive hotel at 443 Eddy Street, close to the Academy, which was then downtown, and began to learn a new city and a new coastal geomorphology. He learned that a heaped plate of tiny highly flavored Bay shrimps accompanied a beer and preceded an order for a meal; that a decent meat stew with bread and coffee was to be had for two bits, a full course "French" dinner for six bits. He found his way to Fisherman's Wharf where he ate his first sea-fresh Pacific crab, Bay oyster, abalone, and sanddab.

The city lay under its usual blanket of summer fog which meant that Kroeber discarded seersucker for wool and a spring overcoat. The unheated and poorly lighted hotel room was neither a comfortable nor a cheerful place in the evening. He went often the few blocks to the local opera where a balcony seat cost two bits and steam beer was brought in to balcony customers from the saloon next door. A repertory company sang an opera nightly, and here it was that Kroeber supplemented his childhood listening—which had been at the Metropolitan Opera House in New York City and largely Wagner—with some Russian and French operas and almost the full Italian repertoire. Well sung for the most part, the operas were often badly staged and acted, but like the folk-tales and songs of childhood, Kroeber remembered them and could recall their plots, themes, characters, some words and arias (which he hummed in a sort of tuneless rhythmic monotone). He had a life-long taste for opera, which is interesting in view of the classic cast of his aesthetic preferences.

The Academy collections were not large—within six weeks Kroeber had them fairly in hand. He knew there were Indians living along the coast to the north: he asked to be allowed to begin an ethnographic study of those people and to enlarge the Academy collections of Indian baskets and other artifacts. Jordan consented, giving him one hundred dollars for train fare, stage and livery-stable costs, purchase of specimens and informants' fees. Kroeber took a northbound train the next day, arriving at Rekwoi at the mouth of the Klamath River a day later, having spent the last hours of the trip in a horse-drawn stage. In 1900, few permanent white settlers lived so far north: there were lumber mills at most river mouths; if there was shelter from the open sea, lumber schooners put in to take on loads of redwood. Lumbermen were already slash-cutting and destroying the virgin stands of coastal redwoods which then extended along the coast and inland for many uninterrupted miles of climax forest; there were a few mines upriver that had survived the Gold Rush and were being worked, and there were some stock ranches.

The Indians of northwestern California had escaped the Spanish-Mexican invasion but were caught in the later Anglo-Saxon conquest; many of them were killed outright or sold into slavery; the independence and way of life of all were interrupted and destroyed beyond restoration. But of those who survived, some, unlike most western Indians, were still living on their own ancestral land when Kroeber first reached them, their life physically much as it had been before the Gold Rush. Their rivers were yet to be preempted by sportsmen; they were still fishing their salmon streams except where mine tailings had polluted the water and killed the fish.

A salmon cannery at Rekwoi was working to capacity when Kroeber arrived, the Indians selling their surplus fish there. He stayed at first at the small hotel which housed the cannery workers, but within a few days he had outfitted himself with two army blankets, a coffee pot, fry pan and stew kettle, a small ax and a machete, lacking only the flat gold-washing pan to have looked like another "prospector." He was now free to build his fire and camp beside the open ocean or on one of the splayed banks of the river mouth, or to go upriver into its gorge. The bounty of the cold Pacific was his: surf fish, mussels, crabs, clams, with salmon from the river. Along the shore of the sea and on the gravelly spits beside the river and up the terraced sides of the river canyon were Indian villages and living Indians. They spoke a language which intrigued him and they lived according to an aristocratic formalized mode which caught his imagination.

The view from Parnassus, first glimpsed with Boas, had seemed to hold much promise. Its fulfillment for Kroeber lay not in the Arctic from which had come his first informants nor on the Plains where he made his first Indian friends and began to communicate in their language, but here, a continent's width away from home and facing another ocean. Fifteen years later he would sit down at his desk to write the *Handbook of the Indians of California*, the opening sentence of which reads, "This history begins with an account of the Yurok, a nation resident on the lower Klamath River, near and along the Pacific Ocean, in extreme northern California, surrounded by peoples speaking diverse languages but following the same remarkable civilization."

Even in 1901, one hundred dollars would not stretch indefinitely. Kroeber returned to San Francisco with full notebooks and some exquisite examples of Yurok carving and basketry. He was allowed a second one hundred dollars, and the shabby room on Eddy Street saw its tenant again only several weeks later when the money was gone and the Christmas holidays were at hand. By this time the language and customs of the Karok and Hupa peoples, neighbors to the Yuroks, were appearing in the notebooks, and their baskets and flint knives were among the specimens he brought back to the Academy.

The full board of the Academy held its annual meeting during the holidays, at which time Kroeber was told it was not their policy to give a curator field funds beyond his salary. Most collectors, he was reminded, did their collecting on their own time and money: the Academy collections were largely gifts. In short, an ethnographic curator, hellbent for the field and informants, was a luxury the Academy could not afford—his position would not be continued after the first of the year.

How to pay the railroad fare back to New York City? Kroeber wrote Boas who arranged for him to return via Montana, to buy an Indian canoe which the American Museum was anxious to have, and see to its transport to New York City in good condition. He could do a few weeks' work with the Atsina Indians while the canoe was being made. So ended the first phase of Kroeber's life in San Francisco. It seems a quaint episode at this distance. There was nothing quaint or amusing about it close up. It is never pleasant to be fired, however pleasantly. (Hard as it may be to believe when one regards today's impressive and impressively budgeted Academy, four or five hundred dollars a year to an ethnologist for field funds was a luxury it could not then afford.) But relations remained good, and some years later Kroeber would choose one of its youngest curators as his first assistant at the University Museum: Edward Gifford, fifteen years old when Kroeber first knew him at the Academy as a passionate collector and already a specialist in Pacific conchology.

BENJAMIN IDE WHEELER

While he was in San Francisco Kroeber had met Benjamin Ide Wheeler, President of the University of California. In the late spring of 1901, back in New York City, Kroeber received a letter from Wheeler making him a formal offer of an instructorship in the soon-to-be-created Department and Museum of Anthropology at Berkeley. Kroeber accepted at once. The Field Museum in Chicago had indicated an interest in him, but he wanted to return to his new friends at Rekwoi, and at Weitspus where the Trinity River flows into the Klamath. By early August of 1901, one year after his first coming to San Francisco, he was back in his old room on Eddy Street. He was also literally on Parnassus now—Parnassus Heights in San Francisco.

Kroeber's story at this point becomes a part of the story of the beginnings of anthropology on the West Coast, and this story centers on two non-anthropologists who were crucial to its early years and hence to much of its subsequent history: Benjamin Ide Wheeler and Phoebe Apperson Hearst.

Before coming to California as president of its state university, Benjamin Ide Wheeler had been a professor of Greek and Indo-European linguistics at Cornell University; as president, he continued to teach linguistics at Berkeley. He was popular with the students who found in him a culture hero figure as well as a cordial and good friend. To meet him in one of the then woodsier parts of the campus, aristocratic-looking in his long blue cape, erect and elegant astride his clean-stepping horse, to have him stop to chat, was a coveted experience. He knew an astonishing number of students by name and often something of their background and interests, or if he did not, he knew how to elicit such information in a conversational, easy way. The door of his office stood open on Friday mornings, during which hours no secretary intervened between him and the empty chair beside his desk; students could bring their troubles or problems there; they were encouraged to come just to pass a brief and to them memorable few minutes talking with him. Besides the sense of personal aquaintance, students appreciated the wit and style and feeling he brought to the large and small occasions of his appearances on campus. Then came 1914. Wheeler's Ph.D. was from a German university; he knew and brought to California permanently or for a year or a semester German and other European scholars; signed photographs from Europeans, among them one of the Kaiser, stood on the mantels of the president's house and office. President Wheeler was appalled at the spectacle of war with Germany; Germany meant to him what it meant to many traveled people of his age and time—the country from which we drew our music, our scholarship, our standards for museums and libraries, our pattern for the Ph. D. degree. He refused to panic when the early atrocity stories began to circulate; he disapproved, and said so plainly, the intemperate rabble-rousing speeches made in the university's Greek Theatre during student and faculty meetings held there each week; he wept openly upon conclusion of the ceremony with which he said *au revoir* to the first ambulance unit to go to France from the university. To Kroeber as to the students, all these things did not add up to "pro-Germanism," an epithet which was to dog and sadden Wheeler's later years.

President Wheeler was less popular with the faculty, many of whom considered him high-handed and arrogant. Kroeber, to be sure, knew him better than did most young faculty members, but aside from that and before he knew him well, he found him to be a good administrator, definite, informed, brief, and as unvacillating in his loyalty and his affirmations as in his refusals. Kroeber said of him, "He gave me my head; when he did say no, he meant it; he did not waste his own time, or mine." Kroeber once told me of going to Wheeler with his first request for a new person on the staff, having drawn up a list of good reasons for the request. Wheeler stopped him before he had begun on his list, saying, "The time has come when a third man is needed?" "Yes." "It is Waterman you want?" "Yes." "Well—I know the young man. Get him." Wheeler's strength lay in being himself a research man and a scholar, in having a wide acquaintance with people in academic subjects in Europe and the Americas, and in his intimate familiarity with each bright and dark corner of the university, having himself selected many of its faculty and having molded or watched while its complex and innumerable aspects were taking permanent form. He knew Boas; he knew something of ethnography and ethnographers, something of ethno-linguistics, enough to realize there was work to be done in California, exciting and important work. His problem was how best to implement such a field-research subject in a young university and in a social environment which clung unthinkingly to the pioneer attitude toward the local Indian population. People who should have known better were still calling these Indians "Diggers."

PHOEBE APPERSON HEARST

It was through Phoebe Apperson Hearst that Wheeler finally arrived somewhat circuitously at a beginning in ethnographic research at the university. Mrs. Hearst was a personal friend of Mr. and Mrs. Wheeler. Her husband, George Hearst, had been U.S. Senator from California from 1886 until his death in 1891. A mining magnate, he was one of the early barons of the Far West whose houses and hospitality suggested the early Spanish American hacienda with vast empty grazing land and a luxurious *casa* presided over by its almost princely *hacendado*. By the time Kroeber knew Mrs. Hearst she had been ten years a widow. A small person no more than five feet in height, modest in manner, there was something regal in the walk, the set of the purple bonnet, the swish of the black and purple silks. She was a regent of the university and when she came into the Greek Theatre on President Wheeler's arm for a Charter Day ceremony, or stood in the reception line for some university occasion, she gave a certain air and tone to these gatherings. She was serious-minded, with none of the flamboyances or ego-drives of her husband and son, generous to those who worked for her, to her friends, to the projects and institutions which she supported.

She had a passion for collecting, for discovering and possessing objects of beauty. She had always collected. What began as dilettante amusement changed as she became more knowledgeable in her selections. She thought of collecting on a large scale, systematically, through expeditions which she would finance. She consulted with the Wheelers; she had already built for the university its first women's gymnasium. The question now was: would the university be willing to house her specimens and collections if she initiated an ambitious program of archaeological exploration? This was the point where Mrs. Hearst's and President Wheeler's visions of a part of the future of the university blended and clarified into a program. She would one day build a museum for her treasures which would eventually go to the university;

meanwhile her collections would be housed on campus; she would pay the housing costs.

By 1899 Mrs. Hearst had been financing field expeditions for some years: George Reisner in Egypt and Max Uhle in Peru. Also, Alfred Emerson, father of the biologist of the same name at the University of Chicago, traveled to Greece and Italy for her, where, because of laws prohibiting excavations by foreigners, he sought out good pieces of early Greek and Roman art *in situ* or in antique shops or from private owners, which he was able to buy.

There was on campus a cottage which predated the settling of the university there, known as Myers Cottage from its original owners, a one-story redwood house which Wheeler assigned to Mrs. Hearst for storage of her collections. Myers Cottage, enlarged before it finally came down to make way for Cowell Hospital and other buildings, was in later years made into the first university hospital-dispensary for students. But for the present it sheltered, unopened, the boxes and barrels which arrived in Mrs. Hearst's name. The boxes and barrels came in increasing numbers. Great crates were delivered which held marbles and stone sarcophagi: they would have broken through the floor of the cottage: they remained perforce outside on the ground. Something had to be done. Early in 1901 Mrs. Hearst authorized the building, next door to the cottage, of an eighty-by-sixty-foot warehouse, fireproof outside with corrugated iron walls and hangar-type roof. It was a mere shell, a provisional home for the specimens which remained in their original packing but were at least off the ground and under lock and key of sorts.

MUSEUM AND DEPARTMENT OF ANTHROPOLOGY

President Wheeler talked with Mrs. Hearst of some time considering work closer home—the study of California's own native Indian cultures. She took to the idea, and the year 1901 saw the appointment by her of four men in the California field along with the creation of the Department and Museum of Anthropology at the University of California. The appointments were F. W. Putnam as over-all coordinator and director; Phillip Mills Jones, a physician and radio specialist much interested in archaeology, to begin archaeological excavation; Kroeber to study living Indian languages and culture, to be in charge of collections and to act as executive secretary under Putnam; and Earle Pliny Goddard, a student of linguistics with Wheeler, to give one course in Berkeley and to do linguistic field work. This was the first formal appearance of the subject in a university curriculum west of Chicago. Putnam's and Kroeber's appointments preceded the actual initiation of the department; Goddard's followed closely thereafter. The first move toward making some sort of center for anthropological instruction was to run a partition across the north end of the warehouse, separating from storage a twenty-foot space within which area a cubicle eight feet square was further set off as an office. A cast-iron, pot-bellied stove was placed outside the partition—the only heat in the building. The first occupant of the office was Gerald D'Aquin, a Hollander of charming manners who was Mrs. Hearst's foreign secretary. He served for a few weeks as a temporary executive secretary of the projected department and museum. Than Kroeber came. The cubicle was his first office on campus.

The crates continued to arrive: a gallery was added around the warehouse area doubling the storage space. An airtight room which could be filled with formalin was built across one corner of the gallery, for moth and worm-prone specimens. This became known as the mothproof room and in later years was valued more for its privacy than its mothlessness and used as a storage place for picks, shovels, trowels, sleeping bags, and other equipment used on field trips; for the manuscripts of theses and other valuables; and for saddles and all manner of department and private objects.

But now the Tin Building was bulging, the gallery stacked to the roof—it could hold no more. Casting about, the regents recalled that on Parnassus Heights in San Francisco alongside the University Medical School, stood an empty building which had been intended to house the Hastings Law School. It had never been occupied, the faculty of the law school preferring a location downtown close to the courts. By moving Mrs. Hearst's collections there, the Tin Building would, with its office, gallery, and stove, do for a few months or even a year or two as the Anthropology Building.

It "did" for almost sixty years. More partitions yielded a classroom, a seminar-laboratory, offices for teaching staff including teaching fellows, a private corner somewhere for a visiting teacher or research student. As the staff grew, the cubicles became smaller. The building's arrangements were what the British call cosy, everyone more or less on top of everyone else. And flexible; a student or professor handy with saw and hammer could put up a set of shelves, change the angle or direction of a partition, or add another one. Its occupants liked the Tin Building and were fiercely loyal to it. Inside its main entrance there was placed for all those years an Etruscan sarcophagus, its lid an hieratic carved figure. The nose of this figure darkened over the years as day after day students came and went, each brushing a hand lightly, curiously over the nose, almost as if they were performing a ritual act. At last there had been so many layings on of hands, the orders to the staff were not to try to clean the nose, but to leave untouched its historic patina. Even today, as it lies in state below stairs in the new museum, the old smudge is there, by now an indelible part of the stone.

The collections, making their second move, left Berkeley, reached Parnassus Heights across the Bay and were deposited in the empty three-story-plus-basement brick building next door to the hospital of the Medical School. The new quarters were now officially the Museum of Anthropology. Here was room for everything; crates, boxes, and barrels could at last be opened, their contents catalogued, classified, and properly stored. There was office and work space. The museum dream appeared close to becoming a reality: for the present there was a storage museum and a center for anthropological activity other than teaching, which would stay in Berkeley. Mrs. Hearst paid all salaries and expenses during the first years of the museum and department—for research, expeditions, museum and office staff from director to janitor as well as for the teaching staff in Berkeley. The university supplied only the museum building; Mrs. Hearst saw to its furnishing.

It was on the advice of Julia Nuttal, the Mexican archaeologist and personal friend of the Wheelers, that Mrs. Hearst had engaged F. W. Putnam, director of the Peabody Museum at Harvard, as over-all director. The arrangement with Putnam was unusual as were many of Mrs. Hearst's arrangements and, like the others, humane and workable. Although a distinguished scholar, Putnam was under the necessity of seeking suppementary appointment since his Harvard salary came from the Peabody endowment which provided only a nominal income. The arrangement was that Putnam should direct the new museum from the distance of Cambridge for nine months of the year, coming to San Francisco for the summer months. This insured for Mrs. Hearst the best advice in the new venture and for Putnam a living without the former necessity of going weekly to New York City where he was curator of anthropology in the American Museum. Putnam came to San Francisco for the summers of 1902 and 1903. Then a severe angina kept him home for the next five years; his 1908 trip was his last as he retired the following year. During the years 1901-1908, Kroeber, in *de facto* charge, reported by mail once each week to Putnam who answered him with equal regularity. Whenever Kroeber was in the East he went to Cambridge where he would be the Putnams' house guest and where for two or three days, whatever time there was, the young museum man and the old one conferred, discussed, made decisions. It was a peculiarly harmonious accommodation which most administrators would assume would not work. But it did work, and in allowing it President Wheeler showed his wisdom. He expected Kroeber to be the eventual director of the museum; the Putnam years would give him time and experience needed before the multiple responsibilities of a research and teaching institution should be wholly his.

The beginning setup of the museum and department lasted only a few years but those beginnings were different enough from the usual university pattern to deserve some description. Their tone determined many later attitudes and habits long after department and museum were wholly incorporated into the university complex and were become as regular almost as a philosophy or history department. The museum was unlike any other museum: its first preparator and first guard were two men who had for a lifetime been part of the Hearst household staff. They were Mrs. Hearst's pensioners, loyal to her and to the possessions under their care in the museum. Mrs. Hearst was particular that they should live as comfortably as they were accustomed to with her: she paid for heating the museum building for several years after she had had to withdraw all other support. The rooms were decently and adequately furnished with sleeping space for the two museum employees and occasional overnight guests; and there was a small kitchen. It was a rule of the museum, which was neither earthquake-proof nor fire-proof, that it be continuously occupied day and night. This was no hardship to the two who regularly lived in, because it was more economical and pleasanter for them than living out.

During those years on Parnassus Heights, the museum was not open to the public. It was nonetheless the frequent scene of Mrs. Hearst's and the Wheelers' receptions, occasioned by the arrival of specimens of unusual interest. The Hearst corps of butler, cooks, and maids catered these parties, using the museum kitchen for coffee-making and for keeping food hot. Swank carriages and automobiles would be parked outside at such times, and the rustle of Mrs. Hearst's purple taffetas and the silks and ruffles of other San Francisco ladies swished among the packing boxes, while crystal, candles, and silver sparkled on the deal tables brought out from the preparators' rooms.

Kroeber's title was that of instructor, but he was brought to the university in the first instance as curator-custodian of Mrs. Hearst's collections and as a research scholar to specialize in California Indian languages and cultures. During his first weeks he spent part of his time at the Hearst home in Pleasanton—Hacienda del Pozo de Verona—where he catalogued and identified Mrs. Hearst's various collections, this early visit to be followed by later ones. President Wheeler thought it might be good if Kroeber were to give occasional public talks in San Francisco, or perhaps a regular course at the university. Kroeber should decide which he preferred. After thinking it over alone in the Eddy Street room, Kroeber said he would like to give a course at the university. The president showed some disappointment over this choice, but the choice stood, Kroeber offering a two-hour seminar once a week for one semester of the first year of instruction in the new department.

Wheeler's preference for having at least one straight research professor reveals a canny foreknowledge that he would meet resistance in the years ahead in persuading some of the regents and the legislature to such appointments, which nonetheless would have to be made if first rank among institutions of learning were to be sought and held. Since Mrs. Hearst was for the present paying Kroeber's salary, Wheeler saw an opportunity to get the principle and concept established.

Despite the one course, Kroeber was almost wholly a research professor during those early years. His notebooks indicate he was in the field well over half of the time between 1901 and 1907. But his decision to teach, to have undergraduate student contacts, to learn teaching in a situation so different from that of Columbia's graduate school, was sound. Boas had shown him that an anthropologist could and should do both teaching and research; Kroeber was a conscientious curator, but the monklike retreat of the preparator's room, a refuge for the wholly introverted, wholly committed museum man was not for him. It was the ethnological field of face-to-face contact, not the archaeological field, which drew him, and he wanted also the experience of student confrontation. It was in the classroom he honed the edges of his thinking and it was there he discovered anthropologists of the future.

Goddard took the daily responsibility for the department in Berkeley, since Kroeber was regularly at the museum. Each began his career teaching a single course one semester of each year. In 1906 Kroeber was made assistant professor, and a third man—Thomas Talbot Waterman—was added as instructor at Berkeley. Waterman was a linguistics student of Goddard's who went on to get his Ph.D. under Boas at Columbia; his interests and training were also linguistic-ethnographic. His appointment meant the teaching department was growing; it also meant a third man was in the field as much of the time as he could manage.

Meanwhile, on Parnassus Heights the collections continued to be unpacked, and shelves and racks of trays were built to hold the specimens: the housekeeping of a museum was under way, and a particularly demanding sort of housekeeping it was. Dust, grease, sun, too-moist air, too-dry air, rust, moths, woodworms, basket beetles, too-strong soaps, chemicals and disinfectants, too-coarse brushes, breakage, mislabeling—these were a few of the commoner hazards to be guarded against. Requiring a combination of deftness with repetitious patience, not everyone is suited to museum work. The best preparator in the early days was Robert Warburton, a retired petty officer of the British Navy. Cleanliness and orderliness had become second nature to him in the service where he learned also to turn his hand to carpentering, sewing, repairing anything from steam pipes to chair legs, and, as he found in the museum, even to Greek amphorae.

He once shook his head over a young man who visited Kroeber and declared his intention to become a Peruvianist. Warburton stood impassively by while the young man examined the finest Nasca pots in the collections. When he was gone and Warburton was putting the pots away, he remarked to Kroeber, "That man will never be an archaeologist. He picks up a specimen in *one* hand; he sets it on the *edge of the table*."

Specimens in a scientific museum must be stored so they are available for study; they must be catalogued and cross-referenced. Automation has probably changed the old accession routine which went in this fashion: upon arrival, a new specimen was at once entered in the accessions catalogue, thereby receiving its first and ultimately identifying number no matter how many later data it might accumulate. This original entry was handwritten, in a strong and legible hand and in India ink, the writer initialing his entry, as a permanent record of the person who signed it into the museum. The original numbers were in chronological order indicating sequence of accession regardless of provenience and other relations. There followed the accession date and a briefly identifying phrase, and last the name of the donor or expedition or field trip by which it had reached its museum destination. Kroeber regarded the accessions entry as being to a specimen what a birth certificate is to a person, and the accessions catalogue as the museum's Bible.

Since the museum had no exhibition halls, the specimens were stored on open shelves where they were most available. The numbers of shelves and trays increased; the specimens stood ever closer. There was a light earthquake one day, enough to rattle the windows and knock over a piece or two. Inquiry by Kroeber discovered to him what he had not known: that the main San Andreas earthquake fault runs only a little way out to sea, close to the Western Addition in San Francisco, hence close to Parnassus Heights at the westernmost edge of the addition. Warburton and his assistants spent the next several days stringing copper wires in front of specimens from support to support of the shelves, and the next several weeks whenever they had time, anchoring individual pieces by copper wires to shelf and wall.

Nearly two years later came April 18, 1906, and at 5:12 A.M. the San Francisco earthquake. The Eddy Street hotel withstood the shake, but downtown San Francisco was a shambles. Concerned over what might have happened at the museum, Kroeber could not get through by telephone, either to the museum or to the hospital next door. He went to Market Street—no streetcars were moving. He started up Market on foot. It is not much more than three miles from downtown San Francisco to the Heights, but walking over heaps of rubble, wary of toppling cornices as the earth continued to quiver from its great convulsion, and encountering distraught people in need of help or who wanted to talk, did not make for speed. It took him two hours to come in sight of the museum. All buildings on the Heights were standing; the museum had suffered only some displacement of its front stoop and a tumbled chimney. As Kroeber went up the flight of steps leading to the building, he heard the tap tap of a typewriter inside. He called: didn't they know there had been an earthquake? In answer, the museum secretary appeared at the window. She had sent the two old guards next door when she arrived and had then gone calmly on with her work. With Warburton who came soon after, Kroeber went from attic to basement. A few stone pieces had fallen over, there was some breakage in the trays where each piece was not separately secured—nothing irreparable. Their earlier precautions had saved the collections for the present; as for the aftershocks and fire, there was little they could do. Before leaving, Kroeber saw both secretary and Warburton out. They promised to stay out until the earth had settled once more. Parnassus Heights was fortunate; the western addition did not burn, at least not beyond Golden Gate Park, and no following shakes were severe enough to further damage building or specimens. The less fortunate Academy of Sciences burned to the ground and with it its library and collections; and before Kroeber returned from the museum to his downtown room, his hotel and all his personal possessions and his professional library had become part of the city's ashes.

With the earthquake in mind, Kroeber suggested to Mrs. Hearst that enclosed cases would have many advantages over open storage, for earthquake protection and general preservation of the specimens. She authorized him to begin the building of hardwood cases. They were made to the measure of the specimens they were to hold, could be locked when not in use, were dust-proof, and almost invulnerable to other specimen enemies, thus reducing the frequency of handling and treating. Piece by piece as Warburton got to it, whole collections found a place within the new cases, most of them visible behind clear plate glass fronts or tops. As this job of housing the materials of the museum neared completion, Kroeber began to wonder why the public should not be allowed to come to the museum to see these remarkable objects of new and old world art and archaeology. Why not, indeed?

In October 1911 the Museum of Anthropology opened its doors to the public, the opening preceded by a formal reception to regents, faculty, friends of the university, directors of some eastern and European museums, official government representatives, and personal friends of Mrs. Hearst and the Wheelers. The reception was a happy augury for the museum, which was open for public exhibition from that day in October 1911 to the summer of 1931 when it closed, the building having been preempted for the growing Medical School next door.

As the museum was opening its doors to the public, its private doors were closing on its first and crucial era: Mrs. Hearst's support and influence were at an end, which ending came gradually and was not of her choosing nor President Wheeler's. As early as 1904, the Home Stake Mine in South Dakota, a principal source of Mrs. Hearst's fortune, was shut down for some months while an extensive job of retimbering was done. Some retrenchment in spending, begun then, became more severe. These were also the years when Mrs. Hearst's only son and heir to the Hearst fortune, William Randolph Hearst, was spending prodigiously, building his newspaper empire. By 1908 Mrs. Hearst was no longer financing foreign expeditions. She relinquished all salary payments except to Putnam, who had only one year more before retirement, and to her own two employees still in the museum.

Kroeber and the rest of the academic and non-academic staff in anthropology became regular and full employees of the university.

Between 1908 and 1911 the university assumed financing of local field work originating within anthropology and appointed one research fellow each year, usually a local student, sometimes one from another college or museum.

By 1913 Mrs. Hearst's support was a thing of the past—not so her interest. To the end of her life—she died in 1919—she held to her dream of sometime building her museum; she died confident that her heirs would do so; provision and instructions to that effect were in her will. (Her son decided instead to build for the university its present women's gymnasium, replacing the original one built by his mother which had burned down.) Mrs. Hearst's interest and financing brought anthropology—department and museum and research-directed staff—to the West Coast years earlier and on a more broadly programed scale than could have happened without such assets. Her warm and immediate enthusiasm for everything Kroeber and the staff undertook launched the new department in style and with brio.

There were lean years following her withdrawal, but the museum as well as research and teaching were sufficiently established to survive the lean years without too serious loss of momentum or enthusiasm or work results. From the time it took over, the university gave some research funds each year, however small; those who received them learned to economize, expecting nothing beyond bare living expenses and an opportunity to do field work. Under such terms, five or six hundred dollars were enough to put a young ethnologist in the field for a good part of a year; and a few hundred dollars

Alfred, 1911.

kept Kroeber, Waterman, and others of the staff in the field during the summers and month-long Christmas recesses of the old university calendar, or brought an informant to live in the museum, occupying the quarters fitted out by Mrs. Hearst, where the staff and students could work with him during the school term.

Back to 1906 and to Kroeber. Like most San Franciscans, he stayed in the burning city after the earthquake. With thousands of others, he slept out, or rather kept vigil to help stamp out the sparks which blew from the heart of the fire, threatening to start new blazes and to incinerate the camping grounds in parks and cemeteries. He took temporary rooms close to the museum. As fast as military sanitary and fire departments allowed them, squatters' huts appeared among the ruins. Here families lived who had no other home—few chose to leave their old neighborhood. Before the winter rains of 1906 came, and despite land and building speculation which ran up the price of food as well as of materials, the city was being raised from the rubble and ashes of its destruction with all the élan and frenetic enthusiasm of the old gold-rush days. Faster than could have been predicted it became itself once more, a white peninsular city with ocean to the west, bay to the east, and the Golden Gate at its northern tip; a place of baroque chateau-like inflammable wooden houses, built narrowly wall to wall up and down the steep hills; each house set to catch its private bit of ocean view and precious sunshine through bellied bay windows.

HENRIETTE ROTHSCHILD

Kroeber's life, too, was expanding and building. Two

months after the earthquake, in June 1906, he and Henriette Rothschild were married. Their new address was 2848 Washington Street, the lower floor of a duplex whose own bay window looked south into the western addition and whose back door opened into a small enclosed garden. Kroeber and Henriette had become acquainted some months earlier at a Folklore Society meeting where Kroeber was the speaker for the evening.

Hugo, Henriette's father, was born in Rottweil, Württemberg; Fanny, her mother, in London. Hugo owned a flourishing candy factory and was beginning to invest in city property. In the old pictures, Hugo looks benign, Fanny has the English heartiness and durability, and Henriette does not resemble either parent. She was a person of temperament whose slim fragility and passionate cast of features must have come down to her from some eastern ancestral strain. An only child, she had gone to a San Francisco school for girls and then to the Academy of Music to study piano. She had been to England and Germany to visit relatives, and in Germany she took some further instruction in piano and musicology. Twenty-nine years old when they were married, Henriette was considered to have talent and dash. The auguries for the marriage were happy ones.

The Rothschilds, their relatives and friends, were predominantly Jewish but no one worried that a Gentile was married to one of them; they did not think seriously in such categories. Henriette herself moved in the company of the city's artists and intellectuals among whom were some Berkeley and Stanford professors. This was Kroeber's group also, not too unlike that of his New York years, one difference being that the young intellectuals of San Francisco, a small

Alfred, 1906.

Henriette Rothschild, 1904.

city, tended to be a single not a multiple entity and of more varied ethnic makeup—the Jewish and German only two of many strains, Anglo-Saxon, Spanish, French, Chinese-Hawaiian. San Francisco has always drawn her people from various and faraway places.

During the summer of 1906 Henriette went with Kroeber to the Klamath River; she accompanied him on other field trips, collecting folk tales sometimes, some of which were later published under her name. At home, the modest salary of an assistant professor allowed for a part-time maid; Henriette continued with her music study and there was time as well for old and new friends who found the Kroeber dinner table a place of good food and good talk. Life was interesting and the future held much promise. So passed two years.

In July 1908 Hugo Rothschild died suddenly of a stroke, and a few months later, Henriette became seriously ill. The doctor thought it was the tiredness of a not robust person, the result of the strain of her father's death, and her concern for her mother who took his death very hard. The extra rest on which he insisted and some weeks away at a quiet resort with Kroeber did not help; she lost weight, coughed, was tired. By the end of the year her illness was diagnosed—she had tuberculosis.

Thus began a cruel five-year-long agony for Henriette, for Kroeber, and for Fanny. Henriette was taken to one sanitorium, to another; she was brought home where she wanted to be; she was taken to the pure desert air of Arizona; she kept to the recommended diets and regimes, all the hopeless round familiar to anyone who has been in the heart of a family when the killer strikes. Fanny, who could be emotional and unreasonable when nothing too much was at stake, was everything one person can be during illness or other disaster: she was nurse when Henriette was home; she was the person who kept some meaning and order in Kroeber's life when Henriette was hospitalized away from home.

Hugo had left a comfortable estate to Fanny, but it was not yet settled when Henriette became ill nor could it in any case have borne the burden of the medical costs. James Rosenberg and Joseph Proskauer, Kroeber's old friends in New York, helped; Mrs. Hearst's personal nurse came from time to time to give Fanny relief; the doctor in charge was a close friend who did what he could to mitigate the cost burden. For the rest, Kroeber went heavily into debt.

There were times of seeming recovery when hope ran high, but Henriette died in the early spring of 1913. She was thirty-six years old; Kroeber would be thirty-seven in June.

Services were at Temple Emanu-el, burial in the Home of Peace cemetery. Kroeber took Fanny home and then, by himself, took a streetcar which went along the bluff of the south side of the Golden Gate to the ocean. He walked down the beach on the wet sand where the surf breaking over the rocks and against the shore drowned out other sounds; within the rhythm of the reiterated ebb and return of the breaking waves the solitary man pondered the multiple patterns of the universe. As for the pattern he believed each life must have, he saw his own as torn, disordered, without design or meaning. He turned inland away from the wet shore sand, back over the dunes, on into Golden Gate Park, walking, walking. At last he reached the museum. Inside his office, buffeted, weary, he sat at his desk, his hands idle, his mind blank.

ISHI

There came to him as he sat there the silken sound of tiny particles of falling flakes of glass from the next room where someone was at work—Ishi. Kroeber went next door. A barefoot but otherwise ordinarily dressed Indian sat on a piece of canvas tarpaulin, expertly fashioning an obsidian arrowhead with a chipper made of the antler of a deer. Ishi smiled a greeting but did not stop the rapid flaking stroke; he was used to having this friend of his sit beside him, watching him at work.

Ishi and Kroeber had been friends for almost two years; the beginnings of the friendship were strange indeed. On August 29, 1911, the city papers headlined the taking into custody of a wild Indian found naked, emaciated, and lost outside Oroville, a mining town on the Feather River in northern California. Kroeber telephoned the sheriff at Oroville who confirmed the story; the sheriff had put the Indian in jail not knowing what else to do with him since no one around town could understand his speech or he theirs. Kroeber arranged to have Professor Waterman go to Oroville the next day. With the help of a vocabulary gathered some years earlier, Waterman was able to make himself understood. It was as he and Kroeber had surmised before he left; the wild man was a Yana Indian.

Within a few days the Department of Indian Affairs authorized the sheriff to release the wild man to the custody of Kroeber and the museum staff. Waterman arrived in the city with him and Ishi was soon settled in one of the museum rooms furnished earlier by Mrs. Hearst. The whole staff concentrated on learning to communicate with him, meanwhile trying to reassure him and to protect him from the curiosity of the crowds who daily tried to get a closer look at him. It was during those first days Kroeber gave him the name Ishi, which means *man* or *one of the people* in Yana, thus satisfying the popular need to call him by name and saving Ishi the embarrassment of telling of his actual private name to a stranger and hearing it used by other strangers, such use of a personal name being taboo to California Indians.

Ishi was the last of his tribe, the others having been exterminated by the white men who first penetrated Yana land at the time of the Gold Rush, either killed outright by shooting or hanging, or indirectly by forcible removal from their villages to die en route or to be sold singly as slaves and to lose all identity. With a handful of his people—all that were left—Ishi had spent forty of his some fifty years of life in hiding from the whites, three of those years wholly alone, the last of his companions having died, probably, in 1908.

Ishi was the last wild Indian in North America in the sense that his life up to 1911 was passed wholly within a Stone age culture. Living in the brushy foothills and deep canyons of his own old land, barely fifteen miles from the nearest white settlements, he was without white contacts or tools or foods or animals and with little knowledge of their customs other than their use of the gun and the noose. His tools were of flint, obsidian, wood; his weapons the bow and arrow, harpoon and sling; he was a hunter and gatherer; his way of life was the Yana Way. He was also a remarkable human being. Despite the lonely, frightening, and tragic years behind him and despite the extreme contrast between the old life and the new one in San Francisco, he made an adjustment to the Iron Age and to the white man's ways, which continues to confound and intrigue people. And however fearful and timid he was in the strange world where he found himself, Ishi never lost the sense of his own identity. He always knew who he was: a well-born Yana to whom belonged a land and Gods and a Way of Life. These were truths learned in childhood; one lived by them and according to them and at the end one would travel the trail to the west out of the white man's world to the Yana Land of the Dead, there to rejoin one's family and friends and ancestors.

Since coming to the museum he had learned many things. He knew—no one better—that a match is a firelighter superior to the fire drill; that from steel and iron could be fashioned tools which enormously lightened and speeded many familiar tasks. He had believed all white men to be murderers, the killers of his people. Now he knew this was not so, that many white men regarded a gun as he did, as an instrument of violence, of bad hunting practice, and of disruption. He used freely the white man's matches, saws, fishing tackle, money, and artifacts; he never touched the white man's gun. In the museum and after a while outside it, he made friends with white people whom he knew to be good, whose ways he could comprehend and accept. Kroeber, Waterman, and Saxton Pope, head of surgery in the Medical School next door, were his closest friends. Ishi taught Dr. Pope to shoot the Yana bow and arrow, from which beginning the doctor went on to the English bow and other bows; to writing several monographs on hunting with the bow and arrow; and to big-game hunting in Africa with Art Young. Pope began the renaissance in archery in this country as a present-day sport and hobby.

Kroeber and Ishi saw each other daily. Between Ishi's gradually learned English and Kroeber's Yana, they talked, worked, laughed together comfortably and, before long, intimately. Ishi was at the reception which opened the museum to the public. Kroeber introduced him to many white men and women that day, and in the days after the party to many more. They came, young and old, to see him, to touch him. He did not much like the touching but he courteously shook hands, this being the custom. Sometimes on Sunday afternoons, with Kroeber to introduce him and interpret for him, he sang Yana songs or chipped and flaked an arrowhead or made fire with his fire drill for the people who continued to come to see him at the museum. He no longer feared these people so long as his friend was beside him.

Sometimes he went to Kroeber's home for dinner; he knew Henriette; he knew of her illness, of her death; he would never speak of these matters, his sure tact reinforced by inexorable Yana custom; neither would he forget them.

Sitting beside him that day in 1913 while Ishi worked, Kroeber thought of Ishi's first coming to the museum, of their growing friendship. He recalled that after a few days Ishi was at work making Yana objects for the museum so that outside worlds would know something of his own Yana world; how almost at once he began the fashioning of a new life pattern suited to himself and his new friends and surroundings. And he thought, humbly, how much then and now Ishi was dependent upon his, Kroeber's, strength and friendship and interest in this new life.

Through the few words they exchanged, through the comfortable silences between the words, he felt Ishi trying to help him in his own loss, to comfort him, to transmit to him something of the strength and wisdom of his own Yana faith. There was much unfinished work for him and Ishi to do. There was other unfinished work in the full notebooks next door and, farther away, with people about to disappear from the earth as had the Yana, their customs and language unrecorded.

Kroeber returned to his own room, to his desk. He took from the safe one of the Yurok notebooks. He worked for an hour, for two hours, the stubborn grammar imposing order on the writing hand, the directing brain. He put his work aside at last. The sun had set long since. He was exhausted, but relatively at peace. He had discovered, with Ishi's help, an anodyne—work—which from that day would rescue him when grief, worry, the agony of living threatened to engulf and overwhelm him.

The chapter in Kroeber's life which opened his professional career and brought him to the West Coast was now finished. Henriette's death marked its ending with an emotional jar which it would not otherwise have had, but the end would in any case have come, her death making it appear more abrupt, more absolute than it in fact was. Many of the personal and professional commitments of the years 1900-1913 were of course a continuation of earlier ones but they were distinctive and some of them were new. Nor is it always possible to say this one was personal, that professional, the nature of the work of a field anthropologist being such that the distinctions are not helpful to an understanding of his personality. Personal and professional, the period was marked by gradual absorption in a new environment and people, culminating in marriage and close family and friendship and professional ties at the core of the immediate and local life. The ties held for the most part, but never after 1913 were they exclusive and all-embracing as in the early period.

HEGIRA

The year was 1915, the first of a long hegira, as Kroeber once characterized the period in his life from 1915 to 1922. The frightening symptoms accompanying an ear infection jigged dizzily through them; Ishi's death darkened them; psychoanalysis profiled them. The museum and Washington Street were the Mecca from which he set out, but where lay his Medina he was not sure.

ILLNESS

As for the ear infection, its symptoms, commencing during Henriette's illness, included vertigo, nausea, buzzing in the head, fierce headaches, and impairment of hearing in the left ear. Because the doctors who examined him, both in San Francisco and in New York, knew that the first appearance of the disease was under conditions of prolonged and continuous nervous strain and exhaustion, they diagnosed it as a neurasthenia. They were not successful in doing anything to prevent or ameliorate the seemingly random presences and absences of the various symptoms. Kroeber realized that there was some tendency for a remission of symptoms to coincide with a vacation period, and this along with alarming accompaniments of the vertigo almost persuaded him he either had a brain tumor or was going insane. When the vertigo was severe he moved sideways although he thought he was going straight ahead, and onlookers assumed he was drunk. One of those times, he stumbled and fell to the gutter outside a corner saloon. The saloon-keeper and a policeman carried him into a room behind the bar and when he "came around" gave him coffee and fetched a cab to take him home. After a while he learned that by watching his feet whenever an attack caught him on the street he could walk fairly straight, but it looked peculiar.

He learned to live, albeit uneasily, with his malady, with the sometimes long periods of almost total remission of symptoms and their inevitable return, until at last the day came in 1922 or 1923 when the hearing in his left ear was wholly and permanently gone. Gone were the vertigo, headaches, and all other symptoms. He remained alerted for the beginnings of the same progression in the right ear. Nor was he free of this worrisome expectation until sometime in the thirties when he at last learned the name of the disease—Meunier's—and that its course was such that having lodged in an ear and completed its destructive cycle, there was an end of it for its present victim.

ISHI'S DEATH

It was Ishi and Fanny, Henriette's mother, who bound Kroeber to the city after 1914. Between him and Fanny there was the strongest familial-affectional attachment and as for Ishi, Kroeber was his *Majaupa*, his headman, despite his being the younger of the two, and he was Ishi's closest white friend.

Ishi, 1914.

Alfred, 1914.

He worried about Ishi who, never ill until he came into civilization, was now often seriously unwell. Having no earlier exposure to disease he had no immunity and he caught frequent colds which sometimes turned into a pneumonia. Kroeber and Dr. Pope both feared tuberculosis, and Pope gave Ishi tuberculin shots which were new and I believe experimental at that time.

Ishi seemed entirely well in the spring of 1914 and he, Kroeber, Pope, and Waterman chose this time to satisfy a wish to go together for a month to the old Yana country in the foothills of Mount Lassen in northern interior California. Spring was at its height, an Indian spring with edible roots ready to be dug and lightly cooked, with fruit needing only to be picked, and with the early run of steelhead coming up the rivers and into the creeks, which flow full and broad in that country. They fished with Ishi's harpoon and nets, hunted with his bows and arrows. They mapped the old trails and villages of Yana days, recording their Yana names and the names of caves, canyons, hills, streams, animals, and plants. They had a marvelous time, living as nearly like Yana Indians as Ishi considered it safe for these white friends of his to do. They came home reluctantly, and with full notebooks and a precious picture record. The photographs show that Kroeber, a year and more away from Henriette's death, was beginning to move out of his twilight zone of pain and loss.

A year later, in the spring of 1915, Kroeber had a full sabbatical year ahead of him. He hesitated to spend it away from home because of Fanny and Ishi and because it seemed to him an extravagance. Saxton Pope, his physician as well as his friend, was adamant: he must go and for the full year; there were no barriers to his going except his own doubts; there was work for him for as much time as he wanted to put in at both the Natural History Museum in New York City and the Smithsonian Institution in Washington, D. C.

Thus it came about that he saw Fanny off on a trip with friends who were taking her to the Hawaiian Islands and said goodbye to Ishi in Berkeley. Ishi was living for the summer with the Waterman family where Edward Sapir, the linguist, would be coming in a few weeks to work with him, recording Ishi's Yahi dialect of the Yana language. As soon as classes were over Kroeber boarded a Santa Fé train bound for the Southwest where he spent the summer, going in September to New York and then on to Europe, to return in February 1916, to Washington and the Smithsonian. He wrote Ishi and sent him pictures and souvenirs from wherever he was, and Gifford or Waterman answered for Ishi. But after Kroeber was back from Europe and settled in Washington for the last months of his sabbatical, Pope wrote to inform him of what he had not known—that Ishi was seriously ill. He had in fact not been well since the end of summer, which had begun so happily with the Watermans. They noticed that he was eating very little and appeared listless and tired. Interrupting the work with Sapir, they brought Ishi to the hospital where Pope found what he and Kroeber had most dreaded, a rampant tuberculosis. Pope did not say that he scarcely expected Ishi to last till summer, but emphasized rather that Kroeber was not to cut his year short, that everything possible was being done, and that the patient was as cheerful and comfortable as could be expected; Pope was even able to report several weeks of seeming improvement. When Ishi became worse in March it was too late for Kroeber to come home before Ishi died on March 16, 1916.

Kroeber was in touch by letter, telegraph, and telephone, following from a distance with grief and sometimes bitterness the events of those last days. There was a strong feeling at the hospital that there should be extensive examinations and autopsy, the brain preserved, and the skeleton kept. Kroeber was passionately determined that in his death Ishi's body should be handled according to Yahi custom and belief. He wrote to Gifford, "If there is any talk of the interests of science, say for me that science can go to hell. We propose to stand by our friends." Gifford did what he could: there was a simple autopsy and Pope made a death mask, a very beautiful one. The body was cremated, which was according to the custom of Ishi's people. The ashes were placed in a Hopi pottery jar, which was as close as Gifford could approximate to the Yahi custom of deposition in a rock cairn. Pope, Gifford, Waterman, and two anthropologists from the East who were Ishi's friends attended the simple commitment service.

Kroeber, reading Gifford's letter giving these details, glanced at the calendar on his desk: it was six days since the burial. Ishi had once explained to him that it took the Spirit, released by the funeral flames, five risings and settings of Sun to travel west down the Trail of the Dead to the Land of the Yahi ancestors: Ishi would already have traveled that trail; he was indeed gone from Kroeber's world.

(In the fifties when I undertook to write Ishi's biography, Kroeber was the only person still living who had been close to him; he was my principal informant, supplementing with his own accuracy of memory and personal knowledge of the facts the meagre and sometimes contradictory source materials. He answered fully and patiently the questions I asked and corrected my own wrong interpretations, but did not otherwise participate in the work. This was, to be sure, the teacher keeping his finger out of the student's pie. It was more than that: the old sense of pain and hurt returned with these recollections as readily as the indubitably happy and comic and fulfilling memories. I knew then that Kroeber would never have written Ishi's biography. He had lived too much of it, and too much of it was the stuff of human agony from whose immediacy he could not sufficiently distance himself.)

CHANGING PERSPECTIVE ON HIS PROFESSION

Until 1914, Kroeber had been doing field work in California and nowhere else. Between 1900 and 1908 the recording of ethnographic data and languages at the village, face-to-face level took precedence over any other activity. By 1914 he knew this land, these people, more intimately than had anyone before him or has anyone after him, more intimately than he would know any other land and people. The Indians of California were in his bones: the tensely beautiful coastal northerners on their wild and wooded seacoast; the most typical of Californians, round-faced and even-tempered, in the long interior valleys and the hills; the tall, heavy-boned, expressive people of the Colorado River.

Beginning in 1908 with Putnam's retirement, Kroeber was given full responsibility for direction of the museum, and after 1911 for exhibition of its materials. In 1912 Edward Gifford joined the permanent staff and began to learn from and with Kroeber how to display the materials of ethnographic collections. Task by task, week by week, Gifford took over the housekeeping of the museum and was soon organizing the talks and tours of exhibits for adults and school children.

It was with a sense of relief that Kroeber saw his young assistant assume the museum routines which had been his: he left its daily running to him increasingly, for Gifford was by temperament a museum man. Kroeber was not: he was meticulous in his care of the collections, orderly and businesslike in its bookkeeping and administration; he respected and advanced the role of the museum in the university and the community; and he enjoyed setting up exhibits that were aesthetically satisfying and scientifically and historically meaningful. But for him the daily confrontation must be of people, and as humanist, not as administrator. He would remain the active director of the museum until his university retirement, but the years of intimate daily involvement were the San Francisco years.

In 1911, and again in 1914, Kroeber taught summer session at Columbia University and during both of these years he visited in Cambridge, Massachusetts, at the Harvard Peabody Museum, and in Chicago at the university and the Field Museum. Roland Dixon, Chairman of the Department of Anthropology at Harvard, offered him an associate professorship there, and the Field Museum was in correspondence with him about a curatorship. In 1911, Kroeber was still deep in California ethnography; in 1914 he wavered. In a letter to Dixon he says, "I could close out honorably in California: the museum's prospects are not large and it is being well run under Gifford's curatorship; a sabbatical year or a summer now and then would suffice for my future field work in California, besides, I am thinking of work beyond California." In the end, he stayed.

Pacing the growing community role of the museum was the growing university role of the teaching department in Berkeley. Kroeber's original teaching load of a single two-hour seminar one semester of each year was increased to one course each semester in 1907 and from that time he regularly spent Tuesdays and Thursdays in Berkeley. With Waterman added to the teaching staff, the numbers of students taking anthropology grew as did the variety of courses offered; the activities in Berkeley absorbed more and more of Kroeber's time and thought. He was chairman of the department as well as director of the museum, and by 1910 was spending three days of the week in Berkeley. The catalogue of courses for the years under discussion shows Kroeber's changing orientation. For example, course 103A-B was called in 1910 *Descriptive Ethnography* and covered Asia, Europe, Africa, and Oceania. In 1912 it became *History of Civilization.* The same countries were included but the emphasis was changed from ethnographic-geographic to that of culture history. By 1913 the course was expanded to four semesters and ancient Egypt was added to the list of special areas. Beginning in 1914 he was spending four of the five teaching days in Berkeley.

Two courses which Kroeber offered in those years were *Anthropology of the Bible* and *War.* The course on war did not survive long: by the time the United States was at war, analysis of the anthropology and psychology of war was probably considered ill-timed if not subversive, and Kroeber discontinued the Bible course in 1921 as he began to develop the fuller aesthetic-historic approach which he would refine in *History of Civilization* and in later courses.

1914/15

Kroeber began and ended his sabbatical year 1914/15 in Zuni, New Mexico, with two summers of work—his first departure from the California field since the commencement of his work there. These were good summers. Elsbeth, his sister, joined him; they lived in two houses in the pueblo, rented from one of Kroeber's informants. They slept on the roof reached by way of an inside ladder and a hole in the roof; they bought a pot of beans and a loaf of bread and fresh garden vegetables from their neighbors, making their own coffee and cooking the fresh corn and squash and beans over an open mesquite fire as did the Zuni.

Leslie Spier and Elsie Clews Parsons, anthropologists whom Kroeber had known only slightly until then, were in the Southwest part of this time. During the second summer Kroeber recorded the beginning words and phrases of a twenty-two-months-old baby, who was his informant for the monograph "Speech of a Zuni Child," the first linguistic study of the sort. There were Navaho silversmiths at work in Zuni. Kroeber came to know them and through them others of their tribe, and he visited the Hopi pueblos and made friends there. But the peoples he would know best and most feel for in the Southwest would be the Zuni. Years later he and Clyde Kluckhohn, an anthropologist and Navaho specialist, would argue their separate preferences, rationalizing them and revealing some of their own temperamental biases.

IN EUROPE

In late August of 1915, Kroeber sailed from Hoboken to Rotterdam on a Holland-America liner, traveling first class on a third-class ticket, which his cousin Clara Grelle was able to arrange, her husband Johan Wierdsma being an owner of the line and the ship sailing half-empty because of the war. The Wierdsmas met him at the boat and took him to their home in Rotterdam. Sitting over dinner exchanging family news, Kroeber was conscious of a continuous distant noise, like the thunder storms over Zuni or the composite roar of the city of New York, sharp enough at times that conversation stopped until the noise lessened. The cousins shrugged —it was the Boches, they said, the bombardment of German guns shooting into France along a line forty miles distant from Rotterdam at its nearest point. Kroeber had gone to Europe partly in an attempt to understand what history was in the making. Close up, it seemed to him that the whole of Western culture was in process of a violent undoing, that this war was the beginning of the end of the pan-European humanism into which Goethe's incandescent genius had drawn Germany, late but surely. It was now being blown to the dust of a dream with each deeper thrust into France of the guns of the Prussian *Wehrmacht*.

He went to the Dutch cities, universities, art galleries, and museums. Then he continued on to Germany where he visited relatives in Munich and elsewhere. In Berlin he met ethnographers whom he had known by correspondence only. Here he studied the magnificent museum collections of ancient Peruvian material—his own museum had equally fine Peruvian collections gathered by Max Uhle for Mrs. Hearst. From Germany he went to Austria. Vienna was the intellectual center of Europe in those days, imbued with a sense of urgency and excitement, particularly in medicine, psychology, and psychoanalysis. Despite the war, these subjects and ethnographic theories, some of them bizarre, could yet be discussed endlessly in cafés over coffee or wine. He left Vienna reluctantly to go to Basle, thence back to Rotterdam. France accepted no visitors coming from Germany or Austria, but England did. So to England he went, after giving assurance to the British consulate that he would not return to the Continent but would go to the United States at the end of his stay in England. He visited in London, at Oxford and at Cambridge.

In Europe, Kroeber's person and baggage were courteously but expertly searched each time he crossed or recrossed a border. Otherwise he traveled without surveillance or questioning or incident across and in five countries, three at war and two engaged in an involved neutrality. His German name, his fluent German, the relatives he visited in each of the five countries—his own and the Rothschilds'—the meetings with scientists and other scholars some of whom were prominent politicians, caused no riffle of concern to any person or government. Such freedom of movement, such universal unsuspiciousness, did not impress him or others then. By the time of the Second World War the entire journey had become in retrospect a never-never-land expedition.

Sailing from Southampton in time to have Christmas in New York with his family, he came home personally refreshed, excited over what he had learned in Vienna about psychoanalysis, and with a renewed attachment to England. He loved the German language with a profound aesthetic response to its poetic beauty and emotional power, but he never liked Germany, never felt wholly at ease there, and he disliked Berlin. Vienna he became attached to with the fondness one can develop for a foreign city. It was London and its people he loved spontaneously and with a sense of identification, of belonging. He did not feel the alienation from the British which so many Americans suffer in England. Perhaps this alienation is a hazard only of Anglo-Saxon Americans.

MOVE TO BERKELEY

Kroeber was back in Berkeley for the beginning of the fall term, teaching both semesters of the 1916/17 academic year. But the restlessness of the hegira was upon him: he arranged to be on leave again for the following year, a leave made possible through a one-year exchange of jobs with Robert H. Lowie, who was then a curator of ethnology at the American Museum of Natural History in New York City. Six years younger than Kroeber, Lowie too, had taken his doctorate under Boas. Through Elsbeth and Lowie's sister Risa, friends since Barnard College days, Lowie and Kroeber were cordial but not intimate friends. The geographic separation of the exchange might have left the bond between them no closer at the end of the year, except that the Berkeley calendar brought Lowie west some weeks before Kroeber was to leave.

Upon Lowie's arrival Kroeber took him to his home for a long weekend, and by the time he returned him to the Faculty Club in Berkeley, where he would be living for the year, the friendship which would last the rest of their lives was already well begun. One day not long after this, Lowie asked Kroeber why he did not himself live at the Club, two minutes from the Anthropology building, five minutes from the Library. It was a reasonable question to which Kroeber had no ready answer; he said he supposed because of his mother-in-law, Fanny. But he pondered the question on the way back to Washington Street that evening; and when he was home he talked of it with Fanny—the first time they had discussed the possibility of other living arrangements.

It was a fact that he was leaving Fanny a good bit to herself, what with the year in Europe and the one ahead when he would again be away. And more and more of his time in residence was passed in Berkeley: Fanny admitted that she was lonely when he was away, despite her friends, her church, and various activities. And she admitted that the housekeeping wearied her increasingly. In her heart Fanny knew—had known for a long time—that Kroeber should not live on at Washington Street. But he was closer to her than any living blood relative, they were fond of each other and enjoyed being together, and there was a mutual dependence; she dreaded a change.

Kroeber too was reluctant to change—he never easily relinquished any close bond. But Lowie's question had brought up into consciousness a dissatisfaction, an as yet unformulated need for more independence, for a way of life which would better square with the realities of his widower status, leave him more time for the new friends he was making in Berkeley, give him scope to discover where he was going emotionally, personally.

Fanny and Kroeber did not crowd themselves, but after a week or two of discussing, planning, talking things out as was their way, it was settled Fanny should go for the year to a residence hotel downtown where friends of hers were already living. At the last moment she decided to take what furniture she could use with her, and they rented the house unfurnished, storing the extra furniture and Kroeber's books and personal effects in the museum. Before he left for the year Kroeber put a hold on a pleasant westward-facing alcoved room with a fireplace on the first floor of the Faculty Club.

As it turned out, neither of them returned to the Washington Street house. Fanny liked the freedom from responsibility and the sociability of the hotel, her one worry being that she would see little of Kroeber. But in their separate residences they saw more of each other than they had during the last years of his commuting back and forth. He made a habit of taking his out-of-town guests to have dinner with Fanny, and in any case he always dined with her on Friday evenings. They went to the theater together; Fanny invited their old San Francisco friends often for dinner with him, and she kept him in touch through her animated gossipy reports. From 1918 to 1926 the Faculty Club room was Kroeber's home.

PSYCHOANALYSIS

Settled in New York in the autumn of 1917 and at work in the Natural History Museum, Kroeber began a psychoanalysis—his urgent reason for being on leave and in New York. The analyst to whom he went was one of the original group around Freud in Vienna. As I recall it, he was a few years older than Kroeber, and they knew something of each other through their writings and correspondence. In any case, during several sessions together their relation remained that of two scholars in different but related fields engaging in a stimulating give and take conversation.

This was not what Kroeber wanted, however meaningful in itself, and they agreed it might be unnatural and difficult for the two of them to arrive at a genuinely analytic relation. Kroeber went instead to his analyst's son-in-law, also from Vienna, trained I think by Anna Freud; with him Kroeber found the relation and experience he was seeking. (Dr. Heinz Hartman confirms my shaky name memory that the two analysts, now both dead, must have been Dr. Jelliffe and his son-in-law Dr. Stragnell.)

Kroeber's reason for being analyzed was neither simple nor single. He had studied psychology under James Cattell at Columbia—it was his minor subject in preparation for the doctorate. And through the years he had followed with interest the development particularly of clinical psychology. He read Freud from the first appearance of his articles in German, and his weeks in Vienna gave this already established interest much impetus. I do not know that Kroeber ever met Freud, although they corresponded, but from all he knew of him Freud reminded Kroeber of Boas: he noted that they looked considerably alike, were within two years of each other in age, came from similar Jewish intellectual backgrounds, had grown up influenced by the romantic-scientific impulse felt all over the Western world and whose axis in their early years was Central Europe; and were alike in their daemonic drives, large capacities, and ultimate limitations. As Boas had attracted and stimulated Kroeber, so did Freud. Unlike clinical psychology, psychoanalysis takes cognizance of "primitive" man and of the primitive in man: how it uses anthropological and folkloristic concepts and materials must be of interest and concern to anthropologists. So much for the intellectual reasons for Kroeber's analysis. They were real, as his curiosity was immense concerning all aspects of psychoanalysis, but these were not the only nor the principal propulsive reasons, for those reasons were personal.

At forty years of age, Kroeber was questioning as he had not at twenty or thirty the where and why of his professional and personal life. Any thoughtful man is likely to stop in middle age to survey and measure his life and what he has done with it against his earlier expectations and his now maturer disenchantments. With Kroeber, the ear trouble was traumatic in the extreme, but beyond that his personal life had not remolded itself in a meaningful way since 1913 and Henriette's death. He had been living in the spent pattern of Washington Street, not having found his way to another street, another sure attachment, another pattern, but knowing these were what he wanted and must somehow find.

The other source of discontent and worry was that his professional life no longer satisfied him, although it had been fulfilling as his personal life had not. This dissatisfaction grew in part from the times, from the changing face of anthropology itself, but there was a pattern exhaustion, which was personal. Before going east Kroeber had turned over for publication to the Smithsonian Institution in Washington his *Handbook of the Indians of California*, all 995 pages of it. For fourteen of his seventeen years in California the materials of the *Handbook* had been determinative of his way of life, whether in the field or at work with field data. In 1917 he felt the need to step back from this close-up view. He had been covering with pointillist dots a canvas which in the *Handbook* became an enormous design, a completed, infinitely detailed panoramic picture. He was now looking, not for a new ethnographic field to dissect and reassemble as he had done with this one, but for a new perspective on his own work and on anthropology. It was, then, around the peripheries of a broken and not yet reconstituted life pattern and a not yet determined professional redirection that Kroeber's analysis begin. It came to an end, having helped him to penetrate both in depth. As compared with the lengths of today's analyses, his was brief, not extending beyond his time in New York, nine or ten months. But it seems to have been the full experience in its ambivalences, intensities, and revelations. He once told me that the analytic period had been for him a serene and absorbingly interesting one; that perhaps he had felt just enough urgency and pressure to give himself wholly to it without being so seriously disturbed as to inhibit him from reaching complete dream participation and positive response to the dreams and to the analyst. "There may be an optimal degree of need for getting the best results" was his speculation. When I asked him what he "got" from analysis, not over-all or intellectually or theoretically, but in immediate, concrete return, he answered half in fun but only half, "I got over my *Sturm und Drang* which had overtaken me twenty years late. I learned not to be so solemn."

PSYCHOANALYTIC PRACTICE

The year's leave at an end, Kroeber returned to Berkeley and to teaching. He felt no desire to be further analyzed but his mind went on playing, unsatiated, around the phenomenon of psychoanalysis and, startling as this was to people in 1918 and to some people today, he practiced analysis for more than two years.

He did not jettison his career as an anthropologist or lose touch with his job, continuing as active director of the museum and as chairman-on-leave of the department. But he did counter his career with a possible other career; he weighed and reappraised, and ultimately he came back to anthropology, as ultimately he resolved the intellectual and personal crises of his hegira.

He started practicing at the Stanford Clinic where patients were referred to him by two medical doctors who knew him well, Saxton Pope and Henry Harris, and later by other doctors when it was seen that he succeeded beyond their or his own expectations in establishing rapport with the troubled, neurotic, but not overtly psychotic people whom he saw. It was not surprising that he made contact with his patients—he was using in a different environment one of his oldest and sharpest tools—winning the confidence and finally the friendship of people who frequently began with a dubious or hostile mind toward him. He saw patients regularly at the clinic two days a week, through 1918 and into the summer of 1919. Another university term loomed ahead, but the psychoanalytic interest was not yet exhausted.

He took leave from the university and opened an office in San Francisco. There some of his former clinic patients came to him as private patients, and doctors sent new patients, more than he had time for. He learned at first hand from his sicker patients, whose need was more acute than his own had been or was of longer standing, that there could be for

Alfred, 1920.

them no such smooth journey as he had made through and out the far side of the heretofore unexplored tunnels of the mind. Daily confrontation of the crippling neuroses of his patients gave him insight into the neurotic personality and a vast compassionate patience with it.

Until sometime in 1922 he was in his office several days a week, or parts of days, having to adjust his schedule to that of some of his patients, men who worked the conventional eight- or nine-hour day. He managed to continue his direction of the museum, to keep in touch with the department in

Berkeley, and to write. It was not only a crowded life, it was a divided one. He was holding in delicate temporary balance two careers, two ways of life, the while he considered giving up his academic career and going full-time into psychoanalytic practice. At the end of two years he knew he could no longer delay a decision, that full commitment one way or the other was necessary to himself, to satisfy the university, and to do full justice to his patients.

Kroeber had always been aware of the limits beyond which a lay analyst may not venture and after two years of practice he had reached those limits, had felt the restriction upon what he might properly undertake. There came a day when the decision was made. He closed his office, storing its couch, desk, chairs, and bookcases in the museum alongside the personal effects from Washington Street. No crisis, no particular circumstance determined the day when Kroeber said goodbye to his last patient. The *affaire psychologique* was at an end, or rather the active patient and analyst participant phases were at an end, and with the closing of the office the long uncertainty which had kept Kroeber from settling and establishing a physical and an intellectual home place was resolved. Medina was just over the next hill.

PSYCHOANALYSIS IN RETROSPECT

This is not to say that the end came in a day, or a year. He had foreseen it in time to plan for it, taking no new cases and preparing his old patients for termination of their analysis. He continued to see those of his patients who needed him—it was months before the last of them was ready to do without him—but he saw them informally, not at fixed times and not in analytic session. For some, it was a matter of settling them with another analyst or in a few cases with a medical doctor. One patient liked to see him for the rest of his life—his transference may never have been dissolved, but it evolved into a friendship.

Kroeber did not manage badly in detaching his patients from a too great or too lasting dependence on himself, but the metaphor, breaking the transference, bothered him. It implied or imposed a harsh and necessary condition which carried a negative value and was foreign to his ethnological field philosophy, by which the informant-ethnologist relation, if successful, is, like a friendship, a growing one, a bond for the years, for life. He did not fully accept the putative necessity for its break in analysis.

As to his own transference, it had followed a fairly classic course, affirmative enough to make the analyst-patient relation workable. He regretted when the year was up that he would no longer be seeing his analyst, no longer hearing his voice which for him had some special quality. And when, a year and a half after completion of his analysis, he was once again in New York City, he phoned his analyst immediately upon his arrival. The familiar voice answered, pleasant as always, but lacking that special something Kroeber had heard in it before. They talked, but Kroeber did not ask, as he had expected to do, to see him again: he knew in that instant that to do so no longer had urgent meaning to him, that his transference had subsided without pain or awareness—also without giving him any formula or rationale by which he could generalize its dissolution.

Other analysts had warned him he must be prepared for a patchwork and partial cure for most of his patients. He found this to be true; also that neuroses in adults go back to a multiple causation: it is rare for the analyst to have a single devil to exorcise. He felt that he helped most of his patients, succeeded in "curing" a few; that some of them learned with and through him to live with their neuroses without destroying themselves or those about them. Some times this was sufficient reward, but increasingly the real limitations in what psychoanalysis may expectably accomplish left him disappointed, dissatisfied. He had no children as patients—he might have felt differently had he worked with children.

Even as it was, his ambivalences were not all negative. Some were nostalgic and lingered on down the years. Five years after closing his office and when he was adding a study onto the house he then owned he included an outside door from the back garden. Anyone using this door would have entered the study without coming into view from other parts of the house. "This door," said Kroeber, "is for a patient in case I sometime take another patient." From time to time he was asked to take someone for anlaysis and always he was fleetingly tempted to do so. He never did, the door was not used, and in the fifties, wanting more book room, he closed it with built-in shelves.

With notable exceptions the stance of most American anthropologists and psychologists at the time Kroeber was practicing was one of turning the back—of shuddering away from psychoanalysis as not scientifically tenable or respectable. Boas considered Kroeber's interest an unfortunate aberration to be borne patiently. Some younger colleagues were less patient and tolerant. Nonetheless, the next years found many of them, or those who followed them, invoking

Freud, not always critically and knowledgeably, to explain and interpret the most varied social and cultural materials from any part of the world and any time in history.

Kroeber never did this. Two articles, "Totem and Taboo: An Ethnologic Psychoanalysis" (1920) and "Totem and Taboo in Retrospect" (1939) state his evaluation of psychoanalysis in its application to the materials and theory of ethnology and ethnography up to that time. This evaluation did not change much, and not significantly in the years intervening between the two articles which differ in that the tone of vigorous indignation of the early one is replaced in the second by a judicious and perceptive weighing and evaluating. The later one begins:

> Nearly twenty years ago I wrote an analysis of *Totem and Taboo*. . . . It seems an appropriate time to return to the subject.
>
> I see no reason to waver over my critical analysis of Freud's book. There is no indication that the consensus of anthropologists during these twenty years has moved even an inch nearer acceptance of Freud's central thesis. But I found myself somewhat conscience-stricken when, perhaps a decade later, I listened to a student in Sapir's seminar in Chicago making his report on *Totem and Taboo*, who, like myself, first spread out its gossamer texture and then laboriously tore it to shreds. It is a procedure too suggestive of breaking a butterfly on the wheel. An iridescent fantasy deserves a more delicate touch even in the act of demonstration of its unreality.
>
> Freud himself has said of my review that it characterized his book as a *Just So* story. It is a felicitous phrase, coming from himself. Many a tale by Kipling or Anderson contains

> a profound psychological truth. One does not need therefore to cite and try it in the stern court of evidential confrontation.

Later in the same article Kroeber continues:

> The fundamental concepts which Freud formulated—repression, regression and infantile persistences, dream symbolism and overdetermination, guilt sense, the affects toward members of the family—have gradually seeped into general science and become an integral and important part of it. If one assumes that our science forms some kind of larger unit because its basic orientation and method are uniform, these concepts constitute the permanent contribution of Freud and psychoanalysis to general science; and that contribution is large.

So much for the positive side. On the negative side, Kroeber says:

> There is a further set of concepts which in the main have not found their way into science: the censor, the superego, the castration complex, the explanation of specific phenomena. To these concepts the several relevant branches of science—sociology, anthropology, psychology and medicine alike—remain impervious about as consistently as when the concepts were first developed. It may therefore be inferred that science is likely to remain negative to them.

About the Freudian myth of the beginnings of human civilizations, he says at the end of the article:

> It is indicative of the largeness of Freud's mind that, although the sole founder of the movement and the originator of most of its ideas, his very ambiguities in the more

doubtful areas carry a stamp of tolerance. He may persist in certain interpretations: he does not insist upon them; they remain more or less fruitful suggestions. Of this class is his theory of the primary determination of culture. As a construct, neither science nor history can use it; but it would seem that they can both accept and utilize some of the process concepts that are involved in the construct.

I trust that this reformulation may be construed not only as an *amende honorable* but as a tribute to one of the great minds of our day.

It was typical of Kroeber's active experience of psychoanalysis that he kept it in a category apart from anthropology. People are always asking me why he did this. I can only say, he felt them to be properly separate. Anthropology was his public profession; psychoanalysis an intensely private and emotional experience. Nor did he ever pretend to speak as an analyst with the authority he used when speaking as an anthropologist. For a definite and definable period the one offered itself as a substitute for the other: why should he not then have kept them separate? The simile of the permanent marriage as contrasted with an intervening, passionate, but passing *affaire* suggests itself. I offer it in no jocose sense—the separate emotion which each discipline evoked in him, the amount of real and important feeling, the extent of the influence each had on the man, were the stuff of any deeply felt and lived experience. In their so different ways, anthropology and psychoanalysis were two of the most telling confrontations of his life, and in their first impact were antagonistic one to another, calling out different impulses, appealing to different facets of his personality, incompatible one with the other and each more than a little jealous of his interest in the other. In the creative scientist, as in the artist, the grip of his subject is the grip of passion. It is as if personalized in its hold on him, in the emotion it arouses, and causes him to expend as he becomes in turn its discoverer, servant, voice, hand, and at last its master, creating something of his own from its inspiration and materials.

In affirming that Kroeber kept anthropology and psychoanalysis separately compartmented, it would be misleading and inaccurate to say or to imply that psychoanalysis did not change his anthropological thinking. It did, as surely as his view of psychoanalysis was deep-dyed from the anthropological spectrum.

For instance, all American Indians dreamed, but the Mohave and the other Yuman Indians of the Colorado River whom Kroeber studied so understandingly were dreamers *par excellence.* You might say of the Colorado River Indian that his whole life was made manifest through his dreams. His long epic stories with frequent song-cycle interludes were dreamed piecemeal throughout most of the dreamer's life, reaching completion only when he was an old man. A shaman's power, a hunter's prowess, knowledge of the world even to its geography, was revealed in dreams. These Indians began dreaming in the womb and they knew of events, even of the creation of the world, through having been present at them in their dreams. Uninhibited, as full of sexuality as a "Freudian" dream and fuller of history and geography and coherent event, many of the difficult areas of feelings, impulse, and desires were probed by way of the dream. And their dreaming left them in waking life open and friendly, liberal toward divorce, relaxed toward sex, healthily obscene, unpuritanical—it must have been a benign dreaming.

There was a different sort of dreaming with the Yurok Indians along the Klamath River many worlds away from the Mohave. Yurok dreams were directed to the gods of wealth, the keepers of shell money and obsidian. In their dreams as in their prayers the Yurok concentrated their thoughts and emotions on these gods, invoking them with long ritual weeping. The dreamer was hedged about with prohibitions, particularly sex prohibitions. It was through puritanical self-control and self-denial that one acquired power—and wealth—that one's dreams "worked." Tension, taboo, and stricture accompanied the dreamer and his dream and spilled over to affect behavior throughout the whole of the waking world. The Yurok was not released by his dream: it was rewarding in its own Yurok way, but it tended to fix the retentiveness, puritanism, and suspiciousness which were part of the Yurok personality. Psychoanalytically speaking, the Klamath River was closer to the the Danube than to the Colorado River.

Known also to Kroeber, as to all anthropologists, were the Arctic hysteria of Siberian peoples and the endlessly varied dreaming and interpretations of dreams from many places and peoples far removed in space and time from Freud and Vienna, each of them sharing intimately in the development and behavior patterns of their own cultures and personalities. Inevitably, Kroeber felt the impact of Freud differently than would a person less aware than he of the endlessly varied culture adaptations to which man has bent his dreams, his symbols, his myths, and his sexuality.

Over the years there were changes in Kroeber's feelings and attitudes, some conscious, others not, which brought him to his last reactions to psychoanalysis. There was a relaxation of the thinking which insisted on the separateness of anthropology and psychoanalysis. He made comfortable use of the vocabulary and metaphors of analysis when it suited his linguistic and ethnographic purpose. The appearance of the 1939 article "Totem and Taboo in Retrospect" may indeed have triggered the change. Before that, as early as the late twenties, he and two Berkeley psychologists, Edward Tolman and Jean MacFarlane, had experimented with joint seminars in anthropology and psychology. They succeeded in confusing the students while demonstrating to themselves the need for more work in the separate disciplines and a greater store of classified and available data before either subject could be of much use to the other. This is beginning to come: psychoanalysts, psychologists, anthropologists, sociologists, economists, and historians do communicate more fruitfully than they used to.

A few years after these seminars, the analyst Erik Erikson lived for some time in Berkeley. From him and through reading the later literature, Kroeber resolved somewhat his opaqueness of understanding toward the phenomenon of the transference, discovering that fogginess regarding it had been general until long after he had stopped practicing; that Freud, having isolated, named, and more or less defined it, had dropped it for other concepts which interested him more. Freud came back to it along with younger analysts in the twenties and early thirties, and only then clarified its function and use.

Kroeber took Erikson to the Klamath River and to the

Yurok and Karok Indians there. When he questioned some of Erikson's explanations of Yurok personality he did not hesitate to do so in terms as Freudian as Erikson's own. George Devereux, who took his doctorate under Kroeber, went at about this time to the Mohave Indians to collect dreams. Kroeber differed with Devereux in some of his interpretations, but his own understanding of the dreams was enriched by Devereux's psychoanalytic insights. One can find other evidence of this sort in his writing, but more important to the change, in the opinion of Kroeber's psychologist son Ted, was his friendship with Clyde Kluckhohn. Ted believes it was largely with and through Kluckhohn that Kroeber came to a view of culture highlighted and shadowed with psychoanalytic perspective and a critical but ready use of certain of its tools in the unraveling of some puzzling culture knots.

To this Indian summer of Kroeber's more sophisticated synthesis between anthropology and psychoanalysis was added a completion, in the year 1955/56. Kroeber was one of the Fellows of the Center for the Advanced Study in the Behavioral Sciences at Stanford when Frieda Fromm-Reichman was a Fellow there.

For her it was the first time in forty years that she was on leave from her patients; it was her first time on the West Coast. Instead of being on day-and-night emergency call from her room on the sanatorium grounds, she was living for the year in a romantic little house in the country outside Stanford. A garden wall enclosed her in privacy while giving her a view over wide rolling hills dotted with an occasional huge old oak tree. By the custom of the Center, she was without duties or commitments. She sat in the sun for hours every day; she talked with writers and historians and psychologists at the Center. She talked most of all with Kroeber. She began to write; she had always written, but only by snatching time between patients or late at night. She now realized what she must do: when this year of total freedom was over she would for the rest of her life carry only half her former patient load; she would keep her mornings free to write what she had learned and felt in her long years of psychoanalytic practice. And so she did—for the two years she lived after the Center year.

Frieda Fromm-Reichman was not a static coterie Freudian analyst. Analyzed and trained by Freud, basing her theory and practice on the dynamic aspects of Freud's teachings and discoveries and with an imagination toward treatment greater than Freud's own, she had gone on from what he taught her. She was different from any analyst Kroeber had known. She agreed with him that the couch is not an essential prop to analysis. Kroeber had not used a couch in his own analysis and many of his patients preferred to sit across the desk from him, talking face to face as in other confidential conversation. She also agreed that a patient who does not pay for his own analysis can still benefit from it: some of Kroeber's most successful cases had been clinic and nonpaying and hers were of all sorts. She shrugged her small shoulders—Fromm-Reichman was barely five feet tall, if that, with delicate little hands and feet. "Perhaps," she said, "the neurotics need always the couch and the paying." As often as she could she left the treatment of neurotics to others. She saw in neurosis a noncreative, life-refusing, negative state with which she did not readily identify, nor did the partialness of the results from treatment of neuroses—all that it was usually possible to achieve—much appeal to her.

What Kroeber found so world-renewing in Frieda Fromm-Reichman was that she gave the whole of her dynamic imagination, physical courage, incredible patience, and intuitive skills to the person suffering from a psychosis. She discovered in the psychotic person a great strength and integrity, someone possessed of and by a positive idea or vision, but so sensitively organized he must narrow his awareness to a small field where, with terrible creative intensity, he concentrates everything of himself. Fromm-Reichman's role was to make herself a familiar to her patient, until his trust in her was such that she was accepted within that narrow field, gradually allowed to share its special ideas, vision, vocabulary, and values. It was only after this that her patient might trust her and himself to share in her world and, if she won him completely, in the "real" world beyond himself and her. It is to be hoped that someone will one day write Frieda Fromm-Reichman's biography; perhaps one of her former patients will do it.

WRITING DURING HEGIRA

The years of the hegira were crucial, yet their totality can easily be misunderstood. An obvious but wrong guess would be that the hegira was a period when Kroeber's writing tapered off or took psychoanalysis as its chief subject. The evidence of the bibliography for those years forces the conclusion that on the nights of the days spent in the office with patients he wrote a surprising amount. Three of the eight hard-cover books Kroeber wrote during his lifetime were composed in these years, all three anthropological:

the *Handbook* (written during the years 1915-17); the *History of the Peoples of the Philippines* (1919), written for the Museum of Natural History in New York City during the year of his analysis; and *Anthropology* (1923).

In 1918 Kroeber reviewed for the *American Anthropologist* the first authorized English translation of C. G. Jung's *Collected Papers in Analytic Psychology* and *The Psychology of the Unconscious.* In 1920 he wrote "Totem and Taboo: An Ethnographic Psychoanalysis." Between 1915 and 1922 he wrote as well some thirty reviews and more than sixty articles and monographs, none of which except the two mentioned above are about psychoanalysis. Some of them are concrete data presentations in ethnology and language; some are theoretical-ethnographic; some are on race, on archaeology, on physical, societal and social anthropology. They range widely in space, time, and subject matter. To these years belong the *Eighteen Professions* (1915); *The Speech of a Zuni Child* (1916); *The Superorganic* (1917); and, in 1919, his longest title: *On the Principle of Order in Civilization as Exemplified in Changes of Fashion,* i.e., women's formal dress fashion. That Kroeber never left anthropology is the sense of his writing record for the years of his psychoanalytic involvement. The tensions of the hegira were many and serious but it becomes plain in the writing record that they were not without their creative rewards.

MEDINA

In the late summer of 1925 Kroeber was home from a field trip to Peru to resume teaching in the fall term. He and I were at a party for Margaret Mead who was in Berkeley returning from Polynesia. He remembered me from a year

Theodora, 1924.

Alfred, 1925.

ago when I had consulted him briefly regarding graduate work in anthropology. He enquired how my year had gone and told me something of what he had done in Peru. We met again at a dancing party at the Faculty Club a few nights later, and the next day he came to my house to see me for an hour at the end of the morning.

I was then a widow with two young sons. Kroeber met the children that morning and, as it happened, both grandmothers.

Before he left, he arranged to take me to dinner and dancing in San Francisco. During the next weeks we saw each other at friends' houses or had dinner together; or he took me and the children driving and for a picnic; he came to tea with me and my mother-in-law or to go walking, sometimes to stay on for supper with me and the children, to sit talking by the fire after the children were in bed. We saw each other almost daily on the campus.

From our first evening together we were aware of a mutual liking but were reluctant to recognize, to admit, we were falling in love, each of us remembering the heartache from our similarly blasted marriages. In December Kroeber was going east for Christmas. We agreed that during the fortnight of separation we would each try to come to some decision as to our future. Upon his request I met him at the train when he returned. We had made our decision; a few weeks later we were married. There was a twenty-year span between us, and we had grown up culturally as well as geographically a continent apart, but neither of us was much aware of these seeming discrepancies.

MY FAMILY

I was born a Kracaw, the family name an aberrant spelling of Cracow, acquired between the time my paternal ancestors left their home city of Cracow in the eighteenth century and reached America early in the nineteenth century, after some years' sojourn in England and Germany, where a "von" was tacked onto the name. They settled in Maryland where my father, Charles Emmett Kracaw, was born in 1860. A strongly Protestant and religious branch of the family insisted their ancestors had left Poland in flight from some of the Catholic persecutions, but Charles considered this romantic embroidering, believing the Protestantism to go back only to residence in Germany.

Charles was graduated from the Academy in Baltimore, then regretfully left school to follow his father's craft of portrait photography. He was a studious and ambitious young man, but he was not particularly robust and showed early signs of a consumptive tendency. "Roughing it" was then believed to be the best way to combat the tendency, or even the disease, and the doctors recommended that Charles go west. Never averse to traveling, he went first to relatives in Iowa and then on to Colorado and Wyoming. In Cheyenne he met and married Phebe Jane Johnston, born in 1864, the daughter of pioneers, her mother Bostonian by birth, a school teacher from a family of teachers, her father from Pennsylvania farming people. Phebe grew up on her parents' stock ranch, called the E-7, the eldest of six children and a favorite with her father, her uncles and the cowboys on the ranch, who taught her to ride and to shoot "like a man." One of the uncles gave Phebe and Charles matching pearl-handled target pistols as a wedding present. Phebe was a somewhat better shot than Charles. I remember my mother as she looked in starched white shirtwaist and tailored "divided" skirt and well-shined boots, sitting her elaborately carved Spanish saddle and riding a spirited stallion with authority and grace.

The fumes of the darkroom were bad for Charles' lungs. He gave up photography to go into business and mining and was by way of becoming a wealthy man except that much of what he made in merchandising and banking found

Phebe Kracaw.

Charles Emmett Kracaw.

its way down the hungry shaft of one or another of the mines in which he was always investing.

Phebe and Charles had three children, two boys, Austin and Forest, and myself, born in Denver in March 1897. When I was four years old my parents moved to Telluride, a gold-and-silver mining town in the San Juan mountains of southwestern Colorado. Here we lived until I was eighteen.

Phebe early resigned the housekeeping routines to "Aunty Norton," a German housekeeper who was with the Kracaws from a time before I was born until the family left Telluride.

Free of housework, Phebe went with Charles, becoming in effect his first assistant and right-hand man. Their marriage was a mating of congenial opposites: Phebe was outgoing and robust, Charles introverted and somewhat fragile; nonetheless they enjoyed the same people and the same sort of life. I felt secure and comfortable with my mother whose strength and dependability I took as a natural condition, without impulse or competence to emulate her. I would have been terrified, for instance, to ride my mother's stallion, my own horse being an imperturbable Indian pony "hand-raised" by the Navajo Indian from whom my father bought him. If overtaken by darkness or not sure of my directions, I gave my horse his head and he took me home; if I dismounted to pick flowers or to wander on foot he was almost on my heels; if I drank from a stream he too drank, his reins dragging in the water. I loved to be a silent companion to my father, to take long walks with him or go riding or to have him read aloud to me poetry, plays, history. Later when his eyes were troubling him, I would read to him. If I did not understand most of what we read it did not matter; I absorbed something of his feeling for literature and understood at least intuitively his almost mystic fascination with all religions, his commitment to none.

TELLURIDE

Telluride in its nature excites the senses. Its situation 9000 feet above sea level is in a serene Alpine meadow bowl surrounded by snow-capped mountain peaks from whose melting packs pour three great waterfalls, the triple source for the San Miguel River, a mountain torrent which boils and spills over huge boulders as it races westward to its union with the Colorado. There is the intemperate speed of the high-altitude spring and summer which must complete its cycle of growth within four months. There is the dry thin air, the red mineralized earth, the unscreened sun, indigo sky or sudden black skies, and fierce thunder storms; the bright brevity of autumn; the powdery blue-white blowing of snow of the long winter; the exaggerated profiles of vertical cliffs and canyons.

There were the times of man-made terror when, following a strike of the mine workers and violence on both sides, the town was under martial law for two years; times when man and nature combined to create disaster—the infinitesimal movement of a glacier into which the Tomboy Mine was tunneled caused the timbering to collapse and trap workers a thousand feet from the tunnel entrance; or times, when the brush of an eagle's wing, a man's cough, or the step of a mule dislodged a formerly stable snowbank, causing it to break off, carrying with it men and mules, a power house, high voltage wires.

There were for me the remembered sounds and smells of Telluride, the throb of the stamp mill, so close to town that it reached down the streets and into the houses, a giant heartbeat. Only on Christmas, the Fourth of July, and Labor Day did the mill shut down, lending those days a special strangeness, the frightening din of silence, of the stopped heart. I woke daily to the constricted primitive cry of burros, long trains of them in single file being led uphill through town toward one or another mine from which they would return late in the afternoon, burdened with their loads of gold, and still protesting. The smells were of ozone penetrating the sheets which were spread on the grass to dry in good weather, ozone all but tangible and mixed with the resinous pungency of fir and pine, the ammoniac acridness of horse manure steaming outside the stable in the morning sun, and the tanned leather of saddles and harnesses and boots. There was the dry smell of bare red rock—not an earth smell, a rock smell.

Benign or threatening, the mountains were part of my daily experience. I rode and hiked in them in summer and sleighed and tobogganed and snowshoed in them in winter. Across the Ballard Range and past Red Mountain were Ouray, Silverton, and Durango; farther south and west, the Mesa Verde and Shiprock, accessible then only on horseback. This was Ute and Navajo Indian country; it was as well my country.

Denver, four hundred miles distant, was reached by way of the Rio Grande Western (narrow-gauge) Railroad: it was the place to which one "went out." Two or three times a year I went out to Denver with one or both parents to visit, to shop, to go to the theatre. The Chicago Opera came to Denver for a short season, and the winter before I was twelve I went with my father seven straight nights to the Tabor Theatre to see Robert Mantell in his repertory of Shakespeare plays and afterwards to eat New Orleans oysters on the half-shell at Pell's Oyster Bar, my first Shakespeare and my first oysters.

By 1914, Austin, my elder brother, a surgeon and living in Denver, was married. Forest, my younger brother, also a physician, would go directly from his internship into the army ahead of our actual participation in the war. For several years, our father Charles had been having to spend a part of each winter at sea level: the combination of altitude and cold was wearing him out. His months away from home grew longer with each year. Phebe meanwhile acted as head of their businesses with the aid and advice of Charles' regular Saturday evening telephone call to her. But she liked doing it less and less—it was alongside Charles she liked to work, not alone. They decided they must sell out and go to California to live. They waited for me to be graduated from high school the spring of 1915, then the three of us left Telluride for the Coast.

Charles tried some new businesses in the Sacramento Valley in interior northern California where private irrigation projects were developing and where he found engineers already there from Telluride. But irrigation has not the aura of success which clings to gold mining; he was, besides, ill and threatened with blindness. In 1917 he took his life. Phebe lived until 1936, never quite the same, deprived of her role as balance wheel to the seeking romantic imaginativeness of Charles.

THEODORA

I have returned to Telluride only twice: once during the summer following my father's death in 1917; then in 1958, when my brother Forest and I made a sentimental journey there for a few weeks. It has been a ghost town for many years, but it was from its remote, hierarchical, and living state, with its overtones of social sophistication strangely interwined with mining camp custom and primitivism and violence of the old West, that I arrived in California, in a small town in the Sacramento valley, the summer of 1915. Until that day it had not occurred to me that my life and outlook had been different from that of any other middle-class small-town American girl; not even that the Western idiom of my pronunciation was overlaid with Britishisms, unconsciously acquired from my friends in a community whose larger mines were owned and staffed by Britishers, a community where the cricket field was alongside the baseball diamond and the polo grounds abutted on the rodeo compound.

I scarcely knew "where I was" in the flat town which had grown up along the highway and then back from it without social or physical definition of its parts. By contrast, Telluride was as distinct in its parts as a city: its main business street bisected the town into "lower" and "upper" whose reference was at once geographic and social. In the upper were the homes and churches, banks, assay offices, and better stores. In the lower, the high-license businesses: saloons, gambling "parlours," and bordellos under the surveillance and protection of the sheriff and his deputies.

Nor had my experience prepared me for the social life I found in the Sacramento valley. It was strictly age-graded: boys and girls chose their friends and their dates from those of the same age as themselves and at their own school level. At parties there was a strong preference for "couples" to divide off; a party was a sort of honeycomb of separate cells, semiprivate, semicommunicating. The only society I had known was shaped by the physical and social stratification of Telluride and towns like it; by its remoteness, its self-dependence; by the cosmopolitanism and the old-worldness of many of its people and customs; and by the statistic of there being three men to each woman. Any party, any social occasion, was mixed in age; married or engaged couples or those "going steady" did not keep to themselves, which would have been considered bad manners. The emphasis was on the occasion, which was gay and intercommunicating. At sixteen a girl was allowed to "date" within a wide age and nationality range, the elders being concerned as to the particular person, not his age or his likeness to themselves.

I was so homesick for the mountains, for people whose ways I understood and did not transgress, that I became physically ill; before there was time for any real adjustment—within a few weeks—I contracted a severe malaria from swimming in the then mosquito-infested Sacramento River. I was brought to a hospital in San Francisco where I recovered quickly although there was a tendency for the malaria to flare up again for several years afterward if I stayed for any length of time in the interior valleys during the intense heat of the summer. Beyond a doubt those early, full, strange years had done their job of imprinting me. The small-town girl from Colorado would never breathe as easily at sea level as at an altitude and she would remain a self-conscious alien in the agricultural or suburban American small town.

I was enrolled as a freshman at the University of California in Berkeley in the fall of 1915, was graduated *cum laude* in 1919, and received my M.A. in psychology in 1920. That summer I was married to Clifton Spencer Brown, the son of a San Francisco judge, Charles Brown, deceased, and Lena Brown. Clifton was continuing in college toward a law degree, but he was not well. He had served in the war, first with the French, then with the American army. In the wake of a severe pneumonia contracted in the trenches he was left with a chronic bronchiectosis which was once thought to be cured but which flared up and grew steadily worse. He was in sanatoriums in California and Arizona, and finally he and I moved to Santa Fe, New Mexico. Despite this move, he again became very sick, and in the fall of 1923 he died. With my two small sons, Clifton Junior, two years and one month old and Theodore, four months old, I accompanied my husband's body back to Berkeley for burial. I went to live with Lena Brown, my husband's mother, in North Berkeley.

It is hopeless to give a picture of one's self, particularly of the stranger who was one's self sixty, fifty years ago. I have written at some length of Telluride, hoping to use the place as a mirror reflecting the person. I begin to recognize myself more nearly from the time of my return to Berkeley as a widow; it seems to me I got adulthood as another person gets religion—violently and overnight. I felt rather as if I had gone through the maw of the rock crusher I used to gaze into with horrid fascination in the Smuggler Mine in Telluride and had come out from under the stamps dazed, another shape, but not disintegrated.

The tangibleness of two small sons is, I suppose, a discouragement to disintegration, as is one's own youth, but it was my earlier friendship with my first mother-in-law and my daily association with her in 1923 and 1924 that was crucial to my future. We called her "Brown" following the baby Clifton's practice of calling his grandmothers by their last names, "Brown" and "Kracaw." (After Kroeber and I were married, Clifton puzzled some people by his reference to "My three grandmothers.") What Lena Brown offered me besides her sympathetic understanding was her passionate belief in living at a steep pitch of commitment and feeling. With her help I learned to build a new and different life from the one Clifton and I had begun. She crowded me back to graduate work at the university, welcomed the new friends I made there, and warmly approved Kroeber as the new father of her two grandsons. She lived long enough for all four children to know her well: their reaction to her was one of hilarious delight. She and Kroeber shared one trait—they both found funny what young children find funny, an endearing quality in a man or a woman.

With the recognition of self I find there comes an awareness of period—the twenties—and before leaving them I should like to suggest that the stereotype presently being created is one I recognize only faintly, nor do I find compelling the parallels drawn between then and now. We of the twenties were not revolutionaries but the inheritors of a revolution which had destroyed the values and the way of life of the prewar Western world into which we had been born. We had not given up; we were trying, however ineptly, to pick up the pieces of the destruction, to put them back together again, somehow. And if the idiom of dressing and dancing and making music and poetry and love was strange to the American scene, it was neither shallow nor debased as I knew it. And if it was bohemian it was also gay and gallant. I observe today that we Old Ones are less put off, less frightened by today's young than are the men and women whose decade of first maturity was the thirties or the forties.

The twenties were the fateful decade of my life, when I came of age, married, bore two sons, faced the specter of my husband's illness, and the reality of his death. By the time I knew Kroeber I had become as cognizant as he of the fragility of human expectations, of the ruthlessness with which such expectations can be brought to nothing. Before the twenties were over, Kroeber and I were married and two children were born of that marriage: Karl, and a younger sister, Ursula. It is not for the crash of the stock market, which shortly preceded her birthday, but for her birth on St. Ursula's Day in the autumn of 1929 that I remember the closing year of the twenties.

As to how Kroeber saw me, I can only say that when his mother, Mimi, wrote asking him to describe his new wife, he was much puzzled how to do it. This is what he finally wrote her: "You ask me what Theodora is like. Well, she has pink hair and is left-handed. And she is amiable."

The earlier introverted and diffident Kroeber was in retreat, it seems to me, from the time I came to know him well. I had heard him lecture a few times in 1916 in the only course I took in anthropology as an undergraduate—Waterman was responsible for the course that year. He looked then much as in some of the earlier pictures, and I recall him on campus, hurried and thoughtful, wearing a soft Stetson hat decorated by a snakeskin hatband. (The hat is now among the attic treasures of the grandchildren.) It was only when I went to talk to Kroeber about doing some graduate work in 1924 that I began to know him as a person, by which time he had an individual style of which as a young woman I was at once conscious; pleasant if reserved manners, and a quiet professorial distinction. I noted the smoothly brushed-back hair and closely trimmed beard, both streaked with gray; the sensitive and elegant hands; the quick but undramatized motions and gestures. I was to learn that the gray tweeds and the plain ochre-red tie were usual, except the tie might be turquoise or occasionally black. And there was the pipe which was always requiring relighting. I was also aware that the man across the desk from me was giving me the whole of his attention although what I was asking could not be of much import to him. He skillfully led me around my nervousness and self-consciousness during which he in some fashion took my measure, for he urged me to take Lowie's seminar which I would not have presumed to ask to do, recommending as well that I take two lower-division courses "to make your reading mean more," and then added, "especially as you can do this all on two days a week—probably as much time as you want to be away from home just now." I would come to know how characteristic of his thinking and his advice was this small practical last clause.

He remembered me from the interview but had a block on my name. Lowie liked to tease me about Kroeber's having asked him when he came back from Peru, "What about Mrs. . . . what *is* her name—you know, the one with the bracelets." One of the first times I was out with him he said something revealing: the occasion was a Faculty Club dance, and Kroeber and a colleague of his and I were sitting on the floor in Kroeber's room in front of an open fire. Some moments of easeful silence were broken by the third person who asked archly, "What do the wild flames say?" There was a pause when neither of us spoke and then Kroeber said with a certain asperity, "The point is, they do not *say* anything."

Kroeber had always thought of himself as one day having children—even though he was fifty when Karl was born. He seemed most contentedly involved in a complex, many-generationed family and household. For there were the children and my own Aunt Betsy, who lived with us for many years; and there were Lena Brown and my mother, my great-uncle John, my brothers and cousins, and Mimi, and Alfred's sisters and nieces and nephews from time to time. He could—and did—retreat to his study where he was secure from interruption, but he went there to work and usually returned from it promptly when he was through working. He thought of himself in the context of wife, children, and extended family: his letters, his decisions as to what he would do and where he would go demonstrate that. Nor was he passive in domestic matters. He was not interested in household chores, and there was no need for his doing them—except gardening which he enjoyed—but he wanted to be consulted on all plans great and infinitesimal and was the initiator of many of them. He had talent for the role of father, advisor, and confidant; he liked children and got a kick out of them. I recall a time during the Second World War. Clifton was in the South Pacific on a destroyer; his brother Theodore in summer-school preparatory to joining the Air Corps. We had gone, the two of us with the younger children, Karl and Ursula, to Lake Tahoe for a much overdue rest. A young couple with two children of runabout age sat at a table next to ours in the resort dining room. We were aware that they listened, observing whatever the four of us said or did, and at last the father apologized to Kroeber, saying, "You have such a good time with your children, we are looking forward to when ours are as old as yours so that we can enjoy them." Kroeber hesitated for a moment before replying and then said, "Take some advice from an old man: Enjoy your children now. Don't wait."

[A year ago Kroeber's son Karl was talking to me about his father and about the biography. I asked him to give me a memo of what he was saying. Here it is:

"I am reminded of Wordsworth's lines from his 'Tintern Abbey':

> That best portion of a good man's life,
> His little, nameless, unremembered acts
> Of kindness and of Love.

"The lines are appropriate to Alfred as a father because no large, single actions or attitudes of his stand out in my memory. It was the continuity and one might say reliability of his behavior which made him a good father. What Wordsworth does not mention are Alfred's knowledge and his humor, or good humor. Alfred was never the least a pedant, but he was a mine of information: a father who knows a great deal is useful and interesting. I remember Alfred angry only two or three times—I never remember him as resentful or hurt or self-pitying. I recall him as being almost continuously good-humored, full of fun, focusing on and enjoying the amusing aspect of everything. I do not recall him as serious or solemn—one reason I suppose I was very slow to wake up to the fact that he was a distinguished scholar. His light-heartedness had the simple earnestness of a child's playing happily: that enjoyment was the most important thing in the world. This is all part of a certain simplicity in Alfred because his was, I think, a simple rather than a subtle personality. With this, Alfred had an unusual ability not merely to single out the essential in books, social situations, ideas and so forth, but also to see in an unusual original way. This was an important part of his dealings with his children—he could be interested in them and interesting to them because he was alert to surprising aspects and peculiarities of things that most people miss."]

Shortly after we were married, Kroeber found a house for sale on Arch Street in Berkeley. He went through it, took a week's option even before bringing me to see it, and before the week was out had bought it. This is one of the few occasions I can recall when Kroeber set his heart on ownership of a particular material object, but this house he wanted from his first moment of glimpsing it through its redwood-tree screen, nor did his satisfaction with it and his possessiveness toward it lessen over the years. When a thrombosis put him in the hospital, he began to worry lest he would not be allowed to return to his house of many stairs. His doctor, an old friend, assured him that if he took the stairs slowly enough not to raise his blood pressure or become breathless, he could live there. From that day, although he naturally moved quickly, Kroeber held himself down by counting devices, by never forgetting.

The house was built in 1906 by Bernard Maybeck, the architect who, around the 1890's and early 1900's, built many houses in the Berkeley hills area, fixing a style which is generally referred to as "Berkeleyan." The Arch Street house is built of untreated redwood inside and out, without finish or painted trim on the exterior or interior wood. Sturdy, ample, it is now weather-worn from age, the wood oxidized from the sun and darkened from the laying on of many hands. John McLaren, the man who made Golden Gate Park in San Francisco, planted the original garden of which little remains today except the low-growing Sierra juniper on the front slope

The Kroeber children, 1931.

and the clump of redwood trees which partly screens the house from the street.

A way of life—to Kroeber and me, the Way—patterned itself within the redwood walls of our home, the mold of the pattern holding until the war caused the first cracks. Even now, the mold has not broken wholly. These notes are being written in the upper front room of the house whose western windows look across San Francisco Bay and through the Golden Gate;

Clifton.

Ursula.

it was the first grandchild's home for his first year, and all twelve grandchildren have lived in the house intimately and long enough to regard it as an old and fond possession.

The couch, desk, chair, and bookcase from Kroeber's psychoanalytic office were brought from museum storage to Arch Street along with such furnishings as I had—these were few because a fire in 1923 had burned most of them. Kroeber's Morris chair, desk, and bookcases from his room in the Faculty Club, all of which are still there among the pieces which have since been added, completed the original furnishing of the house.

Theodore.

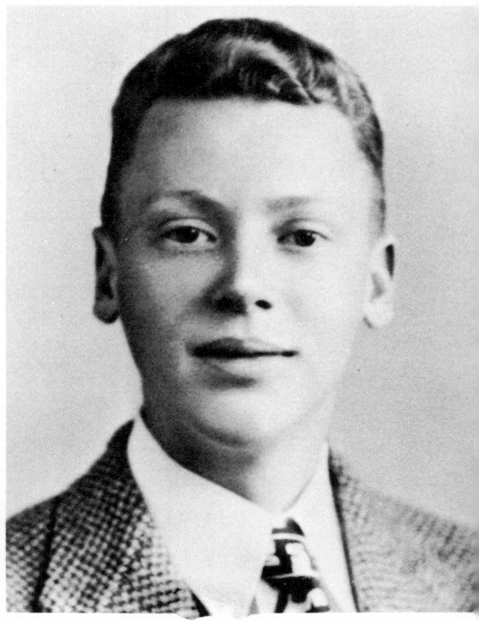

Karl.

KISHAMISH

In 1930 Kroeber and I bought a piece of land which in its own time and fashion became as intimately a backdrop for Kroeber's life as was the Arch Street house. Kishamish is its name. It comprises forty acres in the hills of the west side of the Napa Valley, sixty miles north of San Francisco and once part of the Spanish land grant, Carne Humana. The redwood house and barn lean somewhat downhill and creekward; dry-rock walls as old as the buildings, built by a French vintner many many years ago, incline also toward the creek.

The land, once in grapes, has returned long since to pasture or brush; the hills of winter are green with wild grasses and clover, flower-covered in spring, dry-grass yellow in summer. The sun burns the grass ever darker as the warm dry season advances, four or five months without rain, during which time the grapes in the vineyards on the valley floor below ripen, ready for the wine vats before the winter rains begin. St. John's Mountain, the highest point in the ridge separating the Napa and Sonoma valleys, is at the center of a serene prospect from Kishamish of worn-down hills covered with digger pine, chaparral, manzanita, madrone, California maple, buckeye, and some yellow pine and fir.

Kishamish is not an Indian name. When Karl, the youngest of the boys, was in his myth-making period in imitation of Greek and Norse myths, he saw the two nearer knolls as being Thor and Kishamish (the latter an invented giant), the two recumbent after a fight to the finish: hence the name Kishamish's Place, which became shortened to Kishamish, and later to Kish.

The day after school closed in June the family moved there as a somewhat unwieldy unit: parents, children, my aunt Betsy, and Marciano the houseboy, along with pets, books, and toys, to return to Berkeley the day before school reopened in the fall. There was neither money nor strong inclination to make over the old house—it looks today much as it looked forty years ago. Kroeber and Marciano with the help of Clifton and Ted made a crude baseball diamond and track course in the field below the barn, a dirt croquet court by the barn, and a badminton court above the house. The concrete irrigation storage tank belonging to the only near neighbor served as swimming pool. There was pasture for a horse or donkey. The barn became a place to sleep and to play, its loft the stage of the Barntop Players of Kishamish as well as headquarters for the *Red Bull*, the Kishamish weekly news sheet.

As they learned the old trails or made new ones with the help of Juan Dolores, a Papago Indian who spent his summers with us, the children ranged farther and farther afield. From the floor of the valley to the top of St. John is open land broken by small streams and by canyons, brushy or tree-covered. You could ride or hike for hours encountering only a squatter and his family occupying a deserted farmhouse, one or two deer fences, and the remnant trees of an orchard beside the cellar of a former house. For the rest, there was silence, broken by the rustle of deer and smaller brush animals and birds.

To children and adults alike, Kishamish's forty acres were illimitably expandable, becoming for us a complete world. Much as the California Indians, in their long occupation of the land before the coming of the white man, lived within adjacent but separate worlds, tiny, complete, self-sufficient, of known and near boundaries. What lay beyond his own world interested the Californian very little; what lay within it was for him of cosmic variety, complexity, and passionate concern. So it was at Kishamish: a world without phones or doorbells or the tyranny of close schedules; a world for exploration, for reading, for one's own work, for swimming and playing games, for sitting by the outdoor fire until late in the night, talking, telling stories, singing; for sleeping under the stars.

The Kishamish guestbook kept during those years can be read as a roster of graduate students in anthropology stopping by, to and from the field; of California Indians and other Indians; of visiting writers and scholars; of the children's friends; of family. Among the names are those of the friends who came and came again, who stayed for days or weeks and whose repeated names tell the story of the circle of intimacy which completed itself there—very California Indian, very Kishamishian.

CONFIGURATIONS

The personal configuration we have been tracing is seen to have completed its pattern in 1926. Going back up the time track, we now pick up the strands of Kroeber's professional activities and direction, discovering the beginning pattern of a new configuration which had been quietly forming since 1915 and which concerns archaeology.

ARCHAEOLOGY

The earliest strand of this pattern takes us back to 1901, to Phoebe Apperson Hearst's archaeological collections, to Kroeber's first year with the university, to his curatorship of Mrs. Hearst's collections. At his suggestion, President Wheeler and the regents set up in principle an 'Ethnological and Archaeological Survey," and from that time individual ethnological and archaeological research and field work was sponsored by the museum.

The Survey as an entity with organization and budget and program remained a dream until 1946 when the regents established an independent Archaeological Survey with Robert F. Heizer as director and with authority to go anywhere in the state to develop, protect, or map archaeological sites. Making the Survey an actuality was one of Kroeber's last administrative tasks for the university, it becoming official on July first, 1946, the first day of his emeritus status.

His bibliography shows that almost one-third of Kroeber's published works are archaeological, in part or whole, or have reference to archaeology—a high proportion for a person whose years of intense concentration on the subject were between 1922 and 1930. Kroeber never dug in California nor did he take students on archaeological fields trips. For himself, he felt that archaeology must wait, that it would keep better than the living informants who would be irreplaceably gone tomorrow. But it must also be remembered that he was director and custodian of a collection which was in its most significant specimens archaeological, and that before 1922, he studied all the collections. He studied with deepest interest the remarkable Peruvian materials which belonged to the museum: he went for the first time to Peru, not as a tyro but as a person probably as well-informed about archaeological Peru as any scholar of his time. Let us trace the steps which brought him at last to Peru where he made his single large contribution to original archaeological field investigation.

Kroeber's first archaeological field work was in Zuni and came about by chance. He says of it in his monograph, *Zuni Potsherds:*

> In the course of a study of family life made at the pueblo of Zuni during the summer of 1915, I recorded the native names of a number of ancient villages in and near Zuni Valley. A late afternoon walk a few days afterwards brought me to where Mattsakya [one of the villages] once stood, a mile and a half east of the town of Zuni. The wall

> outlines which Mindeleff [the archaeologist] still traced have mostly disappeared in thirty years, save for two rooms and where a prairie dog hole had laid bare a few feet of masonry that otherwise would have been hidden. The quantity of broken rock on the surface, the sharp rise of the knoll, and the maintained shrine, or rather two, on its summit—the last, as it proved, an almost certain evidence of former occupation of the spot—all . . . indicated a ruin, even to the novice in archaeology. A few moments revealed a pottery fragment or two. At first the sherds were difficult to see and harder to distinguish from the numerous minute slabs of stone. A quarter of an hour, however, practised the eye; and the short time remaining before darkness sufficed to fill my pockets.

Kroeber's work with informants was interrupted from time to time by Zuni family or ceremonial matters, particularly with the summer rain dances coming up. He took advantage of these breaks to walk or ride to one after another of the old villages whose names and approximate locations he had learned and, as he found and identified them, made a sherd collection from each in turn. Back in Zuni, he spread his sampling of sherds out on the roof where he completed a seriation from fifteen old villages—some three thousand sherds in all—with another thousand gathered from the roofs and floors of the living pueblo of Zuni itself. His seriation yielded three phases or periods, datable with reference to native oral history and published historical data as Present, Historic, and Prehistoric. On the basis of stylistic differences, he extrapolated one further phase for the Historic and one for the Prehistoric period. This rich return from the sherd analysis taught him something of how to begin an archaeological-site study. He says,

> The problem of prehistoric Ẓuni and of the earliest Southwest will be solved only by determined limitation of attention. . . . It is fatal for the investigator to exhume pottery in the morning, note architectural construction at noon, plot rooms in the afternoon, and by evening become excited over a find of turquoise or amulets. . . . One feature at a time, then another, then correlation, is the method that will convert Southwestern archaeology from a delight of antiquarians into a historian's task. . . . At present five thousand sherds can tell us more than a hundred whole vessels, and the bare knowledge of the average size of a room in a dozen contiguous ruins may be more indicative than the most laborious survey of two or three extensive sites.

Some years, the psychoanalytic years, would intervene between the Zuni work and Kroeber's later archaeology. Kroeber knew where he wanted to work—in Peru. To this end he was in correspondence with the Field Museum in Chicago and with Julio Tello, Peru's principal archaeologist, in Lima, Peru. Kroeber had met Tello in 1915 and again in 1923, when they were both at Harvard for a scientific meeting. They were beginning to make plans looking to Kroeber's coming to Peru, but back in New York City, a telegram awaited Kroeber telling him that Fanny, his mother-in-law, had died. He took the train to San Francisco without having seen Tello again. It would be two years before he would return to the Peruvian plans.

MEXICO

Before the opening of the spring semester following Fanny's death, Kroeber found a substitute to teach his classes and was granted special leave. There remained in the museum budget some four hundred dollars of research money from Mrs. Hearst for Latin American studies, which money was available to him. It would not suffice to take him to Peru but it would take him to Mexico. Kroeber had moved out from the California field; for the next several years he would leave aside also linguistics, during which years archaeology would interrupt more completely his early and abiding interest in language than would any other anthropological area of investigation.

By early spring of 1924 he was settled in a native hotel in Mexico City within walking distance of the Museo Nacional de Mexico, where Manuel Gamio, custodian of antiquities, whom Kroeber already knew, was most helpful. He it was who suggested that Kroeber might do his first digging in San Angel, a suburb of Mexico City where Gamio could lend a hand as needed.

With Gamio to introduce him, Kroeber made the acquaintance of numbers of people living in San Angel. They were intrigued to have a "dig" run under their property, particularly when he chose to begin work directly under the *pulquería.* He selected the *pulquería* for its extensive cellars which made it accessible to deeper digging, but the well-disposed Mexicans were not at a loss to think of other sound reasons for the choice. This site was, as well, under the *Pedregal,* the enormous old lava flow which lies across the southern end of the Valley of Mexico. And below the *Pedregal* Kroeber was in archaic culture layers. It was a "good dig," as archaeologists say, that is, it exposed old materials in good condition. Kroeber dug at Copilco, another site in the valley under the *Pedregal,* and there he turned up the first archaic Mexican adobe brick to be found by an archaeologist.

He went on to work at Teotihuacan where he made a cut

into the north side of the Pyramid of the Sun. He visited other sites in the valley, making sherd collections from each, seriating them as he had the Zuni sherds. On the evidence from his excavations and seriations Kroeber hazarded a tentative chronology for the valley that John Rowe, the archaeologist and Peruvianist, calls a *tour de force* because it stands up in the face of the full background knowledge and extensive excavations of later Mexicanists.

PERU, 1925

Kroeber went twice to Peru for the Field Museum, in 1925 and again in 1926, traveling both times by boat from New York City, a voyage of twelve days to Callao, the port for Lima.

During his first weeks in 1925 Kroeber dug at several sites to the north and south of Luma, close to the city, since heavy rains in a part of the country where it usually does not rain had made rivers impassable and travel in the provinces out of the question. In April, the rivers having returned to their banks, he went south to the Cañete Valley where he turned up a new pottery style which John Rowe rates as Kroeber's most important single find in Peru.

He went inland and farther south, and, ultimately, north, this reconnaissance revealing the correctness of his surmise from his specimen study in the museum at home, that the first area of concentration should be in the south and on the coastal plain where some of the important early art culminations had taken place—not in the areas of dramatic cyclopean ruins which are in their monumental way the glory of Peru.

During this reconnoitering over the land, perforce at low speed in those pre-Pan-American Highway days, and usually alone, Kroeber began to observe something besides sea and sand: "desert markings" as they are now called, not reported by earlier travelers so far as Rowe knows. Kroeber decided, correctly, that the long sweeping scars on the desert floor were prehistoric, not random, not of nature. Examined closely they are seen to have been made by the removal of the surface pebbles, but no one knows what was their ancient purpose.

Another discovery or rediscovery as he moved south, was of the ancient necropolis at Paracas. William Curtis Farabee reached Paracas in 1922, but becoming ill soon after, did not mention the site in print and it was otherwise unknown to archaeologists. Kroeber, having found it, meant to dig there when he returned to Peru in 1926, but meanwhile, Tello and Sam Lothrop (Harvard Peabody Museum), seeing a new sort of ancient embroidery on sale in Pisco, got a local *huaquero,* a pot hunter, to lead them to its source—Paracas. Tello had already begun digging there by the time Kroeber returned, so he contented himself with revisiting the site.

Kroeber was also the first archaeologist to go to the anciently sacred spring, Wari-Willka, above Huancayo. Even Tello had never been there. Spanish sources tell of it, giving its location correctly; perhaps latecomers never quite believed it existed. But it is today much as it must have been in Inca times—a gushing flow of purest snow water, its natural rock basin enlarged and strengthened by pre-Incan herculean masonry.

PERU, 1926

In June of 1926 Kroeber went again to Peru, Egbert Schenck the archaeologist, Sara his wife, and I accompanying him, on what would be a somewhat longer and more ambitious expedition than the previous year's with an uninterrupted eight months in the field.

On this second trip he spent his time digging, principally in various sites in the Nazca valley, which he supplemented with some far-northern digs undertaken with Tello. The Nazca Valley proved to be as crucial to an understanding of the Peruvian archaeological-historical panorama as Kroeber had judged it to be and was rewarding in the elegance as well as the significance of its yield of specimens. The sites of ancient towns, larger than most towns today in provincial Peru, are along the rivers; the ancient burials on the first terraces above the river bed and close to the towns. In sand whose mineral content has not been diluted by rainfall, previously unopened graves yield perfectly preserved mummies, and textiles and pottery whose textures and colors are as brilliant and unspoiled as on the day of burial thousands of years ago.

By the time the year was out, Kroeber could project a systematic informed concept of horizon styles for all of Peru. His chronology has been superseded or corrected and amplified by later work and his discoveries are today's commonplaces, but his work remains, says Rowe, basic to an understanding of the archaeology of Peru.

He came home from Peru weighing a light 135 pounds, the least he had weighed since he was grown. He was not ill, but he was weary with a special archaeological weariness compounded of trying to do more than it is reasonable to undertake in a given time span, responsibility for the work itself, for the workers, the camp, the finances, the transportation of valuable and fragile specimens, and the social-official aspect of such work—indispensable, often pleasant, sometimes trying and always time-taking.

But the fascination of unearthing history lingers longer in the memory than the weariness, the strains and the disappointments. Kroeber would probably have been back at another camp in the Peruvian desert or mountains within a year or two had he not, by that time, been at work on a book which partook of aspects of his archaeological interests. As it was, after two years of digging in Peru, Kroeber unregretfully resigned trowel, brush, and tamping rod to others. However, the pattern of the full story of prehistoric Peru never ceased to fascinate and engage him: the elegantly intricate use of design and color in Nazca and Paracas pottery and textiles; the monumental Chavin sculpture; the realistic humanistic Mochica ware with its makers' prodigious obsession to commit to a permanent clay record not only the aristocratic beauty of its people, but the minutely accurate details of each of their deforming diseases, each sexual perversity, each personal foible, each animal and fish and flower and vegetable which crossed their observant gaze.

Kroeber would have liked to sit down in one village after another with notebook and pencil, to discover what living Peruvian Indians are like and what insight their memories and remnant cultures might add to what is known of the cultures of their ancestors, as anthropologists are now doing.

PERU, 1942

It would be fifteen years before Kroeber returned to Peru. Nelson Rockefeller was implementing with deeds the increasing United States government's concern over the bad state of our relations with Latin America. To this end he was able to get State Department support for an Institute of Andean Research, and by late 1941 and in 1942 at least four expeditions from the States were at work in Peru. Kroeber was asked to go there by the Committee on Inter-American Artistic and Intellectual Relations. Henry Allen Moe of the Guggenheim Foundation, as well as Nelson Rockefeller, was serving on the committee, and since Moe and Kroeber were old friends Kroeber wrote him personally and freely. In one of these letters, written toward the end of 1941 but before Pearl Harbor, Kroeber said in part:

> I believe actual archaeology (i.e., digging) should be done by young people. . . . As to social contacts and junketing I dislike it and am no good at it. . . . In short the only way I have any faith in serving my country and the world in this mess (the war) is by remaining a scholar. . . . If my presence in Peru were really considered of any moment, I can see only one thing I might do which would perhaps have intrinsic significance: a visit to ruins, sites, collections and results made accessible since I was last in the country in 1926, to enable me to interpret and advise and plan with the men who will be on the firing line of Peruvian archaeology during the next generation. This would mean a minimum of time in Lima and a maximum touring the provinces by car.

In January of 1942, when the invitation was renewed in somewhat more urgent terms, he wrote,

> Since my last letter to you, we've got into war, and looking out from my home over the ocean where an enemy fleet might loom up, I have to remember my four children. . . . I continue to ponder whether all this is really worth while. . . . But you can better decide. . . . So far there is

> no sign of anything here I could contribute . . . so I am at your disposal.

Kroeber decided to go and that I should accompany him. His letter of acceptance ends,

> Your letter is most generous. I appreciate it doubly because it leaves me feeling less superannuatedly useless than I have of late.

Once arrived in Lima, Julio Tello and Luis Valcarcel, also a Peruvian archaeologist, and the North American anthropologists who were in Lima with the Andean Institute met us. Supplied with car and chauffeur, we left for the provinces where we spent most of our time, traveling far north and south, living sometimes in a village hotel, sometimes as house guests in a hacienda. Kroeber wrote to Moe:

> Back yesterday from northern trip—4000 kilometers—have seen many ruins and sites, some new culture types, and met . . . everyone who is in any way active in archaeology. My torch is relit for handing on to the next generation. I want . . . to write an illustrated report which summarizes the status of the problems, . . . Relations with Peruvians have been excellent. . . . My suggestion is that if future work is planned, by Rockefeller, Carnegie or Guggenheim, Peruvians be given a larger hand in it. I did what I could—took Gabriel Escobar [anthropology graduate student from Cuzco] with us for the southern trip and Jorge Muelle (later director of the Museo Nacional of Peru), for the northern. Muelle and I are to bring out in the *Revista del Museo* a joint paper on a new pottery technique.

Two permanent records came out of this expedition: a talk which Kroeber gave at San Marcos University, "Los Métodos de le Arqueología Peruana," which was printed in *Letras, Universidad de San Marcos*—his single generalized statement of archaeological method. (Clyde Kluckhohn who delighted in gentle teasing, chided Kroeber for having written and delivered his one statement on method in a foreign language, to which Kroeber retorted, "The Latins appreciate method.") The second paper was a report written after his return from Peru and published by the Viking Fund, "Peruvian Archaeology in 1942," which gives the results of his reconnaissance and his vision of future work to be done in Peru. Rowe says this is in his opinion Kroeber's "most brilliant archaeological work."

Reviewing Kroeber's predominantly psychoanalytic and his predominantly archaeological periods, they are seen to have overlapped in time especially in the earlier years and to have interchanged one focus for the other now and again. They were even more intimately interrelated: psychoanalysis helped Kroeber to look outward from California and to move out from it scientifically. Archaeology helped him to deal explicitly for the rest of his life with the aesthetic component of whatever he studied, accustoming him to do this through hand as well as mind.

That the return to anthropology should have been by way of archaeology seems, at least in hindsight, an almost inevitable progression, which would move on in the years ahead from the materials and experience of archaeological prehistory to history in the usual meaning to intellectual history to a broadly theoretical view of all culture.

COLUMBIA OFFER

Kroeber was settled into an academic and scholarly routine, when in February of 1931 Boas wrote offering him a professorship and the chairmanship of the Department of Anthropology at Columbia University. Three letters followed in as many days each ending much as this one, "I do not need to tell you how glad I should be if it would be possible to bring you here." Boas, continuing beyond usual retirement age, had been trying for two years and more to bring about a succession and to make full provision for his department. His idea was to get Edward Sapir for linguistics and Kroeber for general anthropology, but his authorization to do so came too late to get Sapir who had only just closed with Yale where he went that year as Sterling Professor.

An acknowledging note to Boas from Kroeber says, "I find it hard to tell you how much I am pleased at your asking me to join you. It made me feel as in student days when you you gave one of your grunts of commendation." This was a very different offer than could come from another person and place, a much harder one to answer. Behind it lay, besides the professional aspect, the affection of the younger and the older man for each other, heightened for over thirty years by the closest interfamily friendships. Boas was saying, in effect, it is you I want—and need. A first reaction from Kroeber was to do what the "old man" asked, as he would have responded to any personal request from him. And the offer was tempting: the salary was considerably higher than he was getting at Berkeley; after many years at the periphery it would be good to be once more at the center, close to Cambridge and Washington and only a subway ride away from museums.

from Carnegie Hall and the Opera, from his family and his oldest friends. California met the offer; his decision had to be made not at the bargaining table, but in terms of what he ought and wanted to do for the rest of his professional life, and the oughts and wants were so nearly balanced as to make the choice excruciating. Kroeber decided against going. He wrote to Boas,

> They were hard days [of decision]. While I have no dissatisfaction here, the opportunities of New York . . . the prospect of working with you . . . pulled tremendously. . . . I hope I have chosen wisely. There are regrets of course. On the side of New York, there was, besides being with you, ambition; but also consequent greater distraction; and I hope that by staying, my work will gain in quality what I give up in scope. Mentally I have done a lot of liquidating these days, and perhaps some of this loosening of attachments and associations will stay with me. I can see now that I needed it. For all this I am grateful to you. And particularly I remember that it was you who first placed me here. I seem destined to move more independently of you than some of the men you have started in life and at times perhaps seemingly at cross purposes; but I hope you will feel as I do, that that makes me more truly your pupil.

If he was to forego the advantages of Columbia and New York City over Berkeley and San Francisco, it would be to give himself time and room to do work, alongside his teaching, in the light of his own intellectual interests. The decision was as crucial as the one to leave psychoanalysis, in determining his work product from that time, in predicating the person he became over the next thirty-four years, and in setting the quality and incidence of his influence. Neither Boas's nor Kroeber's family in New York ever understood the depth or the nature of his attachment to the West. There was his love of the land. There was his sense of a uniqueness in the life which he had recognized first in the Indians who had preceded the white man there. And he had found, as have others, his own equivalent of that old Indian life.

Boas accepted Kroeber's decision regretfully, asking him to come at least for the next academic year. Kroeber went for the second semester only; even so, there was some apprehension in Berkeley lest he might stay once he was at Columbia, as Boas had hope of persuading him to do. To Kroeber, his months there were not a trial run. He went as he went elsewhere when he could for temporary change and refreshment, with the added urgency on this occasion of bringing to Boas his friendship and affection at a time when he must appear to his old teacher to be niggardly of both.

WITH THE YUROK

Kroeber returned from time to time to ethnological field work, to do a stint of work, to renew contact with people and places he had long since become fond of but rarely saw. To return was always a pleasure to him. These visits were usually to the Yurok Indians who live along the Klamath River and the adjoining coast. For several years, until the Highway Control took it for a scenic rest area, Kroeber owned two acres of the top of a considerable headland thrusting into the Pacific Ocean a few miles south of Orick on the northern coast of California. *Sigonoy* was its name. From the stoop of the cabin he built on Sigonoy, the land dropped vertically several hundred feet to a shallow beach, well stocked with driftwood. The view west was to the horizon line, with two sea stacks, sacred objects in Yurok lore, a bit off-shore, and with coastal freighters passing outside the stacks; to the south were Dry and Big Lagoon and the distant lights of Eureka, while to the north the view was to the lighthouse at Crescent City.

Orick Bob lived about half-way down on the sheltered side of the headland where there was a spring, the only source of water. Together, Kroeber and Orick Bob fished, hauled driftwood, talked, and worked at recording the Yurok language or whatever other aspects of Yurok life occurred to Bob. Old and new Yurok and Karok friends came from the coast and the river to visit Sigonoy. Kroeber returned these visits by car if his destination was the coast, by boat and on foot over the rough canyon trails to villages and people on the river. (Kroeber had liked to canoe since boyhood days; the heavy redwood dugout of the Yurok readily became his western equivalent of the light carrying canoe of the Adirondack lakes.) It was leisurely and sociable to go up the Klamath with three or four Yurok aboard, with stops at each village along the way and at each of the sacred praying places on the river banks.

The Yurok addressed Kroeber as "doctor" and spoke of him as "the doctor," or as "kegeys" the Yurok word for doctor. My Yurok name was *Sigonoy-O-Perê*, Old Woman of Sigonoy, a clever triple-meaning name, which placed me geographically, indicated my status as principal-woman-in-my-husband's-house, and kidded my then relatively young age.

Robert Spott, the Yurok son and adoptive son and nephew respectively of Kroeber's oldest informants and friends on the

At Sigonoy, 1931.

Klamath River, spent his summer vacations with us at Kishamish or came to us in Berkeley, until his death in 1953. We were all fond of Robert, gentlest, most devotedly Yurok-religious and subtly intelligent of men. Robert was in the trenches in France throughout the United States participation in the First World War, where he won a personal Croix de Guerre for exceptional bravery, which neither his family nor we knew until after his death. Throughout his life Robert's mystic Yurok center remained untouched by the white man and his world—he was passionately and committedly interested in understanding and knowing everything which was part of the Yurok world and he was fortunate in having in his family Old Ones—uncles, aunts, grandparents—who were interested and unusually informed and intelligent teachers. Never did teachers have a more perfect receptacle for their knowledge and wisdom than Robert, who forgot nothing they taught him.

Together, Robert and Kroeber published the monograph *Yurok Narratives,* part of the fruit of those summers. And it was from Robert I heard for the first time of the Yurok inland whale, as it was through him I arrived at enough insight into the Yurok world to dare to try to convey some of its feeling in my book, *The Inland Whale.*

THE SERI

During the midwinter recess of 1930/31, Kroeber went on a short field trip to the Seri Indians of Mexico, who live on Tiburon Island in the Gulf of California; he was keen to know something of them at first hand. The Seri have apparently always been, as they are today, peripheral to the people of higher cultural achievement in Mexico. They have had to defend themselves since the Spanish Conquest, perhaps before, against neighbors who were more numerous and richer, and who were cruel, aggressive, and merciless; in this defense,

Robert Spott and Alfred at Rekwoi.

the Seri have a reputation for violence, suspiciousness, untrustworthiness, and a primitiveness scarcely human.

The attitude of most Sonorans along the Gulf was that no man, alone and unarmed, could go safely to the island: the Seri would try to murder him; on the other hand, they would be sure to murder an armed man to get his gun. As Kroeber said, in such circumstances, buying a gun would be a waste of money. He was not dependent on bad counsel, since he had made the acquaintance of Señor Roberto Thomson, Rancho San Rafael, Sonora, who was *Jefe de Vigilancia* for the Seri and as well their good friend. Señor Thomson's picture of these people was quite different; introduced by him, the Seri invited Kroeber to come with them to Tiburon, which he did. The only hazardous hour was that of a rough crossing from the mainland in an open boat, the hazard being a donkey aboard, which the Seri took along to help haul water from a water hole several miles from the beach where they lived. The donkey was understandably terrified and almost succeeded in upsetting the boat, braying throughout the voyage, and once there remaining disconsolately vocal, seeking company at night among the blanket-wrapped figures lined up asleep on the sandy beach.

On Tiburon Island with them for some days, Kroeber learned how monotonous and hard was the Seri marginal way of life. They were delighted to have company, especially someone interested in what they did.

For food the Seri depended upon the seasonally shifting shell and other fish of the Gulf, the midwinter fare when Kroeber was there being oysters. Whenever anyone felt hungry, several of them, men, women and children, hastened to gather basketfuls of oysters from the near-at-hand beds. Not every anthropologist, it is to be surmised, would take as happily as did Kroeber to a straight diet of oysters four or five times a day, day after day: a dreamy look would come over his face whenever he recalled those feasts of oysters.

Altogether Kroeber found the Seri to be friendly and cooperative, competent linguistic and ethnographic informants, resourceful in practical matters, and superb fishermen and sailors.

ELEMENT SURVEY

The year 1931 saw the completion of one book, *Cultural and Natural Areas of Native North America;* the beginning of another, *Configurations of Culture Growth;* and the initiation of an "element survey," a study of culture traits among California Indians.

The depression of the thirties delayed publication of the *Areas* book until 1939, making the date of the actual finishing of the manuscript important in understanding its relation to the later book and to the survey, since, if one were to infer from the publication date, it would appear that Kroeber had gone a straight road from archaeological sherds to culture elements to culture wholes. This would be neat, but is not the actual order: he had been writing the *Areas* book on and off for several years; and whereas the second book grew from the first, the element survey had at most tangential relations to both.

The first goal of the element survey was to compile and organize a body of statistically comparable ethnological data for the whole of California and ultimately beyond California. The technique was to atomize, to reduce to their single element-parts all the known culture traits, so far as this was possible and the traits recoverable; the means, identical element lists to be filled or completed *de novo* in the field or from old ethnological data. (A culture trait would be, for example, the bow and arrow. But the elements of that trait would be its materials, the type of arrow release, whether or not the bow was backed, and with what material.)

In the *Areas* book Kroeber first formulated the idea of an element survey. In the last chapter, "Cultural Intensity and Climax," he says, "it should be possible to determine an approximately objective measure of cultural intensity by measuring culture content—by counting distinguishable elements, for instance. This is a task which no one is ready to perform for the continent, but theoretically it is feasible and it might be worthwhile."

Kroeber had taken Boas' course in statistics and from time to time when it had seemed interesting or fruitful to do so, he had organized ethnographic materials according to one or another quantitative scheme or had directed the work of the rare student who came his way who wished to work quantitatively or statistically. Forrest Clements was such a student. In a seminar of Kroeber's in 1926 in which Sara Schenck and I also participated—without ever quite understanding where the chi-square and six-place probabilities Clements was having us use might lead us—Clements organized a small coherent body of Polynesian ethnographic material with results which were published in a paper called "A New Objective Method for Showing Special Relationships."

Kroeber's most mathematically talented and dedicated student was Harold E. Driver, now professor of anthropology at Indiana University. Driver, somewhere about 1930, had discovered a new coefficient of interrelationships which he called *G* (because it was a geometric mean). Kroeber meanwhile had compiled a list of some 800 separate element traits from California Indian cultures, and he and Driver were at work. A paper of theirs in which they tested and demonstrated Driver's *G* as a tool for analyzing ethnographic materials, "Quantitative Expression of Cultural Relationships," 1932, excited the interest of Stanislaw Klimek, a young physical anthropologist at the University of Lvov, Poland, then engaged in making a series of European population studies. He got a grant which allowed him to come to Berkeley to work with Kroeber and Driver, applying his own formula to Kroeber's trait list. Somewhat in this fashion the element survey was launched. Klimek's years in Berkeley, 1933-1935, more or less being those of Kroeber's most active participation, although the survey continued through 1938, with thirteen people participating in collection and analysis of data and with 254 territorial units included.

As with psychoanalysis, some anthropologists reacted to the survey by dismissing it as another of Kroeber's enthusiasms, which it was, while some accepted it as the scientific wave of the future which it was not. The amount of material accumulated for it was enormous; the quality, as with all ethnographic data, as varied as the skills of the gatherers, the comprehension on the part of the informants of what was wanted, and the quality and kind of older data, some of which could be reduced to meaningful elements, some not.

When he closed the files of the survey, Kroeber evaluated it differently from the way he had thought earlier he might. The human factor he found as immanent in statistical analysis and synthesis as in the nonmathematical; the old lesson was brought home to him once again that a good field person returns with superior materials, an inferior one with inferior materials, even when dealing with something so seemingly depersonalized as an element list. He learned that whereas culture traits and culture syndromes may all be reduced to elements, only some elements yield further significant fact or meaning. In other words, he experienced in

1932.

miniature the computer dilemma of today. There was the matter of the absence of a trait from a particular culture: had the informant never known whether his culture possessed the trait or not; had the researcher failed to enquire; had the element once been present and become lost through culture change? Only a person already conversant with the culture could know or make an educated guess as to which sort of absence it was.

Indeed, all weighting of the lists had to be done by someone who knew the culture. The survey failed to illuminate for Kroeber a single culture-whole; it did throw unexpected occasional light on areas and cultures he knew intimately but in which, without having systematically reduced their contents to their elements, he had failed to see their sometime relationships and patterns, and the directions and nature of certain drifts of elements from one culture to another. He could learn, in other words, from the discrete elements, as an archaeologist learns from sherds, because he knew the whole vessel. He abandoned his earlier thought that the survey might be useful to the novice, the stranger to a culture.

He never went back to the element study or on to another one and he was dubious that any similar study would yield results more significant than his and Driver's until different means, other techniques, had been perfected. Driver remarks of Kroeber's failure to use a statistical means of analysis in the *Configurations* study: "The Herculean task of assembling sufficient data and of correlating it by means of the methods of calculation available at the time . . . would have taken a lifetime."

AREAS BOOK

Cultural and Natural Areas of Native North America is an intriguing book. More than Kroeber's other writings, it has a wide span which includes some of his earlier thinking along with some very late, to be developed fully by him only in the fifties. The *Areas* title and the envelope of maps in the pocket of the book have tended to limit its audience outside the profession to geographers and to the land-environment-oriented scholar far more than the text and its theoretical implications warrant. It is not the purpose here to describe its contents since a new edition, 1966, has put the book back into circulation, but I should like to quote briefly from its opening section, "Objectives," and from the final section, "Cultural Intensity and Climax," to indicate the immediacy of connection between it and the book, *Configurations of Culture Growth,* begun in 1931, and beyond, to later work.

Says Kroeber, in the opening pages:

> This study . . . aims . . . to review the environmental relations of the native cultures of North America . . . and to examine the historic relations of the culture areas, or geographic units of cultures . . . the present work in no sense represents a relapse toward the old environmentalism which believed it could find the causes of culture in environment. While it is true that cultures are rooted in nature . . . they are no more produced by . . . nature than a plant is produced or caused by the soil in which it is rooted. The immediate causes of cultural phenomena are other cultural phenomena. . . .
>
> . . . the present study deals with culture wholes. Culture wholes as a concept correspond in many ways to regional floras and faunas, which are accumulations of

> species but can also be viewed as summation entities. . . . We mean a regionally individualized type or specific growth of culture when we say "culture area," much as a historian may use "the Eighteenth Century" as a short way of referring to the culture that was characteristic of eighteenth-century Europe.

Later in the book the language and content look forward to the interests of the 1950's: "At the culmination (of Greek civilization), organization overtook the mastered content: the value system of the culture was set." The vocabulary later used in *Configurations* is found in *Areas*, increasingly toward the end—*climax, culmination, cycle*—and its final paragraph could almost have been used as the opening words of *Configurations:*

> The tantalizing and fundamental subject of cultural periodicity can hardly be pursued farther here, for a variety of reasons, among them the outstanding one that the exactest determinations of cycle can obviously be made best on datable and therefore documentary materials. What I have tried to show is that both in art and in degree of systematization the more outstanding American cultures seem to conform to a general pattern of cycle the outlines of which gleam through the known historic civilizations. Further, the very concept of climax, or, if you will, culture center, involves not only the focus of an area but also a culmination in time. Through the climax, accordingly, geography and history are brought into relation; or, at any rate, the areal and temporal aspects of culture cannot be really related unless consideration is accorded to climax. This view has guided me in the present work, which in turn, I trust, validates the view by its concrete exemplifications.

CONFIGURATIONS BOOK

With these closing words of *Areas* freshly in mind, let us turn now to the Preface of *Configurations of Culture Growth*, where Kroeber says that "the plan [of study] formed itself some years before 1931; its theme I have been exercised over as far back as I can remember. Many years of specifically anthropological preoccupations seemed for a time to have led me away, but eventually they brought me back to it."

Kroeber sent to Harcourt Brace and Co., publishers of his *Anthropology*, a statement with the *Configurations* manuscript which says of it:

> This is the first attempt by a scholar of standing to grapple with the real problems of human history to which Spengler believed he had found the answer through mystic . . . intuition and dogmatic philosophizing. The flowering and withering of the greater Asiatic and European civilizations, ancient and modern, as expressed in their science, philosophy, literature, painting, sculpture, music and nationalistic expansion, are examined and compared. The recognized but little understood tendency of genius to cluster in limited periods and particular countries is construed as an index of the growth of patterns of culture, upon which in turn the rise and fall of civilizations largely depend.
>
> The author . . . is extending his observation . . . beyond the conventional preoccupation of his profession with the primitives to the larger manifestations of high civilization. The book therefore deals with the materials of culture history, but is novel in that it is not so much a narrative of what happened as a sociological examination of how, and to what degree, the major achievements of human civilization repeat themselves.

Such then was Kroeber's "more historic process line of inquiry," which, seven years after beginning it, became his *Configurations of Culture Growth,* with 846 pages of text, an annotated bibliography, and an index. As with *Areas,* I leave the reader to Kroeber's own explication of the materials he garnered and organized, the discussion here being concerned to place the book's composition in time and vis-à-vis his other writing and to make plain what was his relation to it once the long task was complete and he had written *finis.*

The signature of the preface hints at the story of how the book was written: "A. L. K., Kishamish, Napa Valley, California. August 1, 1938. Final reading in type, August, 1944."

The interval between completion (1938) and publication (1944) was due, not to the war, but to the editors at Harcourt Brace not making up their minds either to print the book, or to release it: they hoped to persuade Kroeber to shorten it, to simplify it. Lewis Gannett, book editor of the *Herald Tribune,* read it, as did Leonard Bacon, professor of literature, their advice being also to adumbrate, to leave out the mountains of evidence: no commercial publisher would risk it as it stood. But, as Kroeber wrote to Leonard Bacon, "I have thought of the ideas presented as resting on the full evidence." He was most reluctant to remove the evidence precisely because this was his first study of the sort: how it had been done was as important as what had been done. He was half-persuaded that he must redo it if it were to be printed at all, when the University of California Press accepted it as it was, bringing it out as one of the university's seventy-fifth anniversary volumes. It was a modestly sized first printing but without cutting or change. That the Press keeps it in print, and that it continues to sell today, twenty-five years after publication, means that Kroeber was right not to cut it. It is the experience it offers in technique and process that continues to find for it new readers.

The reader of *Configurations* participates in the slow accumulation and arrangement of data as they are detailed with relentless fullness and concreteness; he steps with the author among the pieces, seeing how and where the patterns reveal themselves, singly, severally, cumulatively. He is never lost in a mountain of meaningless material, because Kroeber knew and constantly restated for his reader his direction and goal. The dark ways into and out of *cul de sacs* where the findings are negative, are as significant in this book and are explored with detail and demonstration as exacting as the few but exciting highroads it travels to positive discovery.

The reader who persists to the end, to the final listings of negative and positive findings, will have done more than read a heavy book. To the measure of his interest and understanding, he will have gone on an historical-archaeological expedition into the areas of highest achievement of the principal civilizations of the world through time. "By an attitude which consciously recognizes pattern growth configurations in their space-time relations as well as in their value relations" (p. 846), he will understand how "the endless events of history are lifted out of their level of near uniformity into organized relief" (p. 849).

The reader may be exhausted, he may be disappointed that he returns with so few souvenirs from so rugged a journey: no final causalities, no cyclic regularities, no laws by which the acts of man can be predicated. Says the author, "As for findings . . . such as might express a general sociology of human history, this investigation has attained only to approximations." The reader will, instead, have experienced at intimate second-hand, one scholar's slow toil, the sometime agony, the sometime excitement of pursuit of an intellectual theme to its far, exasperatingly elusive end. He will also have been made to think at some length about the phenomenon of genius: never again will he regard a work of genius wholly apart from the culture and configuration which nurtured it.

As to Kroeber and *Configurations*, once it was done he took final leave of it—if not of the questions it asks, at least of its technique of arriving at an answer. He had demonstrated to his satisfaction that the Spenglerian and other visionary statements of finality and uniformity rest upon a mystique for which he substituted the evidence of history; their claim to repetitive and predictable cycles he reduced to the realities of human variability and limitation. And he found a definition for genius which connects it in necessary and inviolable intimacy to the culture from which it takes its being: "Geniuses are the indicators of the realization of coherent pattern growths of cultural value."

The completion of *Configurations* freed Kroeber to use from that time the limpid lucid essay style which became his trademark, already present in many earlier writings but consistently so and with greater polish and ease in the forties and fifties. He would also work and think in a literarily and philosophically freer, in a more wholly asethetic vein. The seven-year experience of *Configurations* could be said to resemble the similarly prolonged hegira period in that he tunneled through much darkness and came out at the end into the light. As with psychoanalysis, so it was with the element survey, with archaeology, with the ethnology of California:

there was no real turning back to any of them once they were done, nor was there a turning away from them in the sense of denial of them. Kroeber carried them along as part of his increasing baggage of work experience, he had them handy for reference, for reworking, refining; they were his treasure dump to be dipped into for new ore if their materials were susceptible of being brought abreast of his then more forward position—they were a part of his life, of himself. But his own course with relation to them was as irreversible as he found a developed culture confrontation to be. (See his "Flow and Reconstitution within Civilizations" in *An Anthropologist Looks at History,* University of California Press, 1963.)

Kroeber's over-all attitude to his former self, his former ideas and interests, was tolerant, humorous-affectionate, as toward old friends or his childhood. This character trait explains why he was so relaxedly candid about his own changed views, his old and his changed self, and why he was so puzzled and bored by attacks upon his own outgrown ideas or the alleged inconsistency in his having changed them. For him, creative science, like the arts, looks to a more humane understanding of the configurations of self, of all life, all matter. A work of art achieved, a scientific truth established, become simply the exciting direction pointers on up the road of possibilities of new creation, further truths.

THE WAR YEARS

Recollecting my way back to 1927, then up the years through 1941, I begin to see that these were the years of a high-noon saturation in our familial, personal "way." Through them threaded depression and the events which led to the Second World War, and both depression and the threat of war incline a close family to live, while it may, inwardly, intimately, self-containedly. They were the years as well when Kroeber's involvement with the four children was intense and continuous. Midway through them and close together the three grandmothers, the great-uncle and the great-great uncle—our nearest Old Ones—died.

The goings and comings between Arch Street and Kishamish were regular, interspersed by summer camp and winter skiing for the children, a few days at Sigonoy, and an occasional weekend in San Francisco for Kroeber and me. Kroeber was in New York teaching at Columbia University during the spring of 1932 where I joined him for the final two months, and he and I were in Mexico for the month of December, 1937, this being the first time he was in Mexico without professional commitment and with leisure for monuments, people, markets, and countryside.

1939 EXPOSITION

In 1939 San Francisco was for the second time staging an international exposition during a European war. (The city's first exposition had been in 1915.) The theme of the 1939 fair was the Pacific Basin, with a ' Pacifica House" its social and architectural center. Kroeber was asked to help plan the exhibitions, using materials from the several museums and borrowing from more distant ones and from private collections as he could. He might have been reluctant to do this except that his own museum was moribund, its contents packed away in odd places since 1931; this was an opportunity to display at least some of its specimens. A further inducement was the presence at Pacifica House of Miguel Covarrubias, the Mexican painter and archaeologist, and René d'Harnoncourt, director for many years of The Modern Museum in New York City. Working with them and the others at Pacifica House meant that for some hours each week for two years Kroeber was deep in talk and thought of art and archaeology and other subjects dear to his heart—interludes in days increasingly full of worry over the opening and dire events of the war.

WAR

The political story of a war is usually told in terms of its diplomacy, its strategy, of how it changed the map. Kroeber told a somewhat different story: he said that war is a form of revolution, a violent convulsion in which people are killed or maimed—or they may go unscathed. War is a time in which art works and cities and the land itself are destroyed or deteriorated—or they may be bypassed; but each person, each familial and customary and humane relation is so affected that the core of the old culture, its accustomed values, its subtle psychic aura which we call "a way of regarding life," does not survive. After a war, the times may be expected to be out of joint indefinitely long—whether for better or worse is a value judgment history will eventually make. A people can no more scrabble together a coherent, stable, *felt* substitute for the slowly accreted body of customary values and ways than can a museum director, starting from scratch, assemble a collection of art objects with inner meaning and cohesion, nor can the president of a university "buy" a ready-made faculty and student body and tradition.

In its nature tradition is cumulative; it takes much time to establish a new one.

I do not go beyond this statement toward a reconstruction of Kroeber's strong views on war. I know that they made the inevitability and, finally, the necessity for waging the Second World War particularly painful to him as to all those whose knowledge of history and whose logicality of mind are such that they understand the present, and a possible future, through the story of the past. Kroeber once remarked of this violent side of man that the old Romans were not special in their fondness for the spectacle of blood-letting, but in the manner in which they had codified it.

Kroeber felt a sort of rage and despair that his experience and learning could in no fashion be brought to bear significantly: he must see his own sons, everyone's sons, enlist or be drafted for military service while he stood by, idle, useless. I speak of this profound discouragement as itself a portent of the times; it was unlike Kroeber to rage against reality however regrettable, and wholly alien to him to lose his sense for the useful niche he always found from which to contribute his characteristic bit toward continuance of a humane world.

Such then was the mood in which he accepted the request to go to Peru in the spring of 1942, as described earlier, an assignment which for a time and to a degree relieved his feeling of having no employment significant to the times. (A curious misapprehension is that Kroeber was an intelligence agent for our State Department in Peru. He was not. He would have refused in any case, but he was never asked.) We arrived from Peru to find home unlike itself, which happens after an absence until one falls again into the old routines, but this time there had been changes. Physically the house was strange because my aunt and uncle who stayed with the children while we were away had tried to follow military instructions: they had black-curtained the French doors and windows of our many-windowed house. It was hopeless to try to black out all light; as soon as the sirens sounded and the street and other lights including our own were doused a neighbor or a policeman would knock at our door—the gleam of a single candle would be showing somewhere. And with all lights out and curtains drawn a stalking mania seized my family, creating bedlam within blackness. They went up and down the front, the back, the basement stairs upon suddenly urgent errands difficult to execute in the dark; they stumbled over furniture, into each other, or opened a door creakingly onto a balcony to see what might be coming through or over the Golden Gate. Nothing ever did come; we were saved having to learn to live with air raids.

Another change on Arch Street was that Marciano, our houseboy and the children's prime playmate for all the years we had been there, was in the Army. He came to see us when he had leave. After the war he stayed in the Philippines to teach school. He was the last full-time help we were to have, and Kishamish particularly has never been the same to any of us without him.

Clifton was already enlisted in the Navy when we arrived home and on the point of being graduated from the university. Within a few weeks he was assigned to duty on a destroyer-escort vessel in the Pacific, and Ted had joined the Air Corps. Karl would enlist in the Navy when he was graduated from high school the following spring. Kroeber was again asking with that desperation which was then upon him, "What can an old man do?"

Within a few weeks he had his answer: he was asked to coordinate and direct on the Berkeley campus a language-teaching program for selected Army trainees.

ASTP

The ASTP or Army Specialized Training Program was set up and directed from Washington by civilian linguist-anthropologists, some in uniform, some not, and was the first planned military use of classroom anthropology. It was born of the uncomfortable awareness which the early weeks of our entry into the war brought, that very few American soldiers spoke Chinese, Japanese, Malay, the languages of the South Pacific Islands, or those of Europe east of Germany. The officer in charge of an attempted landing or penetration with forces and matériel in one of these far places was on his own; and stranger and intruder he was, whether enemy or friend: it was crucial that he, or someone with him, should know the native language. The ASTP would provide some of our soldiers with a speaking knowledge of one of the needed languages, and with as full a comprehension as possible of the nature of the area and its culture. These trained specialists would be seeded among the forward forces, in accordance with the area and the individual language specialization, to act as interpreters and spokesmen upon a first confrontation and as go-betweens and emissaries in ensuing encounters, barters, and exchanges.

I can speak only of the Berkeley program as it was begun by Kroeber, and only impressionistically for the most part. He became ill during the early months of its actual establishment which, along with the war itself, blotted out most of the details, but I do remember his own attitude to it, its particular "feeling tone." Dr. Samuel A. Barrett, Kroeber's first Ph. D.—Barrett was only five or six years younger than Kroeber —was in Berkeley in early retirement from the position he held for many years as director of the Milwaukee Public Museum. He became Kroeber's first associate in the program and took over its direction when Kroeber became ill. Robert F. Spencer, then a graduate student in anthropology and for many years now professor at the University of Minnesota, was his second associate. I am indebted to Spencer for most of the facts here stated regarding the Berkeley ASTP.

Particular universities and Army camps were selected, each to teach a language or set of languages, the only duplications being in the two principal Oriental languages, Chinese and Japanese. The languages of the Berkeley program were those two, the long-established Oriental Department at the university being available as a source for teachers and literature; and for two more languages, Thai and Annamese, which had not been taught anywhere in this country until then. To find teachers, Kroeber scoured the states and brought native speakers from their homeland or from anywhere he could find them and arrange for their coming to Berkeley; and he was able to get Mary Haas and Murray Emeneau, both linguist-anthropologists, to take direct responsibility for the teaching of these languages. Mary Haas spoke a fluent Thai; Murray Emeneau, using native speakers, had developed the basis of a course in spoken Annamese. The trainees selected for the program were college graduates with high academic records and proved competence in a given language; they came from all branches of the Army, were all draftees and noncommissioned. The time allowed the ASTP to turn a young civilian soldier into a facsimile of a field ethno-linguist was thirty (plus) weeks: this was the challenge, to Kroeber an intense challenge.

There were good reasons for Kroeber's intensity: it is rare for an academician aged sixty-seven to serve his country in wartime; it is perhaps as rare for an academician of whatever age in the humanities and natural sciences to perform that service within the area of his own skills and knowledge. More important than this, he soon found that the trainees had been well chosen. For the most part their morale was high; they entered into the program not only with competence but with *brio:* their role as civilian soldiers had become meaningful to them, their contribution was to be both humane and forward-looking. Finally, Kroeber's task was in part creative: he could to a degree shape and direct the program according to his own ideal of what such training ought to be. He fought hard to keep it within sight of his ideal; he had never shrunk from asserting himself over bureaucracy when the end was worth the battle.

Spencer, in a letter to me concerning the ASTP says:

> The Berkeley program was focussed on East and Southeast Asia. . . . We employed a quarter system . . . there were three groups that were trained over a period from mid-1943 until the end of 1944. Originally, the idea was to have these men in language and area training on a three-quarter basis, i.e., three quarters of thirteen weeks each. Group one lasted the full nine months. Groups two and three were given an extra quarter, making their stay at Berkeley a full year . . . group one was involved with the

Japanese and Chinese languages, while group two studied Chinese and Thai, group three Chinese and Annamese, or as it is better known today, Vietnamese.

Spencer continues:

> The students were segregated according to the language which they learned. They did, however, meet as an entire group—that is, group one, two or three—for lectures in geography, anthropology, and related fields. Kroeber's particular innovation was the introduction of the ethnographic informant technique. Here he brought native informants from a given area and drilled the class, using English, in the elicitation of ethnographic and related information. This proved signally successful, as indeed I can attest. Homer Barnett (a professor in anthropology at the University of Oregon at the time, as now) took the initial group, I followed using a Cantonese Chinese, and the same informant was used by Samuel Barrett later. On the language side, somewhat the same technique was employed although in the native language. Here native speakers of whatever language were employed as drill masters, holding the trainees to repetitive, perfectionist practice.

Beyond the rigorous language discipline, it was Kroeber's thought to imitate so far as this was practicable the field-village environment, its essence for the primary purpose of language-learning being that the sounds of the new tongue should bombard the ears of the learners for as many hours of the day as possible. They learned by ear, by speaking, and to this end as many native speakers as could be found were used, providing they spoke with grammatical correctness and the "classic" accent idiom of the language. There was no place for pidgin in this program: the learners might speak only a few words of the new language for some time; even those first words would be in the proper mode. An advantage in having several speakers was that, as no two persons speak quite alike, the ear of the listener adjusts to individual differences and allows for them. Also he would overhear natural conversation between these native speakers: he could become all ears, not having to respond, letting the sounds flow into and over him until he recognized, and more or less spontaneously used, the native word for an object, a person's name or patronymic, a random concept, an action word.

A linguistic "cell" as Kroeber called his unit groups, was perhaps twenty trainees and one to several native speakers. This was a cram-and-crash program: except for the background lectures and reading on the congruent culture, they did nothing all day but learn, listen, repeat, practice, and they did it at an intensity and volume of learning only possible to the young and the scholastically adept. If there were published or hand-written phonetically transcribed grammars or dictionaries or vocabulary lists or folk tales or other linguistic materials, they might study them in the evenings. If there were none, teams of linguists were soon busy in cells of their own, putting together language manuals as phonetic teaching and learning aids, as did Haas and Emeneau for Thai and Annamese.

Kroeber's cells were villagelike in that a single group lived as an exclusive unit in a dormitory where they ate, slept, and studied together. He encouraged them to practice on each other, to communicate so far as possible in the new language. Some of the native speakers lived in, and thus the speaking continued after study and class hours. Kroeber was himself within walking distance of the dormitory. His students liked him and liked to have him come in for dinner with them. The conversations after dinner centered on the language, the country to which it belonged, the people who lived there, the way one "got on" in a strange and exotic land—and then the talk might wander off into more philosophical channels. The details of the programs varied with each group as with each student and each informant and teacher. As it went along, method and technique became codified and formal. But for the brief early time Kroeber was part of it, it was new, experimental, hopeful, positive.

Many of the trainees went on, not to military assignments made with reference to their specialized training, but into a military snafu. They were sent to a language area different from that for which they had been prepared; or they were sent to the correct area but allowed no formal and official opportunity to put their knowledge at the service of the Army, the persistingly hierarchical nature of the military establishment being largely responsible for this failure.

There were no doubt correct and fruitful assignments: the the wrong ones obtrude themselves, but Spencer corroborates my recollections. He says, "At the start of 1945 the movement into Germany was made and the Battle of the Bulge was fought. Many of the trainees were simply sent to Europe as manpower replacements."

There were to be interesting aftermaths of the ASTP and its disappointing war history. Spencer says: "A number of the ASTP students whom we trained went on (after the war) to become professional academicians, either in the social sciences or in linguistics . . . several entered professional anthropology, political science, and geography. In fact, I am still in contact with some of these, seeing them at meetings, and hearing from them from time to time." Beyond this, the ASTP began the revolution in language-teaching which is today's commonplace. The current special language schools are the direct descendants of the ASTP. The informant technique of language learning spread from the schools in modified form to universities and colleges, and is practiced in almost pure form increasingly in primary and secondary schools, where a language is presented to children as a living speaking entity. Young Americans in numbers are discovering they can learn to speak a foreign language, to communicate in it rapidly and satisfactorily by the old ethnological field method. One hears less than formerly of that vague accomplishment, "a reading knowledge"; or of the the copybook drill calculated to get a candidate through his language (reading) requirement. As Kroeber once asked, "How can you read poetry even to yourself unless you know what are its spoken sounds, its music; and what do you really know of a language until you know its poetry?"

ILLNESS

The language program itself was never too exhausting, even though it was exacting and tended to absorb Kroeber utterly, an absorption he welcomed: he saw the program as a step to enlarged human communication, to understanding between disparate peoples, to the saving of human lives. He knew that what he did was worth doing. But the core job which was transparent in its purpose and its means maintained its identity and direction against a barrage of bureaucratic red tape which took such toll in wasted time, exasperation and frustration as to bring Kroeber, by the beginning of the summer of 1943, to a state of near exhaustion: I persuaded him to take a fortnight's rest.

We went to Lake Tahoe in the Sierra Nevada, taking Karl and Ursula with us. We sunned and swam from a private beach, the children rode horseback and hiked, while Kroeber and I paddled or drifted under an August sun on the serene lake.

After some days I became ill with a virulent virus infection; Kroeber told me he too did not feel well, that he thought he should get to a lower altitude; that he would like to be near our own Dr. William Donald. It was a measure of my own fever-vague state that what he was saying did not register with me as to its obvious meaning. I said he should take the children and go home, I would follow as soon as I could travel. Even his answer failed to get through to me although I have always remembered it—my unconscious must have been less affected than my conscious mind—"We must go together; we must not be apart now." Between them, Kroeber, Karl, and the local doctor arranged for us to come home by ambulance. Thus smoothly and swiftly we covered the two hundred miles. Dr. Donald was waiting for us when we arrived.

I was enough recovered the next morning to recall that in the adjoining room a light had burned all night, that Kroeber had not come to bed, and that I had heard his voice, Dr. Donald's and Karl's. For the first time in several days I really *saw* Kroeber. He did not look ill so much as strained and tense, and the color under the tan was not good. When I questioned him he said only that his heart had bothered him at Tahoe, and there was still some pain.

Our first night home the symptoms of panic and unease were again acute; Dr. Donald was at the house half the night and Karl was with his father. After another day I was recovered and Kroeber thought he too was better. I believe, as did Dr. Donald, he was by sheer will keeping the full thrombosis at bay until I was returned to awareness and some sort of functioning. That night, in any case, he went to bed and to sleep, but before I was asleep he wakened in excruciating pain. Dr. Donald gave him a sedative, ordered an ambulance, and together we went to Alta Bates Hospital. There, the doctor put Kroeber under an oxygen tent and arranged for me to stay for the night and to call if anything untoward happened before his return the next morning. Kroeber did not expect to survive the severe thrombosis he had suffered, nor did Dr. Donald pretend to any confidence that he would. In hospital for six weeks, he was brought home by ambulance and carried to the upstairs floor where, for another six weeks, he lived without coming downstairs, a time during which we came to appreciate our house for its upstairs variety of environment: a west bedroom with wide Bay and Golden Gate view; an east room with fireplace which became for the time Kroeber's study; an enclosed sun porch if the day was windy; open balconies when the day was fine. The small room next the playroom was reserved as our dining room: except in the hospital, Kroeber never ate from a tray. He hated it. If he was well enough to eat at all, he sat up at table. Of this preference he said, "No man, at least no man with a beard, likes to eat from his lap or a tray."

After the twelve weeks of strict regime, Kroeber began coming downstairs, at first once a day in time for a before-dinner drink. Soon he was coming down after breakfast for the day, spending some time in the garden, gradually increasing his physical activities. There were a few weeks in this time when I drove him to West Berkeley where the land is flat, and we walked for a half hour or an hour. But Kroeber was recovering from a torn heart muscle not from a stroke: the doctor agreed to his doing light gardening which he much preferred to the formal exercise.

The doctor found that he could give Kroeber his head without concern lest he overstep the restrictions on his activities. He did not like being a patient: he reasoned that the fastest way out of the patient's box was to follow doctor's orders, which he did conscientiously. All smoking was forbidden—a smoker who was used to carrying three reserve pipes in his pocket as replacements for the one in his hand, he stopped smoking overnight and without complaint. Dr. Donald was to say in later years that he was no longer so sure the prohibition had been good medicine: Kroeber's sense of "being really through" if he could not have even an occasional pipe may have been worse for him than the tobacco, but at the time the doctor was afraid to risk it. After a while, Kroeber might take a cigarette at a party, or even a cigar, but he never again touched a pipe.

He "counted" when going up steps to force himself to go slowly; he adapted his former strenuous preferences for tennis and the rapid one-and-a-half mile walk between house and office to shorter walks and milder games. But he never sat for a day without exercise of some sort, if no more than to tie up branches which wind had misplaced, to get the mail or take mail to the letter-box, to walk around the block. The weather never kept him wholly indoors.

At some point during the convalescence, Kroeber asked the doctor when he could "work." I remember the ensuing conversation almost word-perfect since it was for me a sort of eleventh commandment. The doctor wanted to know what Kroeber meant by "work." He meant, he said, getting to some of his notebooks, to a language file, analyzing a grammar—something of that sort. Oh, that—that he could do anytime he wanted to. And for how long? As long as he wished—until he was tired, or tired of the work. But there was to be no administration. No decision-making. No accommodation to someone else's preference or time schedule or decision. "It is the pressure from the other fellow that is the killer. That is why doctors die young." Kroeber asked when he might return to the ASTP. "Never. It damn near killed you once, isn't that enough?"

This was bitter news, to be ameliorated only by his continuing to have some contact with his former students in the program. When he became ill they wrote to him in the hospital and were among his earliest visitors as soon as he was allowed company at home. His hour with them—it would be in the early evening—became one of his happiest during his days of convalescence.

Kroeber returned to teaching in the spring semester of 1944: a "Civilizations" lecture course and a seminar for which the small class came to Arch Street one evening a week.

Kroeber was not fully recovered when he received word from the Royal Anthropological Society in London that he had been awarded the Huxley Medal for 1944—an honor never before accorded an American anthropologist. (There have been two awards since to Americans: to Robert Lowie and to Sherwood Washburn, both of the University of California.) The actual presentation had to await the peace which was still in the future. Under the circumstances of war and near mortal illness, Kroeber received the news with complex emotion: an appreciation of the gallantry of scholars who continued some semblance of humane study in the heart of bombed London, a sense of personal pleasure—it was one of the very few public honors which had real meaning to him; regret that it was for him probably too late.

In the summer of 1944, Kroeber, Ursula, and I decided to try Kishamish, the three of us alone. It turned out to be the final step in Kroeber's recovery. We went, ready to retreat at the first sign of strain. Would Kroeber feel too confined, too invalided there, under the restrictions following his illness? Could we really face, without the three boys, a place which so echoed to their absence?

Ursula and I went to town once a week to market. This left us enough gasoline for close-in drives, an evening or two a week, when the three of us wove slowly up and down and in and out of by-roads of the valley, discovering old vineyards and houses and prospects unknown to us before. Ursula and Kroeber wrote prodigiously—poetry and science respectively—and I made my first tentative beginning toward writing. And far from being frustrated and confined, Kroeber found more and more within his capacity to do outside and each day walked a bit farther. With the help of a neighbor we extended a trail with gentle ups and downs, around the first knoll out of sight of the house and among large boulders, digger pines, and manzanita, where late-summer flowers bloomed and St.

John's Mountain loomed ahead; where squirrels, rabbits, and deer paid us little attention; the only cry was the flicker's, doves repeated their odd lullaby, and quail almost underfoot, scolded their young, Segaga! Segaga!

Here in Kishamish Kroeber was healed: the torn muscle, the tattered edges of confidence.

We stayed the summer.

Back in Berkeley the months of waiting, of listening each night to the ten-o'clock news, of clocking one's day by the arrival of the mails, wore on.

There came at long last the days, May 7 and September 2, 1945. The war was over.

HARVEST YEARS

DIASPORA

We come now to the weaving of the final pattern into the fabric of Alfred Kroeber's life, to the years 1946-1960. He was approaching his seventieth birthday at their beginning and had celebrated his eighty-fourth birthday four months before their ending.

It is autumn as I write, the season Kroeber cared for least. I am sitting in his garden which looks much as it looked when he left it for the last time. It is a spring garden, not a fall one. Unpruned rose bushes put out long thorny branches and a willow tree weeps to the ground across the entrance to the front door. Yet there is order in the line of the dry-rock walls, in the close-cropped grass plot, in the camphor strawberry and liquidambar trees pruned to be uncrowded in the small space. Roses, fuchsias, dahlias, chrysanthemums, and the night-opening tobacco are in full late bloom. In the borders are pansies, lobelias, and begonias along with herbs and succulents. From the plaza the prospect is of distant hills and city, bay, and boats—two-dimensional and Japanesque in the milky-golden haze, framed by two heavy houseposts. Without sentimentality his garden can be construed as a metaphor for

Kroeber's ending years: its tools which are at hand, its weeds which are not out of hand but are present, its intimacy, its window on the outside world, its variety, its unfinished pattern still on the loom of imagination and innovation. Here it was Kroeber read and wrote and gardened whenever we were at home. But most of those years we spent elsewhere, returning like migrant geese to settle in for some weeks or months, then taking off again.

RETIREMENT

The end of the war and Kroeber's retirement marked the beginning of this era. The strident tone of the war years was modulated and the three boys were back, making the family complete, Clifton and Ted with their wives. Families must always have come together at the end of a war to lick their wounds, count their blessings, then start afresh to make some sort of comprehensible life once more. So did Kroeber's family. The boys would return to their books, their uncompleted educations, to the low-income intellectual-proletariat status and life of graduate students from which the war had taken them. They lived at Arch Street during the first months of their return. Clifton's first child, our first grandchild, Jeffrey Alfred, was born there.

Ten years earlier Kroeber had looked forward to 1946, his year to retire, with the pleasurable expectation of release from the load of extra-academic duties asked of senior professors in a state university, and with some apprehension of "being through," of doubt whether he had made adequate economic provision. But long before the time was at hand, both feelings were submerged under the worries and uncertainties of the war. With the approach of the last semester of teaching, he was principally dreading the farewell parties and occasions which are likely to accompany the beginning of retirement. Having been present upon occasions of this sort for some of his friends which had taken on an obituary air—"last suppers" he called them—he asked me to see to it that there should be none for him. But President Sproul, with tact and sense for the appropriate university gesture, quietly arranged for Kroeber to be on leave his last semester. Thus it was he met his last class, attended his last committee meeting, saw the museum staff as its director for the last time, in the spirit and natural relation between students and teacher, and colleagues who expect to meet in the ordinary course after the semester break. On leave in England, and New York City and New England during the spring before his seventieth birthday, the mode and tempo of the coming seven years was set.

ENGLAND

With the end of the war the Royal Anthropological Society set March of 1946 as the earliest possible month for the ceremonies attendant upon presentation of the Huxley Medal for 1945; Kroeber decided to go if I too went, but wartime restrictions on travel made getting permission for me dubious: we were given permission only two days before sailing. We went on the *Queen Mary*, a war-worn queen by then. The passenger list was short, consisting besides ourselves of a few military and State Department people and a few investors and businessmen, carefully screened, we felt, to begin to give England what she then so badly needed: money, machinery, and buyers.

Our small company roamed all over the huge, almost empty ship, talking to her peacetime crew, all of whom had served on the *Queen Mary* throughout the war. The roomy, first-class suites to which we were assigned, without drapes or any movable furnishings were barnlike and rather uncomfortable. All unoccupied cabins and all decks with any roof or wall protection were still hung floor to ceiling with narrow Navy hammocks, separated by aisles equally narrow, and there remained on the open decks the stacks of rafts which the *Queen Mary* had carried as a troopship to supplement the lifeboats. Stopping on a promenade, we would decipher some of the names and home states carved into the railings by American soldiers the ship had carried safely through torpedo-infested waters. The circular emplacements for anti-aircraft guns were bare. Delighted to have some semblance of a normal passage, the stewards set up tables and chairs and made us drinks from the private stores the passengers carried, the *Queen Mary* having no spirits of her own aboard. They also found us deck chairs and blankets. The weather was raw but sunny and, well wrapped and sheltered behind a stack of rafts placed so as to make a windbreak, we were more comfortable on deck than indoors where it was drafty and damp.

We were taken immediately upon our arrival in London to lunch at the Royal Society, and there were gathered many of the people Kroeber most wanted to see in England, among them Julian Huxley—a first face-to-face meeting with him—and Daryll Ford, a British anthropologist who was a friend of many years. We had come, by chance, at the commencement of a five-day bank holiday. Daryll urged us to go with him on his first holiday since the beginning of the war, but when he saw we really preferred to remain in town he left us, having made sure that we had entree to a good physician who was also surely staying in London; a bottle of bourbon; the addresses of his favorite restaurants; and a phone number in Wales where he could be reached.

Our lodgings in London were at 6 Coliseum Terrace, Albany Street, and consisted in the comfortable old-fashioned one-time drawing room of a once elegant house. A shilling fed every two hours to the heater, set in the fireplace, kept us warm. From our windows we looked across to hoardings which hid the destruction, but there stood opposite us at the end of a block otherwise destroyed, an intact pub, The Queen's Arm and Artichoke. We liked this pub, and in its shadow was a fish-and-chips cubicle where we sometimes ate, Kroeber liking to talk politics with the radical Greek who ran it. But we found better food on Tottenham Court Road or in Chelsea or Soho.

There is only the width of the Regency Terraces between Albany Street and Regent's Park; the weather was warm and sunny; the zoo was crowded; everywhere on the grass were children, families, lovers, and solitary persons. One scarcely saw the grass, it was so densely peopled, yet at the end of the the day no flower plot was trampled, the grass did not look overrun, no newspapers or picnic remnants remained to mark the hours of occupation. For five days we saw and spoke to no one we knew, but we talked to many Londoners, men who had fought, women who had done a man's work, old people who had spent their nights in the tunnels of the Underground, volunteer fire fighters, ambulance drivers, first-aid assistants: the survivors. They were keen to talk, to syphon off in words the poison of the remembered terrors, transmitting reality to legend. We were a good audience, soaking up the words like listening sponges, coming to understand the extent of the quiet heroism of these people. It was during those days Kroeber said, "I could live here, feeling at home, not a stranger, for the rest of my life," as he had said in the wartime London of thirty-one years earlier.

We went to Cambridge one week, to Oxford another. The Cambridge week was spent for the most part with British anthropologists, and for Kroeber in informal classroom discussions with students.

Oxford was our most intense encounter, which began in the train compartment we shared with a young Oxonian and two Continental Europeans. Kroeber got into conversation with the student who talked freely and disarmingly, commenting at one point, "We British never talk to each other on the train; it is odd how I do go on with you." He went on until he said something about "the so-called Iron Curtain," at which one of the two men broke into the talk to say in accented, careful English, "Pardon me, my dear young man, the Iron Curtain is not 'so-called.' I, and my friend here, live behind it. I assure you it is real." The speaker was Czech, his friend Polish, both scholars and both going to the meeting Kroeber was to attend. There were other people from behind the Iron Curtain at Oxford, brought there for a first meeting of its European members since 1938, through the efforts of Sir John Linton Myres—historian in New College and secretary of the Congress of Anthropology and Ethnography.

The men from eastern Europe scarcely ate or slept during their days in England. Their hunger and their need was, quite simply, to talk shop, openly, freely, endlessly. The language was the lingua franca of science, of scholarship, of enlightenment; their natural milieu that of men of learning the world over, supranational, cross-cultural. To comprehend the intellectual and emotional starvation of these people, to share even for those few days in the intensity of its brief assuagement, was exhausting, humbling, beautiful. Never, said Kroeber, had the human animal appeared to him more wholly, tragically human.

The awarding of the Huxley medal was a simple ceremony in the hall of the Royal Society, London, presided over by Professor D. T. Fleure, then president of the Royal Anthropological Society, with Julian Huxley assisting. Kroeber's paper for the occasion was titled, "The Ancient Oikoumenē as an Historic Culture Aggregate" and might be said to have been the prelude to much of his later writing and thinking.

We were invited to be present when the doors of the British Museum were opened to the public for the first time since the commencement of the bombing. The wing which had been destroyed by bombs was not yet rebuilt, but in the intact rooms there had been put on display, without reference to provenience or age, several hundred of the museum's most valuable and historic treasures, only just returned from wartime storage in mines or caves. English people came, all classes, all ages, crowding the museum hour after hour. The guards were friendly and responsive and I think no damage or loss occurred throughout the long, permissive day. One saw a hand touch a sculpture or the hilt of a Saxon sword, but caressingly, welcomingly.

We scuffed through the rubble remains of bombing, going behind the hoardings where the old city was already giving way to the new. As we walked, Kroeber mused aloud: To what end this Western civilization, this gift of the Greeks, this so triumphant accomplishment of man? Spengler, with his bizarre view of history, his racism, could not be right that the West was in fact doomed. How truly to understand—not predict—the rise and course and fall of a civilization? History surely is never invariable, inevitable, unchangeable, predictable—whither the civilizations of the world?

On our return trip the *Mary* carried perhaps twenty people from several foreign embassies who were going to Washington. They and Kroeber and I were assigned two suites, one for the women, one for the men. There were also on shipboard 782 mothers each with one or more babies or run-about children, these young women the wives of American and Canadian soldiers who were being brought under United States Army and American Red Cross authority and responsibility to their new homes, to their husbands, or to their husbands' families.

Much about them was touching. They were young, some of them scarcely more than girls; most of them were from small villages and had never been as far from home as London. For them there was morning inspection of quarters, daily medical check-up of the babies, assigned hours for laundry for sunning, for feedings, for meals. The Red Cross did what it could to give them some sort of background: each mother had a long talk with one of the workers who came from an area close to where she would be living. Also, a beauty parlor was opened for them so that they arrived in New York with freshly shampooed hair and manicures. The *Queen Mary* steamed into the inner harbor with her pennants flying, and accompanied by fire boats, tugs, and other vessels with fire and water displays, whistles, and brass bands. The day was one of brilliant sun—it all seemed gay and gallant and of good omen. The ship tied up at her own Pier Forty on the Hudson River. Immediately a giant crane began reaching its great jaws down into the hold, bringing up mouthfuls of prams and depositing them gently for all its noise. Eventually they were all claimed.

Behind a rope barrier on the pier were waiting those who had come to meet and claim the new arrivals. A husband and wife would recognize each other and there would ensue an excited happy effort to converse between ship and shore while the wife held the baby high in her arms for the father to see. There were also those widows and children who must wait while the Red Cross found and identified them to the grandfather, the brother-in-law, the stranger who had come to claim them.

Kroeber's family lived in apartments now, so for the first time we stayed in a hotel in New York. We tried the East Side where the pleasant-seeming hotels proved to be noisy and vastly costly as well as subject to the wartime rule of a three-to-five day limit and to cancellation at any time for military priority. We would have fled the city but we found the late Bernard Mishkin, an anthropologist then occupied with reorganizing the Flying Tigers, living comfortably on the West Side in the Van Dorn Hotel between 7th and 8th avenues on 58th, the pick-up and delivery street for its elegant neighbors to the north and south, the hotel occupied by actors, artists, and models, especially out-of-work or between-job actors. Here we shed our priority troubles onto the concierge, Rosie, who was beyond temptation of cancellation of a paying tenant, particularly a professor whose title, trim beard and walking stick lent an air to her building, according to Rosie's view. We in turn were so taken with our quarters as to linger on for several weeks in the city. For the price of a single small room on the East Side, we now had an ample living room, a bedroom, a large bath—painted purple—and a scratch kitchenette. The only noises which came intimately in our wide-open windows were those of music practice and teaching, of singing and parties in nearby apartments, and of the early morning rattle of garbage collecting. Delicatessens and restaurants were ample and good in the area which served Carnegie Hall people as well as those of the theatre. I loved to lean out our ninth-story windows around eleven o'clock in the morning when the smell of brewing coffee and frying pancakes hung heavy and friendly, countryfying the air.

It was here Clyde Kluckhohn visited us: the friendship which blossomed there is what I most remember about the comfortable disreputable Van Dorn: it was for Kroeber his last close full friendship.

ARCH STREET

Back in Berkeley we were in our last months of having our extended family under one roof. We all went to Kishamish that summer but by fall Clifton and Ted were in separate households. Karl was in his senior year of college, Ursula of high school. The younger children were absorbed in school and friends and engagements away from home, while the older ones, although we saw them often, were busy building their own way of life. Kroeber and I had been alone on

occasional weekends in San Francisco and at Kishamish and on trips, but never on Arch Street. Now we were much alone; we foresaw a near time when we should be wholly so.

We missed the children, their clamor, their variety, their omnipresence. Rooms where we were used to seeing the baby crib and to walking around toys and tennis rackets and the pieces of current projects were become orderly, passive. The house itself heightened the unwonted quiet with its poppings and crackings, the seeming footsteps up and down vacant hallways. All old houses built of wood talk; a redwood house has an astonishing vocabulary, its boards contracting and expanding with explosive noisiness; a copper nail releasing its hold on a panel and dropping with a dry sharp sound; stairs reliving whisperingly at night the comings and goings of the day.

To be alone together here was to be in a new relation to the house—to each other. Almost unconsciously and quite unself-consciously we found ourselves, that early fall of 1946, sloughing an old skin, learning to move in a new and not familiar one. It is hard to put the finger on what was sloughed, what most different in the new. Perhaps it was a change of focus by which the children began to be distanced, to be shifted to a cognitive-emotional plane somewhat off center while the two of us—husband and wife—moved into the close-up precise center of each other's fields.

[When the children were at home I often felt fragmented as if there were not enough of me to go around and with not much of anything left for Kroeber at the frazzled end of a day or a week. I realize that many women escape this frustration; but many women appear to me to have greater resources of energy, of extroverted adaptability, of sheer

Arch Street, 1969

physical strength than I have ever commanded. Neither are all families as impinging, as stimulating to each other as was this one; nor do all fathers and husbands give and receive back such fullness of interpersonal response within their families as Kroeber asked and gave.]

I liked my new skin which I found wondrous free. Would his suit Kroeber as well? In other days he had escaped for awhile when the clamor became too wearing, too insistent, to return refreshed and ready to add his bit. Would the house be to him merely echoing, dull? We studied each other during those autumn weeks. One day, Kroeber speaking somewhat formally and diffidently, said that this was as another autumn many years ago when we came to know each other for the first time: we were now rediscovering, each of us, what the other thought, believed, liked, wanted to do; what he had become.

The crisis passed as such crises must have come and gone since the beginning of human time. A sense of reprieve was some part of the new skins, a reprieve of which we had been conscious in another way since the day of Kroeber's coming home from the hospital in 1943. Now, three years later, Dr. Donald pronounced the torn heart muscle wholly healed.

We dared to forget it, to give ourselves adventurously, never with the timelessness of the young, but intensely, freely—days fast passing as the red clusters of the winter-blooming rose on the back fence of the garden. With the psychic shifts came new ways of doing homely daily routines. Clif and Ted remind me that it was then my way of cooking changed even as the slim green bottle of chablis replaced the squat green pottery milk pitcher on the lunch table, that breakfast was later and more often in the garden, that we tended to linger over any meal, talking, unhurried. We began to use the house differently, changing the steps from the study to come down inside the house instead of into the garden; the card catalogue of a poetry project we had under way was moved into one of the unoccupied rooms; and we spent more hours gardening than had been our wont and more of those gardening hours together. Kroeber liked to fill bowls with roses, putting them all over the house. He liked the painstaking job of gathering seeds of wild and garden flowers, and growing them. There was a ragged clump of carnations: I suggested they might be taken out, but Kroeber shook his head, "They've done poorly lately, but I'm going to feed them up." He once said, "Gardening is for the old, when the children are gone and you feel the want of something growing, needing your care." And he said, "The most satisfying thing in the world—next to children—is a tree you yourself plant and watch grow, measuring it, knowing it will be here when you are gone."

Two or three days a week Kroeber went to the campus for part of the day, to get his mail, books, and materials from library and museum, to dictate for awhile in his office, to have lunch according to old custom with his colleagues at the Faculty Club. In his study at home he turned first to his notebooks and the files of materials he had collected earlier but which had not been put into finished and publishable form. The linguistic and folkloristic data—some of it—went back to his earliest field work in California. To complete these raw data he considered a first obligation of retirement. But there were other obligations: there was his correspondence which was large and varied and, free of the former business and administrative matter, almost all of importance to him or to his correspondent. There were requests for recommendations for positions, for research grants, for appraisals of papers or books, and requests from universities and foundations for confidential opinions on people and projects—these all as numerous at least as before retirement, probably because Kroeber was thorough and conscientious in his responses. Other correspondence was in the nature of continuing conversations between himself and people in a number of scholarly fields, some of them friends, some he knew only by way of their letters. They and the matters of which they wrote were of many sorts in response to his varied interests, and this correspondence was as important to him as to the other parties to it.

The first autumn of retirement passed quickly. Christmas came and the New Year, without Kroeber's having looked for occupation or entertainment beyond home, office, and library. The next sentence might have been projected to read: "And in this fashion, Kroeber's life moved serenely and uneventfully down the years, one year much like another," except that in his own fashion and on his own terms, Kroeber was one of the company of the questing, evolving, impinging, inseminating avant-garde of science and scholarship, and a retirement begun in a new adventure would draw to itself others.

GUEST PROFESSOR

Clyde Kluckhohn visited us early in the new year. A beguiling and persuasive person, he and Kroeber had long talks, entertaining and stimulating each other seemingly endlessly—Clyde must have determined then to lure Kroeber away from his Arch Street retreat; in any case, a few weeks later Talcott Parsons, then chairman of the Social Relations Department at Harvard, wrote asking him to come there to teach for the academic year 1947/48, the teaching load to be light and with the number and selection of students left to him. After some weeks of hesitation Kroeber accepted—it did not occur to him that his acceptance would affect absolutely, not the single year, but all the years ahead.

Hard upon Parson's invitation came another from Duncan Strong, chairman of the Department of Anthropology at Columbia University, to teach there the coming summer. This invitation included the promise of a large cool apartment on Claremont Avenue, half-way between 116th Street—the entrance to Columbia—and Riverside Drive. Kroeber accepted. To be in New York for some weeks was tempting to him and it would take the two younger children east for the first time. (Karl would be going to Keokuk, Iowa, for a year of work in radio, and Ursula would be entering Radcliffe College in Cambridge in the fall.)

Kroeber would be satisfied to be away from Berkeley for a full year for another reason: he now knew that so long as he was within call he was consulted weekly sometimes daily, on some museum or department matter. This was natural enough: his concern for department and museum was not diminished by retirement; the decisions had been mostly his for forty-five years; he was the person to whom Lowie, now chairman, and Gifford, now director, were used to turning for administrative, academic and personal advice and direction as did others in the department and museum. It was hard for them to go elsewhere so long as Kroeber was at hand, and it was hard for him not to respond to whatever the request or need was: one year away would break the habit of many years.

In other words, Kroeber might be said to have accepted his first post-retirement teaching positions despite their involving him in teaching. Teaching accounted for many years of Kroeber's time and energies; he thought of himself as a teacher; when asked to fill out identifications cards I noticed he always wrote opposite the request for his profession, Teacher. As to his attitude to teaching, and to students, he did not feel the compulsive concern so common today; he considered teaching the most onerous of his tasks, the students themselves the task's reward. Kroeber and Lowie perforce discussed teachers and teaching whenever they selected assistants or assessed the qualifications of a prospective teacher to give the large introductory course or to give graduate instruction. Later, Kluckhohn and Kroeber sometimes talked about teaching, it being a more controversial subject by the fifties, particularly in an experimental department such as Harvard's Social Relations. Kluckhohn, Lowie, and Kroeber were in agreement in looking upon teaching, as had Boas, as an indispensable task of a practicing anthropologist and an absolute responsibility to graduate students in the profession. Kroeber recognized a further duty as teacher to give each year if possible one nonprofessional course as his contribution to the humane and broad education which he regarded as a desirable part of a university student's undergraduate experience. The three men were in agreement also, as I suppose are most professors, in considering the specialists in radiation, in computering, in the expensive fringe of modern university activity most closely tied to government and the military, as not engaged in university-oriented instruction or research except by individual exceptional chance.

As to his further responsibility to students, Kroeber posted office hours which he kept, and he made himself available by appointment at other times. His response to the interested, curious, and bright, or to the groping, troubled, and confused young people who came to consult him was unforced, genuine, warm, perceptive. But except for routine business with them, he made himself selectively available: it was to his and Lowie's graduate and upper division major students that he looked first, seeing to it that they went to the field, if possible the field of their own choice—helping them to get money, fellowships, scholarships, permanent positions. He lent himself generously to their intellectual problems and to their personal-emotional problems when this seemed called for. He was aware that time and other personal expenditures which went to them took that much from other occupation and preoccupation as a creative scholar and scientist and from his family. He reserved the freedom to discriminate.

Kroeber had no ambition to be a "great" teacher, or to be a guru to disciples. So far as I know neither students nor his colleagues thought of him in either category, nor does his name come to mind when teaching "personalities" of the university's past are being recalled. What does happen is that a former graduate of the university will introduce himself to tell me how much a course he took with Kroeber fifteen, thirty years ago, still means to him. More often than not it turns out to have been the Culture History course, and frequently it is the only course he really remembers, because it animated a trip up the Nile, a morning in the Uffizi Palace, a pilgrimage to Greece; or the reading of a book. But it is the course content which is principally recalled. He is likely to say simple homely things of the man: "He was plain, like he was talking to a friend." "He was kind." "You didn't have to put a question very well—he was quick to know what you meant."

Over the years Kroeber became disenchanted with teaching—not with students. The small sections of ten or at most fifteen undergraduate students, meeting twice weekly to supplement the three large formal weekly lectures of the basic Anthropology 1A-1B were looked upon with less and less favor by the administration, and their curtailment or abandonment encouraged: the small class in any form was coming to be regarded as an extravagance, while some educators and administrators were fascinated with large "general education" courses for freshmen. Lowie and Kroeber saw these courses as doing little more than unrolling before the young student a too broad map of a too large scholarly terrain for him to manage with accuracy or assurance; untrained in the narrower disciplines of scholarship, he got from the broad survey course no more than a series of vague impressions and a few generalities which he did not know how to confirm or to move out from. Then there were the prolonged faculty committee meetings having to do with the adoption of a new course or a new name for an old course or with other minuscule curriculum changes. I remember the weariness in Kroeber's voice after one of these sessions, "Whisper Curriculum! and a dozen pedants are in full cry." When he accepted the summer appointment at Columbia he was contemplating a final full year of teaching, whose rewards would be largely outside the classroom. But before the summer session was half gone he had discovered a freedom, a creativeness, an opportunity in teaching, which until then he had experienced only during his brief time with the ASTP, a discovery that persuaded him to teach ten full semesters and two quarters of the twelve years remaining to him. His teaching load in these years was light, never more than a seminar and, usually, a lecture course. Within the aptitude and competence of his students and the slant of the department, Kroeber chose courses which were most meaningful to him at the time. He experimented. He learned along with his students, whose numbers and make-up were subject to his control. He found the student-teacher relation to be relaxed and spontaneous except for the first semester at Harvard where he had to accommodate to the abnormal pressure on his students in the Social Relations Department to become equally expert in anthropology, psychology, and sociology—a temperamental and academic impossibility.

Kroeber drew a moral from his post-retirement teaching: American universities would use more fully their senior scholars' skills and experience if, for perhaps the last ten years of their active service, professors were relieved of extra-professorial responsibilities, asked to sit only on such occasional *ad hoc* committees as had to do with grants and research and appointments which interested and concerned them. For the rest they should be left to teach what and how and when they wished, with more time, and a more relaxed time, for teaching, writing, research—for field work if they so desired. Kroeber would have been on the side of the students in the 1964, free-speech protests at Berkeley had he been alive then. But I think neither students nor faculty would, for the most part, have agreed with his teaching attitude which differed from the more common one in its assumption that teaching, like painting or writing, is an art, not a service; that it cannot be stereotyped and bureaucratized; that the soundest foundation for real learning is the old apprentice one: you learn most from the one who is the master in his field, no matter how far his teaching departs from the rules set up for run-of-the-mill teachers. You accord him the freedom and consideration which such a teacher will in turn and as a matter of course accord his students and his colleagues.

Kroeber could have taught full-time and summers from 1947 on; he declined more invitations to teach than he accepted, accepting those he did for reasons which seemed appropriate and significant to him. Besides Harvard and Columbia he taught at Brandeis, the University of Chicago, and Yale; he was scheduled to give a seminar in his old department in Berkeley in 1960/61. He taught enough to keep himself in touch with the generations of becoming anthropologists for another twelve years. He came to know well the various departments and to know personally many people in art, linguistics, and anthropology whom he had known only at a distance and through correspondence; and those teaching years put him at the heart of the social and intellectual currents which flow, even today many of them, east of the Mississippi.

Although it was Kluckhohn who did most to lure him back to teaching in the first place and Duncan Strong in the second, Kroeber took little stock in Clyde's plea that it was more important for young anthropologists to have known him face to face than for him to finish yet another ethnological report. Said Kroeber: "It is the other way around—it is more important for me to know them." Duncan pointed out the importance of a prolongation of the Boas tradition at Columbia, but Kroeber was little interested except as historical fact in any so-called schools of anthropology whether Boasian, Kroeberian, or other; and less interested in their prolongation if the times had outgrown the school.

It was to Columbia he went after one year at Harvard, somewhat to Clyde's dismay and disappointment, and it was at Columbia he taught for the next four years, 1948-1952, much his longest stretch. The preference was natural: New York City had been his home; it is the center, the obvious place if one is gypsying around intellectually, not staying with one's old ideas and habits in one's own study. Kroeber found the Columbia students much to his taste; they were bright, off-center, avid for new ways of regarding cultural phenomena, and in a mood to stimulate and be stimulated by him. What he would most miss, away from Cambridge, was Clyde himself, but he would see a good bit of Clyde in New York, since they were already in the first planning stages of their joint book which became *Culture, a Critical Review of Concepts and Definitions.*

For the next four years our home was an apartment on Riverside Drive, a steep block down from Columbia, our west and south windows overlooking the Hudson River to the harbor below and beyond Washington Bridge upriver. Nor were we alone there: Clifton was with us briefly en route to a research-history year in South America; Karl was taking graduate work at Columbia by then, living near or with us; and in 1951 Ursula came to Columbia for the first of two graduate years she would spend there.

These were full years for Kroeber, varied and intellectually exciting, their direction and content unplanned, unforeseeable. By their end he had come to take as a condition of life conferences on a variety of subjects and with people drawn from Europe, Asia, and Africa; lectures or a seminar at one or another eastern campus; frequent dinner meetings such as those of the Ethnological Society of New York and the Wenner-Gren Foundation; time to spend with his New York family, with his friends, a score of different stimulating possibilities in any week. Opera, Metropolitan and City Center, Carnegie Hall with Kroeber's mother's seats for symphony and concerts, on- and off-Broadway theater were a twelve-minute subway ride distant. One block up to Broadway and between 116th and 110th Streets were our butcher and barber, greengrocer, shoe and umbrella and typewriter repairmen, bank, stationers, post office, pharmacy, bookstore, kosher baker and delicatessen, restaurant-bar, and fish house. At 110th, our village ended and another began where we were not known and which we did not trouble to know. By the end of the first summer we had found the few small westside French, Basque, or Italian restaurants where we went once or twice a week and which we continued to prefer to others.

What set these years apart from all others was not our being away from home during most of them; it was rather that Kroeber reverted to being, and I became New York oriented in the way we spent our time, in the way we felt. Came the spring of 1952 and a letter from Oslo, the university or an institute, I do not now remember which, inviting Kroeber to teach there for the following year; he had already been asked to continue at Columbia. Whether to stay where we were or to go abroad or to go home brought us to a confrontation we had until then side-stepped: what indeed were our long-range plans? In the deepest sense, where were we going?

We sat weighing, considering, while, looking out our windows we saw, spread below, the park drive and the river. It was the time of spring thaw upriver; ice had broken loose and come coursing downstream, one enormous free-form floe sparkling as the sun touched it, followed by others as in a formal parade of holiday floats on their way to the sea. When the year was over in Oslo, we would be very close to the heart of Europe, to Paris, to Venice, to Delphi—east, ever eastward, away from home.

We thought of our home and the garden, which had not been much in our thoughts recently, recalling them as a house and garden deteriorated, seeming scarcely to be our own after years of alien occupation and neglect. We thought of the many demands of property and community identification. The children were fairly launched; we could choose where we wanted to be, what we wanted to do. Were we choosing now—or were we drifting with our tides? Kroeber said, "We could liquidate all our holdings and float free henceforth."

But there was a homesickness in us, a weariness of always packing and unpacking, of lugging books and papers and pictures, always too many and never enough; of being weighted down with indispensable household and study utensils and equipment, but always making do with substitutes for the most part; a distaste for other people's ugly china on our own table, for the cramped space in our rented temporary shelters; for the inadequate dark holes which passed for kitchens in which I had been cooking since leaving home. Thinking aloud, Kroeber mused that he was facing two ways, had been doing so for some time, as he had done back in the early twenties when he was trying to be both an anthropologist and a psychoanalyst. He had to choose. The short-run decision to come east had been good and he might, leaving it, miss it. But for the long run, the healthy deep roots pulled inexorably westward where, undisturbed, they had been digging themselves ever deeper since 1900. The turned tide brought back upstream under our windows the free-form floe, now moving strongly away from the sea, still intact but with its parade of followers somewhat the worse for their bath in warmer and saltier waters. Kroeber said: "We must *reracinate* to Berkeley or close out—we shall go home for a full year—then we shall see."

WARP AND WEFT

Alfred

This old notebook I write in was my father's;
he never wrote in it. A grey man,
all my lifetime, with a short grey beard;
a slight man, not tall.
The other day I saw five elephants,
big elephants, with palm-trunk legs
and continents of sides, and one,
the biggest one, had bent tusks bound
about with brass. They were waiting,
patient, to be let outside
into the sunlight and the autumn air,
moving about their stall so quietly,
using the grace of great size and the gentleness,
swaying a little, silent, strong as ships.
That was a great pleasure, to see that.
And he would have liked to see the big one making water,
too, like a steaming river,
enough to float ten bigots in.
O there is nothing like sheer quantity,
mountains, elephants, minds.

This poem by Kroeber's daughter, Ursula, written the summer following her father's death, introduces my account of Kroeber's final seven or eight years. In writing of those years I found myself necessarily selective in choosing which colors, which threads to use from among disparate and numerous possibilities for completing the ever more complex pattern. For during these years Kroeber's mind and imagination spread, like the delta of a great stream, over the whole plain of culture history, probing its vastness and variety, testing, playing with possibilities; gathering in new data or rearranging, freshly interpreting old data; viewing the phenomena of history in ways as yet not philosophically accepted, sometimes not named. I have contented myself with the barest of outlines, with naming some of the occasions whose subject matter suggest the nature of the interests, with naming some of the people who were part of these interests, and with adding a few of Kroeber's own statements—usually in personal letters, now in the archives of the Bancroft Library of the University of California in Berkeley. Such treatment makes for dispersal. But Kroeber was gathering data and perspective for historical work and was himself as yet in the "dispersal" — the almost abstract stage — of a major undertaking. (I refer to the unfinished *Roster of Civilizations.*)

THE RETURN

In our first months back on Arch Street we renovated and restored house and garden, which we never again rented. Kroeber once wrote: "It is a mistake to rent one's own home. There is always the sense upon return of there having been violation practiced upon something intimately part of oneself, even when there has been no misuse." A letter to Clyde Kluckhohn carries into 1953 when Kroeber wrote in the mood of return and settledness: "It was good of you to think of us for Salzburg and I wish we could come. But this summer five Clifton Kroebers converge on Berkeley from Madison; Karl, after school, comes with Jean Taylor to whom he will be married by then, and Ursula flies in, not to mention the Ted Kroebers, numbering four. We'll be fourteen when we sit down together at Kishamish, the first time and quite possibly the last that assembly will actually happen. So how could we go off for the summer?"

Said Kroeber: "It is good for the soul to have two irons in the fire. . . . A second active interest tends to encourage a third; whereas a man who has only one is in the ultimately retractile position of a monolingual." From the time of the return to Berkeley Kroeber accepted short teaching engagements of a few weeks or a quarter. Twice he went for a full semester, but the absences were now regarded as temporary breaks from a permanent base and from a way of life which left space and time for three or more irons. Time to spend at Kishamish in springtime when the clover is new and green and the floor of the valley chartreuse with wild mustard; in autumn when the vineyards are scarlet and purple and the air acrid from fermenting wine. In winter, to go to the coast where oyster catchers and pelicans and cormorants come to the shore, where sea lions play and where sometimes one can watch a mother sea otter feeding her baby and teaching it to swim in a bed of kelp close to shore. Time to correspond with the Yerkes Laboratory about dolphins and octopuses. "If you have an octopus beak to spare, I should be delighted if you would send it to me. I have never had an opportunity to examine or handle one." (The beak and an octopus liver arrived shortly.) "No, I shall not be attending the psychological meetings in Boston. I would have difficulty understanding most of the papers. We anthropologists are mostly simple folk as regards terminology and abstractions . . . It looks to me as if the octopus beak were specially adapted to crush through crab shells."

Time to make two winter field trips. For the months of February 1953 and 1954 we drove south and inland to the Mohave Desert, to Boulder Dam, then downriver to Parker, the small Anglo-American town set in the middle of the Mohave Indian reservation where the Parker Dam impounds water which goes to Los Angeles. Here Kroeber was back once again doing field ethnology as he had done in the early nineteen hundreds. The Mohaves now had cars and farm machinery; they raised cotton, but they also planted corn, beans, and squash in the red silt of the river banks as had their ancestors.

Within an hour of our arrival, Kroeber was seated on an upside-down washtub, pencil and notebook in hand, while a friendly and mild-mannered Mohave recounted to him the details of how he had recently brought death to an enemy through witchcraft. And within two days Kroeber was deep in the recording of an extended story—the personal property of an old man, Aveyupa by name, his long hair bound up in a net in the Mohave style. This story differed only as each man's story must differ from another's because he dreams its episodes throughout his life, and no two men dream alike. But it was classic Mohave with alternating episodes and song cycles; and with the expectable specificity in matters of geography.

Kroeber himself had sometimes dreamed of checking the geography of a Mohave myth against the actuality from which it grew, but he had never had the leisure to do this until now. With a list of names in the order of their appearance in a story he had recorded before 1907, with a graduate student to drive the car and an old Mohave man as guide, he set out into the desert. The distances between various places, the length of a day's march, the springs, mountains, hills and swales, the old village sites, the places where a song cycle had been sung, could now be pin-pointed on a modern geodetic survey map of the area, except where all evidence had been erased. Thus it was mapped—this long ago myth from a man dead many years, who had lived into old age and throughout whose adult life, night after night, year after year, had dreamed its parts until at last he had come to the end of his dream journey.

Kroeber knew only by hearsay the spot at which the Mohave world had been created at Ha'avulypo in Black Canyon on the Colorado River. At last he went to Ha'avulypo, recognizing the exact spot—the upright slender column of red rock which stands there: Matavilya, the Creator God turned to stone and become a silent sentinel guarding the river which his son, Mastambo, had caused to gush forth with a single plunge into the earth of his powerful cane made of spittle. After making the river, Mastambo had ridden it to the sea, carving out the Grand Canyon and the other canyons along the way by ramming his stone boat against one bank and then the other.

The boat in which Kroeber and I poled and paddled our way

to Ha'avulypo was a weaker vessel than Mastambo's, small in all its dimensions, light and flat-bottomed, thus enabling us to rock it gently over the symmetrical soft cones of red silt which form the river bed. The peaks reach almost to the surface and are ultimately deposited down river, forming the delta, building and renewing the Imperial Valley, a garden which will go on feeding a good many of the world's peoples, unless the greed of cities and power companies is allowed to destroy Mastambo's unique work.

INDIAN LAND CLAIMS CASE

Before turning to Kroeber's other occupations in the fifties, his participation in the Indian Land Claims case, *Docket 31-37, Indians of California vs. The United States of America*, should be mentioned. The proceedings of this and all Indian land-claims cases, the earlier as well as the more recent ones, are a matter of record; here I wish no more than to suggest Kroeber's role in the single case and some of his reactions to it.

An official representative from the Indian Bureau of the Department of the Interior in Washington first talked to Kroeber about the case. He wanted Kroeber, along with other Indian specialists, to "sit down together around a table" with government and Indian representatives, there to arrive at an equitable and common agreement about the just claims of today's surviving Indians and to compensate them for their lost lands.

There was no follow-up to this conversation because the hearings were, by the wording of the enabling act, in the form of suits, and suits are heard in the Department of Justice. Kroeber learned how bitterly the Justice Department was fighting the claims: gone, then, was the perhaps always mythical around-the-table gentleman's effort to find justice in a hard case, and this put a different face on Kroeber's own role and his moral and professional responsibility. He was retained directly by the law firm representing the California Indians, which in turn paid what looked at the time to be a reasonable fee with some expense monies for preparation of maps and the like.

Kroeber, as the principal witness, found his the decisive voice and conscience in a no-holds-barred legal battle. He won the battle: his evidence was indubitable; his testimony was vivid, precise, and interesting. He brought his classroom manner to his court testimony, speaking quietly and reasonably. He spoke also with a contained passion: he was testifying for a people and land which he knew intimately and loved deeply. He had an old way of cutting in, amiably, humorously, but firmly, lightening the mood when discussion at the seminar or dinner table took an unhappy or ugly turn, and he used that old way in court.

Outside the court he was at pains to maintain good relations with his colleagues and former pupils who were giving evidence, some for the government, some for the Indians. So far as I know no friendships were blasted by the hearings; the Berlin Wall of that court was not between the scientists of opposing sides but between the world of science on one side and the world of litigation on the other. His participation in the case was altogether an aberrant and unsatisfactory experience for Kroeber and an expensive one in that it cut across and interfered with his writing and research for five crucial years, from January 1952 to June 1956. Moreover, he considered the act by which the hearings came into being less than adequate or forward-looking or unambiguous. Conceived in guilt, it sought by arbitrary money payment to appease a bad conscience arising from conquest and seizure of a people and their land: scarcely an acceptable solution in the socially aware twentieth century.

After four more years the commissioners appointed to hear the case "found for" the Indians, and eighteen years after the case was opened the Indians of California were authorized in a bill signed by President Johnson to receive the monies of the judgment they had won: eight hundred dollars to each properly identified and qualified Indian man, woman, and child living in September 1968: the sort of expensive-meaningless *dénouement* Kroeber had feared.

ACTIVITIES AND REACTIONS

Turning now to some of his happier and more natural interests, I find that Kroeber's slim vest-pocket appointment books for that decade record symposia and conferences in which he participated, some large, some small, and of considerable variety of subject matter and viewpoint. They range beyond conventional ethnography and linguistics and history into metahistory, mass communication, and theoretical linguistics to such matters as human rights, feudalism, cyclic phenomena, the psychological set of different disciplines, Darwinism today, the unity of knowledge, causality in culture. Two of them were of his own design and direction: a large international conference entitled "Anthropology Today" (New York, 1952, auspices of Wenner-Gren Foundation, eighteen nations besides the United States sending representatives); and a small intensive symposium entitled "Anthropological Horizons" (Burg Wartenstein, Austria; September 1960, also under Wenner-Gren auspices).

Kroeber's correspondence for the same period, now in the Bancroft Library, sometimes reflects reactions to these various concerns, some of which I have included below, where the statement or the manner of it appeared to me to enliven or point up something characteristic of him. I give them without particular comment or explanation.

"How does one decide where one culture, civilization, period, phase, ends and another begins, without getting caught in a Toynbee formula, or working just by common knowledge. Delimitation won't work; will some kind of 'clotting' give an integration?"

"I read and write theory with a good deal of mutual effort—while I have written a good deal of it in the aggregate, it has been sweated out. You'll note it rarely comes pure—I tend to hang it on to something concrete."

"I'm still a determinist, but I think it is impossible to maintain a completely deterministic attitude. I should say the thing to do is to treat the phenomena of history as if they were determined and see how far you can legitimately get by doing that; i.e., how many new insights you reach which would not be reached if one kept injecting consideration of individuals and the random wills of their personalities. In short, phenomena are mixed and who are we that we should think we can find a total causality that will explain everything."

"I am more and more tending to deal less with causality in

our material and more with patterns, significance and the objective analyses or delineation of values. Obviously individuals who really are entirely self-determined are never going to add up into patterns. Any pattern is some kind of an order, and any order is in some way determined. It seems to me this dilemma cannot be escaped. Either we are primarily interested in individuals as personalities, and in that event we shall attain to only a minimum of order, or on the other hand we are interested in order, and in that case the fruitful procedure is to treat individuals as exemplifications of an order so far as they legitimately fit into patterns without forcing—and if there is a residue, which there will inevitably be, not to worry too much about it. In neither case is a total exploration attempted."

"I am skeptical about rhythms in most socio-cultural phenomena, and especially their macro-manifestations. But we've got to try to find out instead of just believing or not believing."

"As a fatalist, I have not too much faith or interest in anybody's solution of the contemporary situation."

"I get on fine with historians and always feel at home with them in the flesh. In fact I consider myself a sort of irregular and unorthodox one. I do wish more of them would compare more; but you are right: there is no use getting impatient."

"I am aware that I am perhaps the only anthropologist who has genuine macro-historical interests. Lowie and Laufer were interested in culture history, but not in its periodization. Almost no historians want to do macro-history, and their profession is against it. Anthropologists are a looser caste—they look upon my predilection as a foible. So it's all very amiable, especially as I learned early to travel alone if need be. . . . You cannot do macro-history without evaluating comparatively."

"I look for contextual relations in time, in space, intrinsic. I don't deal with causes, except incidentally, little ones, now and then, by the way."

"I wouldn't worry about the unsolved or presumably insoluble problems, like the reality of historical organisms, or the minor civilizations. Tell what is definable in space, in time and cultural content, and what recurrences and regularities, whole or partial, speak for themselves."

"I believe that individual human beings are always the immediate causes of events. . . . But in addition I have learned that cultural events have their interrelations and significances brought out more sharply if one focuses beyond individuals on the cultural pattern."

"It was stimulating to meet you [Arnold Toynbee] especially our walks together. . . . I offered two public lectures here [Harvard]. . . . I diluted nothing but the audience followed closely all the way. . . . I called [the lectures] 'Spengler and Predecessors,' 'Toynbee and Successors' and left myself out at least formally. Sorokin's is a very Russian personality. . . . I find him . . . definitely stimulating in the flesh, whereas his writing tends to the inflated if not turgid . . . but he knows a vast deal of actual history. Northrup of course is a philosopher with answers . . . flashes of historical insight."

"Why not stop weighing alternatives and giving explanations, but write with your head and knowledge, like all old-fashioned historians, and lay down the line of what seems to you most likely to have happened?"

Two meetings in 1952 drew comment from Kroeber: a small symposium, "Application of Scientific Method to Study of Human Behavior," with Crane Brinton, Joseph Wood Krutch, and B. F. Skinner participating; and the large "International Symposium on Anthropology" under auspices of the Wenner-Gren Foundation, with Kroeber as over-all chairman.

"I believe anthropology to consist of three about equal components—natural history, humane and social science—I consider my own motivations and interests to consist overwhelmingly of the first two; I am not really a social scientist at all. I had to reach seventy, before I began to discover that, but I think I know it at eighty."

"I have increasingly realized in recent years that I have never been a behavioral or even a truly social scientist, but a humanist with a sort of natural history slant. I am interested in languages, grammars, civilizations, styles, religions, logics—all of which have patterns and forms and are *products* of social behavior, but are not behavior in themselves. I have really been only incidentally interested in the interrelations and actions of groups of people. Yet that is just what personality-in-culture, acculturation, community studies, communications, applied anthropology, and its other contemporary cutting-edge fields deal with: they come truly behavioral."

"For centuries hundreds of thousands of human beings in California have been forming a style, a variety of styles, according to nation and occasion, in which they expressed some of their profoundest feelings; and we cannot yet make a single exact and intelligible remark about their accomplishments."

"I am more and more convinced that the real difference between sociologists and anthropologists is one of temperament. Speaking broadly, anthropologists want contacts and experience and want them concrete. They like sensations. It is one way they have of living—impinging on other people or on other cultures or on other sciences. The result is that their work has in it a touch of the same sort of thing that makes humanists, as well as perhaps a bigger ingredient in most cases of what in science is called natural history. Sociologists, on the other hand, are not avid for impingements and experiences: they want abstractions. Hence they have done so much more theorizing and are so much sharper in their definitions, and altogether seem to live in a more rarified atmosphere. On the other hand, they forego without a qualm, whole areas, such as physical type, biological basis, specific environments, language, almost the whole of archaeology, etc., a whole series of areas that anthropologists resolutely refuse to let go, although many of them do not themselves cultivate more than one or possibly two of these fields."

"One could take the position of social psychologists that everything the psychologist concerns himself with is due to conditioning. . . . I was tacitly assuming on the basis of parallel phenomena in sub-human organisms, that there are such traits or qualities as cruelty congenital in our make-up, and that what conditioning determines is the norm and intensity of their expression. . . . I have noted before that the modern psychologist attributes more to culture than the anthropologist does, the latter being ready to allow a congenital substratum to the manifestations of personality."

"I have been the arch-anti-Frazerian in anthropology. In fact, my view is that Sir James has never really influenced professional anthropologists in their thinking, though his affect was great and real on classical scholars, humanists, Freud and Freudians, people wanting to break away from religious orthodoxy, and intellectuals generally."

"I feel that the need of the anthropologists learning more about art is much more pressing than to have students of art know more anthropology; it seems to me very strange how timid we continue to be about making, I will not say value judgments, but value analyses in the material which we collect and often describe."

In 1953 Kroeber attended a conference at Arden House, New York, "The Unity of Knowledge" of which he wrote in part: "Every field of knowledge has its implications for the study of man, his nature, his life, and his place in the world. Is there any likelihood that a single recognizable picture of man can be discerned among the many detailed and varied arts and sciences? In what ways do the disciplines interrelate in their understanding of the human scene? What obstacles stand in the way of a whole view of man, and what signs are there of the possibility of its achievement?"

In 1954 Kroeber taught at Brandeis University, visited in Florida, and went several times to the Center for the Behavioral Sciences at Stanford, California—his return to Berkeley in 1952 did not take him away from his various interests; it merely changed their focus.

He spent the year of 1956/57 at the Behavioral Sciences Center, to which he returned also in 1958 for a two months residence. He gave the Messenger Lectures at Cornell in 1956, his title "Style and Civilizations"; and the Bernard Moses Lectures on the "Psychology of Sex" at the University of

California in Berkeley. He taught during the fall term at Yale in 1958 and was at the University of Chicago during the fall of 1959 where, with Julian Huxley, he prepared a panel—"Social and Cultural Evolution" in preparation for the Darwin Centennial in November of that year.

Whenever the possibility of a permanent museum building came up in conversation, Kroeber would say, "It will not happen in my lifetime." But it did. And upon the occasion of the dedication Kroeber said, "This consummates a dream of more than six decades." Two aspects of the hall were unique at the time of its completion: it was not a donor's gift but was built with state funds; the regents for the first time named a building for a living scholar. (They have since repeated this amiable custom.) Kroeber Hall houses Anthropology and Art, and of this association Kroeber said in his dedicatory address: "The museum exhibit is Anthropology's, the galleries are Art's; we share the remainder of the building. The association fulfills the cycle of Mrs. Hearst's orginal intention. It is a most welcome partnership to us anthropologists. It will aid us in developing the aesthetic and humane component which we recognize in our subject in addition to the scientific ingredient."

In September 1960, in a symposium at Burg Wartenstein in eastern Austria, entitled "Anthropological Horizons," Kroeber made some statement reflecting his world view. It proved to be his ultimate statement although he expected at the time to expand it in a seminar in Berkeley during the coming academic year. For this symposium there were no written papers. Kroeber introduced each day's discussion with a somewhat formal statement of his own angle of understanding of the subject for the day. This was followed by open discussion. The pattern was that for the first two hours, the talk tended to stay close to the day's subject, after which it took an unpredictable course and direction, one afternoon's discussion being on outer-space ethnography.

Kroeber had expected to do a summing up of his sense of the symposium on the final afternoon, but when the time came the participants contributed their own interpretation of what was said there, making Kroeber's statement unnecessary. Here are the penciled notes he had written as reminders toward a summary:

"The various fields of anthropology, while continuing to specialize, will develop more intercommunications than they now have. Control of the whole field will increase. It should be the aim of young men—universal control. . . . Compare *Biology of the Human Race*, Wells, Huxley, Wells, and *Life: An Introduction to Biology*, Simpson *et al.* . . . The humanistic aspect of anthropology to be treated not as parochial but as metaparochial: existentialism, in some cases also personal experience; concrete, in some cases in addition to existentialist; holistic. All these aspects of anthropology will continue and will be expressed in new ways. This is a faith."

At the final dinner of the symposium, Kroeber said of it, "I tend to judge intellectual activities by the pleasure they give me, and I have enjoyed this one greatly."[7]

RELIGION

Among the strands of a life configuration, some dominate the pattern for a while, seemingly determinative, and then disappear or become secondary, while other strands, appearing early in the forming pattern, continue throughout the design, giving it its ultimate gestalt. Religion is likely to be one of these strands, and so it was with Kroeber in the special sense that he never subscribed to any religion, to any creed of religious belief, public or private. He said, "I began without belief in God . . . hence my 'fatalism,' hence, too, my implicit monism, with nature as the sole basis for understanding life. But since phenomena are highly differentiated, I emphasize levels, emergent evolution, differentialism." In other words, Kroeber had gone on from the ethical training he received and absorbed as a child, to build his own wholly secularized value system, something that had been happening to an increasing number of people in the Western world since the Renaissance. Kroeber's thinking was in line with the scientific-rational attitude of the day, but it was his own, as shall be seen, and except to become more explicit, changed relatively little throughout his life.

Kroeber was not a seeker for mystic explanations of life's mystery; not a yearner; nor did he expect to find any ultimate solution to the mystery: in this area as in others, Kroeber did not much believe in ultimates, nor did he find it profitable to look for them. He accepted the rugged logic and limitation of his secularized-rationalist view of life, but without dogmatism: this was the way it appeared to be; it was as much as he found verifiable; nor did he insist that the vision might not, could not, enlarge. If the human animal were to become more human, a possibility he envisioned as occurring through cultural evolution, man's awareness might expand, his understanding might become such that he could comprehend the universe, the beginning and the endlessness.

He was immensely interested in all manifestations of the

religious experience, both the seemingly personalized one, and those which were plainly culture-conditioned—as curious and interested as was William James, and, like James, he comprehended perfectly that there was expansion or concentration of awareness in genuine mystic experience. He smoked hashish and drank datura and absinthe a few times, but the drug-induced visions and day dreams were less vivid and communicating than those which came into his imagination unaided by anything stronger than reading a favorite poet, pondering an odd thought, observing, or learning from another person's observations something of the life and behavioral patterns of plants and animals, listening to certain music.

The *Handbook* dwells with understanding on the deeply mystic and dream-directed religions of the California Indians. Psychoanalysis no doubt illuminated for Kroeber some of the possible avenues leading into the realities of myth, but the *Handbook* was completed before Kroeber was analyzed, and his real penetration into the mind and psyche of the Indians who recounted to him their own religious experiences made him critical of Freudian or other over-all formulae for interpreting them. He accepted as fact that the outer world—what we call reality—and the inner mystic-directed world were to the Indians a single world, the outer and the inner of equal reality, validity, and immanence.

When he presented the rationalist-scientific view and taught Darwinian evolution in class he kept in touch with his students' reactions. Nor did he ever speak of himself as an atheist or an agnostic; he denied no man's God; he made no God in his own or another's image; but he comprehended that every man, in health and fulness of living, must be emotionally, "religiously" committed. He was anticlerical;

he did not recognize organized religion as part of the religious emotion and understanding; he was untheist; he hated bigotry and was intolerant of intolerant creeds. His own commitment was to creative scholarship and creative communication with his fellow man: the Way of the Humanist, an open and sunny road with all byways unblocked and leading out from the self. Such a way implies freedom to [illegible] choices, and such freedom Kroeber believed modern thinking man to possess. He once gave me this definition of free will: "I mean by free will the freedom to be unpredictable." Nor did he mean unpredictability in any small or mean sense, but in a conceivably cosmic dimension, if, as, and when man were to become aware and wise enough to comprehend his cosmos. Meanwhile he saw the world as full of wonder, of ten thousand things which can be held, each, in the palm of the hand. He said, let us sit and marvel at this mystery. Perhaps penetrate it a little. Let us live at our full stretch—and let others live at equal stretch, and not worry too seriously about those matters beyond our comprehension. Kroeber's own phrase, "cultural evolution," is the clue leading to the heart of the configuration.

In the conference at Burg Wartenstein one day was spent on religion. Kroeber said then what he had said many times before: that culture was his religion; that in culture he found the commitment and faith which another person finds in religion.

Where Kroeber first mentioned cultural evolution and its gradual replacement in importance of biological evolution, I cannot say. The concept is in "The Superorganic," an article he wrote in 1917. I shall not quote from it. It is one of Kroeber's better-known statements, particularly familiar to social scientists. In its author's opinion, it has been overrated, overpraised, overdenigrated. Kroeber was bored with it at least from the time I first knew him. He would groan when another blast of praise or blame arrived in the mail, "Why did I ever write that damn 'Superorganic?' Am I supposed to stand now where I stood in 1917?" Another article, "My Faith," written in 19[illegible], states his commitment to cultural evolution, which I believe he called "cultural drift" there, but it is altogether an atypical piece of work, written for a popular audience, and not in his natural style.

Kroeber's enlarging conviction of the role of culture can be traced through his writing, but I content myself with some description of the men with whom he hypothecated intriguing possibilities for the future of mankind. Culture, creativity, his own strongly aesthetic bent, will be intertwining strands in this account.

I know some of the poets and philosophers Kroeber read and some of the living men he talked with at length, men for the most part in biology and philosophy. A later company tended to be artists, art historians, metahistorians, and philosophers whose interests were aesthetics and creativity.

Much of the early talk took place at a so-called *Stammtisch*, in the thirties, consisting of a mixed bag of about twenty people, more or less intimate friends and part of the "North Berkeley crowd": artists, professors, poets, intellectuals, living by preference in the hills north of the University campus and locally looked down upon or up to, depending, as a Far West sort of Greenwich Village. Theirs was a bastard *Stammtisch*, because some women were included and the shabby Emeryville restaurant where it met was Italian. But it had a stuffy little room off the kitchen to itself on Saturday nights, and the cheap red wine made by the proprietor was tolerable and ample. Imaginations expanded there.

Among the Saturday night regulars were Arthur Ryder the Sanskritist, and Robert Oppenheimer the physicist. These were the years when Oppenheimer was reaching out in directions new to him—toward people, into politics and social movements, into the 'real' world; when he was reading anthropology and psychoanalysis. He was captivated by Ryder, a well-defined man, a New Englander and a Puritan who considered that he knew and lived by the Eternal Verities; erudite, arrogant, inexorable in his scholarship, sadistically ironic in his disenchantments. He became Oppenheimer's *guru,* and he taught him Sanskrit—the language, its poetry, its ancient wisdom. Obviously these early discussions of cultural evolution were slanted steeply Eastward. The Yogi view was in any case immanent in much of the talk and speculation around the *Stammtisch.* Those were the years when we dreamed of a world at peace, when the Eastern contemplative way seemed to some of us a possible twentieth-century way. We were, I suppose, the doves of the depression in our Innocent Bohemia.

During the last years before the Second World War, there were further conversations, extensions from the *Stammtisch* in which the geneticist Richard Goldschmidt sometimes participated. He contributed to them his theory of genetic change and his reassessment and restatement of the meaning and significance of "acquired characteristics," of, as Kroeber would say, "culture." As I understood him, Goldschmidt was saying he did not regard evolution as an ordered step-by-step process whose essence was gradualness, but as the sum of innumerable, discrete, singular flashes of genetic inspiration, of mutations small or large, unpredictable, sudden, and as well benign as malign to the organism experiencing them. Without pressing my uncertainty further or asserting anything of the verifiability of his theory, I do recall that it made sense to Kroeber. To his and Oppenheimer's imaginations this view of evolution freed it from the inevitability and remoteness of the old Darwinian idea of a slogging and mechanistic rhythm, suggesting to them, not so much free will in general as the possibilities of a free creativity, of neurological and psychological and cultural growths and changes. It brought the concept of evolution into the world of sensibility, into the dynamics of modern man. Was this, they asked each other, a lead-in to comprehension of the creative process? To them, creativity was not tangential to cultural evolution but at the heart of it. These were the years when Kroeber had thought and reasoned and written his way through *Configurations of Culture Growth*, and even while he was writing, his mind was leaping ahead to aspects of creativity not touched upon in that book. It is almost inconceivable I should think, that an anthropologist should subscribe to the "great man" theory of history: Kroeber did not, but he came back again and again throughout his life to the knotty problem of the presence in all cultures of genius, of a creativity of extraordinary quality, and of how and why a given culture avails itself of it or denies it its realization. Robert Oppenheimer and Kroeber, perforce, left hanging most of the questions they put to each other: the thirties were drawing to a close and the war was upon us.

In 1949 Père Teilhard de Chardin came to New York and soon after he and Kroeber met for the first time. Kroeber the anthropologist and Teilhard the paleontologist had known each other's work as scientists for many years and they had mutual friends among Chinese specialists in archaeology and paleontology, for Teilhard had spent twenty years in China, most of them in the field, and had been present at the discovery of Peking Man. Now he and Kroeber came to know each other face-to-face and in roles which proved mutually congenial—Kroeber's that of metahistorian and theorist, and Teilhard that of Jesuit priest-philosopher. For the remaining years of his life—Teilhard died in 1955—his place of residence was New York, as it was Kroeber's for much of that time; and it was here that Julian Huxley the biologist and head of UNESCO came frequently and for extended periods. Huxley knew Teilhard from Paris and Kroeber from London, both since 1946. The early fifties became the time when the three of them talked together—or any two of the three—and engaged in occasional discussions at supper meetings at the Wenner-Gren Foundation for Anthropology which sponsored Teilhard during his last four years, and on programs set up, as I recall, as part of the Columbia University Bicentennial commemoration. Their favorite topic was the probable future course and role of evolution in human life.

Huxley is still living, continuing to spell out a dynamic post-Darwinian view of evolution. This account has to do with his earlier speculations which, fluid and tentative as they then were, helped to sharpen Kroeber's view as his own had earlier been sharpened and clarified by his Paris talks with Teilhard and subsequent correspondence. It would be supererogatory for me to attempt to "explain" Teilhard's approach to religion and science—and to life: his philosophical writing, allowed by his Order to be published only after his death, now speaks for itself and its author.

Science and philosophy grow from communication between units of people as small sometimes and as unpresuming as the trio I am attempting here to bring to partial life. They formed one of the seminal tiny culture clusters which are the source of change. Teilhard was four years younger than Kroeber, Huxley eleven years younger. Each was a natural scientist whose base was biology; and a humanist whose concern with evolution was part of his concern for the human condition. Each began in his early twenties to think through the hypotheses of evolution in his own fashion. And now, in old age, and despite the differences in life experiences, background, and vocabulary, they found themselves in such close agreement that one stimulated and drew the other on to greater clarity, to a farther distance than he had gone before. (It occurs to me as I write this that whereas Huxley and Teilhard wrote specifically to the point of their evolutionary conclusions, Kroeber did not, or if so, I have not so recognized it.) Kroeber lacked Huxley's propagandizing zeal and Teilhard's need to square the circle between "given" Christian doctrine and evolutionary science. Kroeber rarely pressed a point. Make it and leave it. Or plant it, let it grow, as it would if it was of healthy seed and in its proper environment. Neither the growth nor its death should be forced. Kroeber's conviction that cultural evolution was central to his anthropology is implicit throughout his writing, but the reference is to be picked up if at all almost as an aside, or as a theoretical and speculative sentence or paragraph between the interstices of concrete description or analysis, which remained

Kroeber's natural way of thinking and of introducing his thinking into his writing.

I heard only a single open discussion at which the three talked of their understanding of the evolutionary process in man today. This was with a number of other people, most of them anthropologists. Huxley was the speaker of the evening. He spoke to this effect: By accepted astronomical measurements and estimates, our sun and hence our planet will last so and so many millions of years. A long time, it would seem, but not of genetic evolutionary time, far too little to achieve a species new and higher than man even if there were such evolution astir. But the evidence is that no such drastic slow genetic change is in process. Rather, the earlier biological impulse to evolve would appear to have spent itself, on this planet at least, and to have gone over long since into the nonbiological area of culture from which would come far-reaching, unforeseeable changes in man himself, supposing the fact to be as he saw it to be. Huxley concluded by saying that such cultural evolution was indubitably the most particular concern of, and opportunity for, the anthropologist.

An hour of open discussion followed during which Teilhard, Kroeber, and Huxley, with Earl Count and one or two other anthropologists did almost all of the discussing. The other anthropologists who were there were either genuinely puzzled by the implications of Huxley's hypothesis, or they were hostile to them, or they were frightened by them. Were the frightened ones those who had "learned their evolution" once and for all and did not wish that learning disturbed? And the puzzled ones those who had not thought in cultural-evolutionary terms of any sort? I do not know. A child rejects the toy he is not ready for, and anthropology in the early fifties, in response to its recent role in the war and to a world convulsed by social change, was in a sociological, meliorative, and applied mood and phase. This would seem to be less true today, despite the continuing revolutionary social changes. Many of today's young anthropologists, equipped with the modern techniques and knowledge of genetics, psychoanalysis, linguistics, and archaeology nonetheless regard their updated field experience as being within the natural-history tradition and practice. Nor are they fearful of ideas and concepts and hypotheses far more bizarre than Huxley's, Kroeber's and Teilhard's, for that trio was saying no more than is within the realm of ordinary philosophical thinking todav: that biological and human evolution are parts of a single process; that motion (process) is or can be toward realization, toward becoming more human; that all aspects of culture including ethics and values are engaged in an evolution ever more significant, and that all these aspects can be studied and scientifically analysed. What Teilhard called *noogenesis*, Huxley called *evolution of mind*, and what Teilhard called *hominization*, Huxley called *psychosocial evolution*; Kroeber used the phrase *cultural evolution* to cover both aspects. All three agreed that they were engaged in explicating a possible *evolutionary humanism*.

STRANDS

Kroeber said that it is in the nature of the humane disciplines that they are cumulative. An achieved scholar in the humanities is likely to be a long-lived one whose stature grows with his gradually accumulating understanding; that the *tours de force* common to mathematics for example are rarely possible to him; that even if he unearths a Troy, a Tutankahmen, early in his career, it will nonetheless be his longtime interpretation of the discovery that will determine his full accomplishment.

The plotted curve of Kroeber's life does not make the even rise and drop beloved of statisticians, for it begins at a central point on the left-hand side of the chart and arcs out, going right off the paper at the far corners of the right-hand side. It fails to follow the classic rules for a play whose middle act exhibts the principal tension of interest and action, the first act building up to, the last act down from the high middle, nor does the pattern project struggle, achievement against odds, a success story. Such turmoil, such achievement as there is revealed, leads into personal realization, an expanding personality, the expansion coming about through the natural opening of the mind and understanding, and accomplished in serenity, with pleasure in the doing, despite the daily grits and grinds.

This account is approaching its last pages: it is concerned with gathering up some of the strands from the far outer unfinished edges of the configuration: a many-patterned configuration held to ordered design by its vertical and horizontal warp and weft. The warp, a natural-history curiosity which came to include any imaginable phenomena, with literalness, the dogged pursuit and recording of concrete data, and their scientific analysis and synthesis at its core. The weft, strong as the warp but showier, glistening with imagination, at home with the generalizing, philosophical, patterning and aesthetic aspects of creative scholarly endeavor.

As soon as he could begin to explore his world, Kroeber brought home samples of it: he made collections. He learned the names of the rocks, the bones, the minerals, the fungi, and the animals of his collecting and to whom and what they stood in close relation. Very early he also wanted to know the why, the purpose of each animal and object he had classified, and its relation to man, to other life on Manhattan Island, on the planet. The child of four, the old man of eighty-four, investigated and pondered and theorized and imagined over the discoveries, but possession as such was never the well-spring of the collecting. To discover all there was to know about it made the object his—it and its kind—Kroeber was not afraid to generalize. The particular object need not remain forever gathering dust, itself forgotten, on some attic shelf of the mind where room was needed for newer, more exciting discoveries.

As an adult, Kroeber made no collections for himself: his home contains no single archaeological or art object of value. He collected for museums and studied specimens in museums where to his way of thinking specimens belonged, available to him, to the world. He was not a book collector. His library contained no first editions as such and consisted only in the volumes necessary to him as a working scholar, nor did his passion for paintings and sculptures carry with it any lust of possession. He liked about him only that which was congruent with his house, his way of life, his family and its tastes. The painting and sculpture, the pottery, metal, and stone objects he found timelessly significant and beautiful would have offended him by their inappropriateness to his home surroundings. Their insistence of form and high style would have wearied him to have always before him: he wanted them only sometimes, and at those times they were imaginatively present to him. One may infer correctly from this temperamental preference to a personality singularly free of envy and jealousy. He was unenvious of others, their possessions, their opportunities, their jobs. His friendships and deep loves flowed without barrier of overpossessiveness, overanxiety.

Many of the detailed and ordered data of ethnology and folklore which Kroeber collected during the first two decades of the century were concrete and descriptive: in the *Handbook*, that pattern is ever-present. The consistent continuum of Kroeber's ethnographic reporting is to be found in one of his last publications, done in collaboration with a young anthropologist, W. W. Elmendorf, a monograph published in 1960 and bearing two titles: *The Structure of Twana Culture* by W. W. Elmendorf and *Comparative Notes on the Yurok Culture* by A. L. Kroeber. In its introduction, Kroeber says:

> It occurred to me that a point-by-point comparable description of the structure of the Yurok, a related culture, with the Twana would be of interest, and I proposed it to Dr. Elmendorf [who was writing *Twana* as a Ph.D. thesis]. He assented, and we agreed that I would prepare an account of Yurok which would follow item by item [his Twana account] . . . ; that the two would be tied or keyed together by a series of superior numbers such as are usual for a system of footnotes; and that, so far as possible, corresponding items would appear below and above on the same page. The result would be two parallel descriptions, marching concurrently, of two cultures—a double-barrelled ethnographic presentation. This we did; and so far as I know, it is the first time it has been attempted.

Kroeber goes on to point out some of the limitations of the method and of anthropological method:

> That our Twana-Yurok parallel presentation is a novelty does not constitute it a milestone. . . . It is rather a testimony to the backwardness of American comparative ethnography—how we have not pulled together and organized what we know and have on record, how sketchy our taxonomies still are on which better understanding of the whole array of . . . world cultures must rest. There is still much synthesizing interpretation to be achieved: probably most of it.

The introduction makes it plain that Kroeber had a very good time doing this task, including its physical organization. And, not surprisingly, he goes on to speculate upon the future possibilities of making a simultaneous comparison of three cultures, of multiple ones, of whole culture areas, of major civilizations. And this led him straight to the concept of his *Roster of Civilizations*, of which only a single chapter was finished, but the whole of which was planned.

The *Roster* had taken form and its ultimate content was clear to Kroeber before 1957, for in February of that year he wrote to Milton Singer, anthropologist and philosopher, at the University of Chicago:

> I was much stimulated by my days in Chicago the end of October and on the train and after arrival home started a monograph which I thought of as a formal and defining and classificatory roster of civilizations and cultures. Then I had to prepare some special lectures, put the finishing touches on the Luiseño grammar, etc. and it remained a very small fragment, but perhaps enough for a sample. . . .

> It is dull reading because I am aiming at something like the 1735 *Systema Naturae,* but I have a feeling it is needed.

That the idea was older than the roster form is indicated in an earlier letter (1953) to the then chancellor at Berkeley, Clark Kerr, in which Kroeber summarizes his general plan:

> A constructive outline, at three points, of all more important civilizations or cultures, namely: (a) distinctive qualities; (b) causal interrelations or influences; (c) course or life history. There will be as much emphasis on uniqueness as on similarities, and no assumption of repetitive or cyclic phenomena. I see this as the crux of the subject, and hope I may live long enough to get well into it. . . .

Charles Le Guin, professor of French History and Kroeber's son-in-law, writes in his preface to the *Roster,* the completed part of which was published in 1962:

> The material here presented is that which Kroeber left in his file marked Roster of Civilizations. . . . Some of the sections, such as the Introduction and that on Minor Civilizations in North America, were in completed form. . . . Other sections such as those on Science and Divination, were scarcely begun. It seemed well to include them because they are pertinent to the more complete material . . . and because they further clarify what Kroeber had in mind.

Kroeber's introduction to the *Roster* begins: "Herewith is submitted a sort of checklist of the known principal civilizations of the world, with such definition as is possible, and a skeleton indication of their character." Even the ninety-seven pages which were printed give some considerable idea of what the book might have become. It grew directly from *Style and Civilizations,* written in the summer of 1956; from contacts and seminars at the Center for the Behavioral Sciences at Stanford; from conversations and collaborations with Rushton Coulborn the historian on various aspects of metahistory; from discussions with Arnold Toynbee in addition to careful readings of his works. It goes back to the Culture Growth course; to the *Handbook;* to a long desire to set down in his own way his understanding of civilizations and their cultures. It is, so far as it goes, a most Kroeberian statement and in a broad sense a most anthropological one. Completed, it would have summed up a great deal of Kroeber's thinking, finished the edges, given a seemly ending flourish.

But perhaps Kroeber is not to be summed up. There were more things in his world than the *Roster;* more unfinished matters in his files. There was, for instance, the projected book, *Hard Bitten and Small,* of which the first chapter, on insectivores, is complete. The opening statement and a sentence or two from this chapter will suffice to give the flavor. Says Kroeber:

> It is the custom in reviewing the animal kingdom to begin either with the lowest or the most advanced forms. But an interest in the variety of forms historically achieved by life in its long course on earth is as legitimate as a desire to reaffirm progress in evolution. A beginning will accordingly be made here by choosing one of the most primitive orders in the class of animals generally considered highest: the Insectivores among the Mammals.
>
> This order possesses the special interest of containing the closest living relatives of the putative ancestors of our human kind. . . .

> The insectivores survive among the modern placental mammals much as their and our Jurassic and Cretaceous ancestors survived among the then dominant reptiles: by their littleness, obscurity, nocturnal habits, hiding or burying proclivities, general inconspicuousness. They never swarm in vast numbers, they never obtrude in shape, color, size, or habits. They are getting by in the world and are satisfied with that.

The tree shrews particularly intrigued Kroeber, as being in most direct line to man. He tells of their diurnal habit of foraging by day and sleeping by night—a shrew habit as it is man's—and of the "habit of their individual members to fight each other fiercely, even to death, on encounter." The chapter—a long one—ends with a discussion of the aquatic shrew:

> It swims rapidly, dives, leaps out of the water, and catches fish . . . [it] thrives also in fields and will enter barns. Its aggressiveness is almost limitless. The elder Brehm tells of how this miniature beast of less than an ounce of weight dived into a tub, seized the heads of two two-pound carp with its paws, bit out the eyes, and then ate into their brains. This seems a fair note on which to end an account of the Insectivores.

WRITING

Kroeber's writing method and volume were conditioned by his education. He had learned in early childhood to study, to concentrate, to follow through. His mother had valued these traits. Dr. Bamberger, his first tutor, encouraged them, Dr. Sachs' school enforced their observance if the pupil were to have any time for himself. He early formed the habit of writing and a preference for a brief article or monograph over a lengthy monograph or a book, and he kept the habit of studying and writing throughout his life, doing a certain amount of writing every day unless he was altogether too ill to write; many hours of a milder indisposition and a convalescence he passed writing on less demanding material. He did not write on days broken by packing and preparations for travel or when driving long hours in a car. But, settled in a train compartment for the cross-country trip of three or four days, he would write for several hours of each day; or on a boat, on an airplane.

Even a day full of distractions would find him writing a little to restore himself to serenity, but he never went directly to bed after writing: he might have a drink and some conversation if someone else were up, or he would read some poetry. His writing did not drive him except in the demanding but rewarding way in which all creative work drives its initiators. For Kroeber, writing, like reading, field work, and gardening, was benign, restorative, fulfilling. In a time of upset he stayed away from complicated theoretical presentation or from a subject wholly new. He would turn to something already framed: continuing work on a grammar whose structure he already knew; translating a folktale from a familiar language; amplifying a notebook-penciled description of some object of material culture or some custom from a known culture.

Whatever Kroeber found of interest he committed to his peers' inspection. He once said, "It is not important that we agree, but it is important that we understand each other." He liked reactions from others while an idea was hot in his mind. He believed that much that was worth saying, should at the first try be said briefly: if the original statement proved worthy of fuller treatment, he could come back to it. He advised his graduate students to form the habit of writing a note or a brief monograph, committing to print at once any fact, impression, idea, or theory which came to them and excited or intrigued them and about which they had some conviction that it had significance beyond their own interest. One should not wait for the whole story to be in before telling the part one knew. Let its unknown chapters turn up when and where they would.

He felt strongly that a Ph.D. thesis should be only the length needed to present its subject and to demonstrate the writer's capacity to make an original contribution to knowledge; that it should in any case not exceed in length one hundred double-spaced typewritten pages. Long theses, in Kroeber's opinion, were padded with secondary or extraneous matter, whose purpose was to bolster the ego either of the candidate or of his sponsor. He said, with reference not to a thesis but to a book of history, "If it comes out short, so much the better. Flinders Petrie said a lot in 1500 words." And again, "Why don't you start writing your history? Books get written by being started. At that, many die incompleted, but more die stillborn in intent."

Kroeber believed ultimate answers or causes were rarely come by, and was not disconcerted when he failed to discover them. His three long books give few answers, few absolutes. The *Handbook* is a collection of histories of peoples, full or brief depending upon the available data. *Anthropology* is an extended essay; it was not written as a textbook although it has served as such. Kroeber wrote no textbook, his and T. T. Waterman's *Source Book in Anthropology* being as close as he came to supplying a text for teaching. He had strong feelings about textbooks: he considered them the prop of the routine and not-too-interested teacher; and a straitjacket for their author, forever fixing and confining his formulations and scope. He never taught the Indians of California course after the *Handbook* was completed except for an occasional lecture, although it was his own course and had been a favorite one. He no longer had the freedom to range, to change directions, to bring to the classroom the smell, the feel, the excitement of the field in which he had found the materials he was presenting. For this reason he never wrote the Culture Growth course into a book—it was his favorite teaching course and he wanted to keep it free-flowing and alive.

Kroeber's writing before *Configurations* is full of germinal ideas which found expression in that book. The book itself bores through treasure tunnels of historical data, asking more questions than it answers, leaving the treasures exposed for further reworking by other hands, other minds. To work as Kroeber did is to accept two certainties. One, someone else may pick up your suggested idea and run with it. So much the better, was his answer; I or someone else may, like a relay racer, pick it up yet again from its farther vantage point. The other certainty is that you will be accused of inconsistency, but only, said Kroeber, by the pedantic, the timorous, the unimaginative. Kroeber preferred to take entire responsibility for his writing; he never passed his manuscripts around to his colleagues for criticism, wishing to stand or fall by his own knowledge, his own view and presentation. As author, and as editor of the three monographic series in anthropology in Berkeley, Kroeber believed, as he said. "in completed manuscripts without loose ends, and ready for final submission to editor or publisher. In other words, manuscripts ready as they stand for the ultimate test. Once carried to that point, the author finds himself out, if he still lacks knowledge or the needed thinking through. The editor or appraiser can give a definitive instead of a contingent assessment. The publisher can accept instead of referring back and waiting for a completion which may never be made."

Kroeber composed in longhand, writing in pencil if in the field or in the garden, and with an old-fashioned steel pen, at his desk. The handwriting becomes readily legible once its peculiarities have been learned, since they are consistent. His is a neat page whose left-hand margin moves inward as the lines progress down the page. There was nothing haphazard or unconscious about the writing or the punctuation. He wrote to one editor, "I appreciate the very competent editing. . . . I have restored to original copy in certain cases. . . . My punctuation aims to bring the sentence structure into relief. Standard modern punctuation is meant for a less contoured or modulated type of sentence, so tends to flatten mine out."

Another editor made changes which Kroeber considered gratuitous. I remember his annoyance, although the letter keeps it under control:

> I formed my English, more than I realized at the time, on the Old Testament, authorized version. I like to write in sentences that definitely balance, in contrast or in supplement. That is why I have so many colons and semi-colons. I want my sentences to show structure. . . . The contemporary way of writing effaces structural form in favor of level continuity—hence all punctuation is bad, except for some commas, and they chiefly set off adverbs—a spot use, local, not concerned with the form of the sentence as a whole. The ideal is that of teletype—as it flows word

5

Nor is the drama unique among the arts in this matter. Hellenic sculpture rose and fell like Athenian tragedy. The apex is unquestionably at the middle of the fifth century, with Phidias. The better known fourth century is more popular with the public, and ranks but a shade below. Certainly and ~~—~~ were worthy successors of the sculptors of the ~~day~~ time of Pericles. The third and the second centuries fairly upheld the [art] old standard with the reliefs of Pergamon, the Venus of Melos, and the Laocoon; and even later, in Roman days, the Niobe and the Bull of , though lacking in inward nobility of taste, are not without merit. Nor are these the end, though late and degenerate enough. Against this senility of half a thousand years or more, there is but a briefly fleeting youth. The eighth century was aniconic — statueless; the seventh was ~~mostly if not wholly so~~ nearly so: motionless, grinning figures of impossible proportions, without either suggestion of lifelikeness or the decorative curves of a totempole, are the product of this age. Not until the following century had nearly passed and the Persian was preparing to threaten Greece — say during the life of Phidias' grandfather — were the first sculptures produced from which a modern eye, however charitable, can derive the least pleasure of any but an antiquarian kind.

> after word. I do not think the two manners can be hybridized, and I'd like to stick to G. B. Shaw's and my own. I began by accepting as many of your comma substitutions as I could, but went back to my own way. Yours is also a style, and a modern one, but . . . Harcourt tells me I'm touchy about my semicolons. I do feel who violates them manhandles my style.

The children were at home the summer he wrote the Messenger lectures for Cornell University which became his book, *Style and Civilizations*. Because they and I were interested in the content, we badgered him into letting us see the manuscript chapter by chapter and we all were generous in suggesting improvements. Kroeber was patient and fairly cooperative about adopting our editing, but a few weeks later, when he prepared another series of lectures, he announced that he was not going to write them out or tell us what would be their content: five eager editors were five too many.

Kroeber said that perhaps his most original work was *Configurations of Culture Growth*, and the best written, in his opinion, *Anthropology*. When I countered with *Style and Civilizations* he replied that that book was a series of lectures, little changed in printed form from the platform delivery. My choice says something as to Kroeber's style in lecturing and in writing; in both he was vivid, immediate and cadenced—a long rhythm which was individual to him and pleasantly literary. He did not edit his writing for style beyond making sure he had been entirely clear and that he had said what he meant to say. He believed that if you truly and thoroughly understood what you were presenting, you could and should say it in language comprehensible to anyone with a reasonable command of English, ordinary intelligence and education.

He hated jargon and was suspicious of the clarity of mind and sureness of knowledge of the person who used it.

When asked for an outline of a projected paper, Kroeber once answered that the reason he did not send an outline of what he proposed to say was that during the years he had gradually drifted away from writing an outline. He said he had a sense, true or fallacious, that it cramped not only his style, but his organization.

It is interesting to discern the pattern of composition of each of Kroeber's books and longer monographs within the outward differences attending upon each. There was for each a long period of gestation—sometimes of many years. Then when he actually started writing, the composition flowed readily—the changes, rewritings, and back-trackings at a minimum. The *Handbook* had behind it fourteen years and more of field work, a mountain of field notes, and published shorter specific ethnographic articles. The writing, as Kroeber told me of it, seems to have been a pleasure for the most part, a reliving of the field experience. It was accomplished without strain, which means that he organized masses of concrete data with satisfaction and pleasure.

Before writing *Anthropology*, Kroeber had planned and taught the beginning courses in anthropology and had considered for long what should go into the book he would one day write: he would cover the field, prehistory, linguistics, physical and social anthropology, but in his own way. When the time seemed to him to have come to write, he gathered together his notes of various sorts and ages, took a bus to Benbow Inn, an English style country inn in northern California situated within an oxbow bend of the Eel River. There he settled himself for the next several weeks. Most days he went out in a flat-bottomed boat with a lunch and a thermos of coffee, poled himself to a shady backwater of the river and wrote. No deadline stared him in the face, no publisher harried him, book and author were under no pressure to be other than themselves. The finished book reflects the circumstances of its creation.

The *Areas* book was done piecemeal as there was time, on weekends and holidays over several years.

Configurations took slow form during seven consecutive summers at Kishamish. Kroeber discovered early in his work on this book, that he could not do it between teaching and administration—it required his full attention and he could give it that only during an uninterrupted summer, hence the program of its writing. Between those seven summers he read with reference to the book's materials and made notes, but did no actual composition.

The over-all pattern suggests that his books were summations of processes of thought over long periods; that they were written in tranquility and because he wanted to write them.

The titles and dates in Kroeber's bibliography reveal a good bit of the man and the drift of his core interest. I have analyzed them enough to learn that, by 1905, generalizing and speculative monographs began to appear among the predominantly data-recording ethnographical and linguistic ones. And that by 1922 the generalizing papers were only slightly fewer in numbers than those of folklore and linguistics, with straight ethnographic reporting still much the most numerous and with archaeology scarcely represented. The twenties were the years when archaeological titles came in, tending to replace folklore and linguistics. After 1946, there are few ethnographic monographs and few archaeological, whereas the philosophical-theoretical ones have become strongly dominant, remaining so for the whole of the harvest years, the ratio about fifty theoretical to twelve linguistic titles. Linguistics was the competitor by then, and many of the linguistics articles were theoretical. A sampling of titles from the more than five hundred written by Kroeber suggests the scope of his bibliography: *The Arapaho* (1902), *The Yokuts Language of South Central California* (1907), *Zuni Kin and Clan* (1916), *Peoples of the Philippines* (1919, 1928), *Anthropology* (1923, 1948), *Handbook of the Indians of California* (1925), *Cultural and Natural Areas of Native North America* (1939), *Peruvian Archaeology* (1944), *Configurations of Culture Growth* (1944), *The Nature of Culture* (1952), *Style and Civilizations* (1957), *Miao and Chinese Kin Logic* (1958), *Parts of Speech in Periods of Poetry* (1958), *Semantic Contribution of Lexico-Statistics* (1961), *Three Quantitative Classifications of Romance* (1961), *An Anthropologist Looks at History* (1963), *Life Against Death in English Poetry: A Method of Stylistic Definition* (1969).

READING

Kroeber's reading preferences and habits were definite and lifelong. He read rapidly, a great deal, and remembered what he read. Besides German, he spoke and read French, and, later, Spanish. He could "get along" in Dutch and Italian; he made his own translation into Latin of those folklore incidents and passages which were considered, earlier in this century, to be pornographic or unfit in other ways for library shelves, when translated into English. He complained he had forgotten much of his Greek; he knew a smattering of any language to which he was exposed and could communicate in several American Indian languages.

Aside from straight professional reading he read more in history and biology than in any other subjects. History fascinated him as literature, as the story of cultures other than those which were the object of his study. In 1958 he wrote to George Macauley Trevelyan, "I am reading your *History of England* for the third time with greatest pleasure. It has the excitement of a novel, with a balance that is almost a rhythm." He said of history: "I read history as a continuum and *feel* it as such. If it is presented with what seems to me coherence and balance of its patterns, I get a conviction that the presentation is fruitful of understanding and therefore 'true.'"

His literary taste did not run strongly to novels, least of all to American sociological novels. However, he said of Sinclair Lewis's *Main Street*, Sherwood Anderson's *Winesburg, Ohio* and John Steinbeck's *Grapes of Wrath*: "Historians a hundred years from now will learn more from these novels about what Americans looked like, talked like, thought about and did and were than from anything any of us write."

He believed a communicating writer or other artist communicated directly with his peers—in most cases. He once wrote to the anthropologist Leslie White:

> As to posterity—I'm not much concerned. A buried talent like Emily Dickinson—or Mendel—may reach greatest renown posthumously. Now and then a personality happens to have kinship with some later period, and is then given a whirl from second to first ranking: Herman Melville or Greco. Sometimes the reverse. Most men of ability have some influence or appreciation in their lifetime. Then there is usually a sag on their death: Anatole France,

> for instance—and watch Shaw. After that they hit a more permanent level.
>
> Back in my college days I noted a type in English literature, Samuel Johnson, Dryden, Carlysle; famous in their day, landmarks still, read by no one, patterned after by no one. I used to wonder. Later, when I had experienced more people, I decided they were massive personalities whose massiveness made them live though their product, through lack of specificity of talent, did not live.

Kroeber's reading, whether in history, biology, or fiction gave him intense enjoyment when the presentation was simple and flowing. He rated the storyteller high on his listing of artists, whether he was historian, scientist, novelist, or shaman. His own success as a teacher was his gift of relating as a story whatever interested him. A well-written child's story held his attention. Björnsen's collected tales were among his favorites. One after another he reread several of the Waverly novels and he reread Stevenson with much pleasure. Rereading books one has liked he considered as natural to prose as to poetry or as listening to familiar music. When his children discovered Dickens he reread most of him during one winter. One of his several rereadings of Tolstoy's *War and Peace* was to read as a continuity only the parts that discuss the author's theory of how war and peace are made. He followed this by reading the novel uninterrupted by the philosophizing and found in both readings a fresh experience.

When Lewis Gannett published his anthology, *The Family Book of Verse*, Kroeber wrote him asking why he had included nothing of Chaucer. Because Chaucer was now read with pleasure only by scholars, said Gannett, to which Kroeber replied,

Dear Lewis:

I remain shocked at Chaucer being left out! The most trouble is from his "e muet," which English in his day still pronounced as German does now, and of course French in poetry. This is easily marked by é; then generally everything scans.

Most forbidding is his spelling. Why can't that just be modernized—as we do Shakespeare and Milton? It's the English profs who want the obsoleteness retained.

Third, a lot of words from French still have their accent on the last syllable: honór, liquór, couráge, governór. Easily fixed by accenting them in this fashion:

A knight there was, and that a worthy man,
That from the timë that he first began
To ridën out, he lovëd chivalry,
Truth and honór, freedom and courtesy.
Full worth was h(e) in his lordë's war
And thereto had he ridden (no man farr*)
As well in Christendom as heatheness,
And ever honored for his worthiness.

---

*farther

Kroeber was selective in his reading preferences. Jahveh, the fierce Old Testament god, fascinated him; he came back over and over again to the high tales clustering around Jahveh, as he did to the tales of the Greek pantheon and its Olympian adventurings. But the New Testament and the Norse and German pantheons did not attract him much. He once read the whole of the Koran (in translation) and the book of Mormon, doggedly, finding them uncommunicating and boring. He read the classic and later philosophers, but I remember that Plato irritated him. He preferred Santayana's novel,

The Last Puritan, and his contemplative volumes, in which Santayana reviews his own life and times, to his formal exegesis on aesthetics. Contemporary French and German existentialists left him unmoved and unconvinced despite his children's and his friends' efforts to convert him. He found Claude Lévi-Strauss subtle and exciting either to read or to talk with; for the most part Kroeber preferred face-to-face discussion with living philosophers to reading what they were writing.

He reread the hymns of the *Rigveda;* the *Upanishads; Book of Tao;* the *Golden Mean;* the *Shinto Way of the Gods.*

In Vienna we picked up volumes of Hugo von Hofmannsthal, Kroeber having become intrigued with him. In his last years he discovered Bertolt Brecht and his poetry, and Kroeber's daughter Ursula introduced him to Rilke. Kroeber read poetry all his life; few ordinary days passed without his taking one or another volume from the shelves of poetry and reading for a few minutes, perhaps for an hour. Increasingly as we were alone, he read aloud to me and we talked about the words a poet uses, or avoids, about the language of his metaphors and whether his choices are conscious or unconscious reflections of his time and culture. We asked, was the poet in fact prophet, the unwitting herald of change? We made some word counts, we pored over concordances. Eventually we completed two studies which grew from this late-evening game. (Both have been published since Kroeber's death, one in 1963 and one in 1969.) Kroeber added a wrinkle to this game—translating poetry from English into German and vice-versa. He never took this entirely seriously but he became increasingly intrigued with the possibilities and problems such an occupation presents. The two lyric poets with whom he worked most were Alfred E. Housman and Heine, Housman being deeply influenced by Heine.

Kroeber's lifetime favorite poets were Goethe, Shelley, Keats, and Homer. Ursula writes me to this effect regarding her father's preferences:

> I most often saw him with Swinburne, counting metrics, or with Keats, comparing versions. He knew Shelley better than most people do. He certainly knew Milton, but I don't think he had a very strong affinity with his poems. Ditto Wordsworth. He reread the *Elder Edda* now and then. I don't recall his reading Greek and Latin classics or the Bible or Shakespeare, but they were awfully handy to his memory—maybe he didn't have to reread them? Once when I was twenty or twenty-two and remarked that I had never read Homer or any of the Greeks, he said, "My God! you have a whole golden age still ahead of you!"

Kroeber was one day recalling the people who had influenced him at different periods of his life. He said John Galton was the first scientist to excite and impress him, and Carl Schurz the first social leader; Hans Bamberger and George E. Woodberry, the two teachers who had most stimulated and directed his interests; Goethe, the poet most important to him throughout his life; Raphael, the painter who first roused his interest in the figurative arts; Homer, in the art of story-telling; and, jumping to the twentieth century, Sidney Griller the musician, who, late in Kroeber's life, gave him a fresh and enlarged understanding and enjoyment of music. He named in this order and without hesitation, Franz Boas, T. T. Waterman, Edward Sapir, and Robert Heizer, when I asked him what anthropologists had influenced his professional thinking.

Kroeber was stimulated by the minds and imaginations of a variety of men with whom he was associated in one way or another: Colutzi Kretz, a friend and half-mad, half-genius painter; Saxton Pope, a San Francisco surgeon; Ishi, the last living Yahi Indian; Juan Dolores, a Papago Indian; Robert Oppenheimer, the physicist; Robert Spott, a Yurok Indian; Erasmus Buceta, a professor at Berkeley; Paul Sachs, art curator of the Fogg Museum, Cambridge, Massachusetts; Harry Lindstrom, landscape gardener; Meyer Shapiro, art historian; Rushton Coulborn, metahistorian; Leonardo Olschki, medievalist; Paul Fejos, director, Wenner-Gren Foundation; Clyde Kluckhohn, anthropologist; Dell Hymes, linguist and poet. The list, if complete, would be very long. Even this short one scatters from gardening to glottochronology. But however long, the common traits linking each one to Kroeber were an original and independent way of thinking and a vivid concern with some aspect of living, of creativity, of humaneness. Eric Wolffe, anthropologist, told me that at the end of the Wartenstein conference he asked Kroeber on what basis he had invited those who participated in the conference and Kroeber said, "Well—I asked people I liked, but what you have in common is you are all mavericks."

Clyde Kluckhohn liked to tease Kroeber sometimes about "his women Ph.D.'s." Neither his colleague Robert Lowie nor Kroeber were prejudiced against women in academic life and in anthropology—among them Kroeber had warm friends: Elsie Clews Parsons, Ann Gayton, Isabel Kelly, Cora du Bois, Dorothy Demetracopoulou Lee come readily to mind, as does Margaret Mead, of whom Kroeber said, "She is the best gossip I know, and no meanness there." Kroeber liked women but he was more discriminating about the women he liked than about the men. These women tended to be "characters," to be interesting and vital, to be intellectual and humane. He was as aware of beauty and sexual attractiveness in a woman as in a painting or a sculpture, but he did not confound those traits nor identify them with others. Two women who best epitomize his taste are Jean MacFarlane, psychologist, and Fanny Flounder, who was the last of the great Yurok Indian doctors. Jean and Fanny share the qualities of strength, humor, vividness and an amiable drasticness.

Kroeber did not like women who attempted to lionize him, or who made a cult of the Indian. He did not like women who "fussed" and he was critical of women's voices: a woman's harsh voice ground his nerves to an unusual degree and he could not resign the conviction that the voice was an expression of the personality.

Kroeber cared not at all for the socially elaborate or formal occasion, nor did he like large parties. The ideal number at a dinner table he considered to be six, and guests at the family dinner table should, by his choice, be limited to one or at most two people, whether children or adults. On the other hand, he was an active and willing participant in the intimate festive celebration: a child's birthday party, the large family Thanksgiving feast, the Sunday evening dinner at his own table, particularly as the children became old enough to be part of it. In fact he felt strongly enough about this dinner that except for an occasional intimate friend it was reserved for the family.

Kroeber was almost unborable, being bored only with those who were themselves bored or with ill-natured or deliberately self-limiting company, which he usually avoided. He liked to come to know a new countryside, a new person and personality, a new dish, a new book, a new idea; or all of these however familiar if newly seen. He sought neither the new nor the old, but coming upon fresh experiences from either direction on the timetrack, he took to them much as he took to the seashore, where he liked to wade out to where he was surrounded by tidal pools, then to sit, quiet but alert, awaiting whatever came under his observation. On the Pacific shore of northern Peru, he once spent most of a day sitting on a rock a few yards offshore, confronting and being confronted by an octopus, perhaps three feet across, who was half-hidden under a nearby rock. The octopus—as curious as Kroeber—became reassured enough to leave his rock and come much closer, even to allowing his tentacles to be stroked with a long reed; but he remained wary, and any motion on Kroeber's part had to be gentle, slow, and quiet. After one of these tidal-pool vigils, Kroeber was heard to complain of history that "it was enamored of the great, and so neglected the small. You never consider, for instance, the history of the mollusks." The response was, "But how does it happen we have never heard of an Alexander or a Shakespeare of the mollusks?" "Perhaps," said Kroeber, "you've never taken the time to look."

Kroeber did not drum his fingers or tap his foot or engage in other nervous motions. He sat quietly except, when he was thinking something through or when he became much interested in a conversation, he would leave his chair and pace slowly up and down the room. For this reason, as well as his preference for simplicity, there was space in his living-room for unobstructed pacing.

(A colleague of Kroeber's confesses to having once suggested that Kroeber "either give up pacing back and forth in the classroom or project his voice more." Kroeber didn't say a word at the time, but months later he stopped the colleague on the campus and said, "I just wanted you to know that I have tried it, but it doesn't work, I can't think unless I walk, and I can't think if I am trying to project my voice. But I believe I have solved the problem—I had rubber heels put on my shoes.")

If music was being played, whether live or not, he wanted to listen to it and disliked talking or having others talk over it. His one stricture when the first radio came into the house was that, if turned on, it should be listened to; it should not become a part of reading or studying. He did not like music intended to accompany or supplement conversation, partly because of having only one functioning ear and partly because he liked his experiences single, with full attention given them, if he regarded them as worth having at all.

SENSE OF BEAUTY

Kroeber and the art historian and critic Meyer Shapiro, discussed art and corresponded at length about it. Kroeber wrote to him in one letter:

> As to taste in art, mine is as is nearly everyone's, founded in his period, and I was born a generation earlier than yours. . . . While I mostly don't like what Picasso sets out to do, my admiration for his genius is compelled. I would not say he (or Joyce) "negate form," but rather that they destroy achieved forms. That is their privilege if they can recreate new forms as good or better. If they don't, I

think they deserve low esteem. I continue to feel that Joyce did not do better (though he did achieve some new aspects); but Picasso justified his iconoclasm even though he could never wholly coordinate his talents into one stream. All in all my schooled taste seems to me to come out not very different in kind from Bernard Berenson's evaluations, though he is of course infinitely more steeped in art and more trained in expressing quality; also more one-culture-bound. We are in the same generation, too, and perhaps equally dogmatic!

On another occasion Kroeber wrote to Shapiro:

Berenson's "tactile values" in painting, which can appeal only through the eye, and never actually to the sense of touch, nevertheless refer to something that underlies the vision which is at the center of visual art: namely, that feeling by touching precedes sight, phylogenetically and ontogenetically in every human baby. We all touch first, learn to see later, and in learning erect a nearby visual world on a tactile base, giving a double quality to all perceptions of objects, first within immediate reach, and later within ultimate or potential reach. All children, and many adults, want to handle a new sight. The two senses of course are disparate; they operate through different sense receptors. But what is seen and touched is always made part of ourselves more intensely and more meaningfully than what is only seen. And so in art representation the representative picture we *only* see but cannot, in imagination, touch, does not carry the same attraction and concentration of interest as the one we can, imaginatively, handle and touch as well as see clearly.

(Kroeber had pursued orally, but had not written, the

logical sequence to this beginning: that perhaps abstractionism of whatever era has a more intellectual, a lesser appeal, the "subconscious tactile aspects having been withdrawn and abandoned.")

To write a history of art according to a method of analysis and presentation which would be an extension of Kroeber's dress fashion analyses was a project he had kept half in limbo, half at the front of his interests at least since 1928 when he signed a contract with Harcourt Brace to write on that subject. It was never written: in the fifties, when there was time to settle down to it, other interests crowded out this older one. In part, matters relating more directly to the Huxley-Teilhard-Kroeber theories of cultural evolution and its possibilities for humanity appeared to Kroeber of increasing importance, as did the various aspects of meta and whole-civilizations history. In conversations with his family Kroeber had already written part of his history of art in the air. I have confessed to the family's responsibility in this matter in my introduction to *An Anthropologist Looks at History:* "[We] lured him into talking with us about art and artists, about theories of creativity and beauty, about everything which might have gone into the book. These conversations were restful and fun for him and exciting for us, but now we feel some sense of guilt at our selfishness."

One far-out subject of these conversations was: The Sense of Beauty: What is it? Kroeber was beginning to write about this. Here is one of his notes:

> I propose to examine, first, the quality of beauty as it can be distinguished in the arts from other properties, such as

majesty, tension, serenity, or charm; and second, how far the qualities of beauty achieved in different arts and separate civilizations are comparable. The first of these endeavors is one of definition, in the wider sense. The second is an inquiry into the question of how far the relativity principle of human culture can be transcended. As a first approach, one might cite some examples.

Karl Kroeber wrote a summary of these notes in which he said:

> The method is inductive; beauty is more subtle than style, more related to experience. The approach would be autobiographical—how and when and in what way he, Kroeber, came to appreciate different painters. In other words, the beauty he was trying to isolate was experiential —something he "experienced" in a Raffaello painting but not in a Rembrandt; in Tennyson's poetry, not in Browning's; a quality related to the whole of the personality of a work of art. It had not to do with the ultimate rating or evaluating of an artist and his work beyond the single particular quality.

Kroeber's last completed scholarly work was the final volume (soon to be published) of a three-volume collection of Mohave myths and literature which he had begun collecting in 1901. The final report was signed by him in late August of 1960, only a few days before we left for Paris. The work will be consulted, ultimately, by folklorists and Mohaveists, but it includes an epilogue, part of which speaks directly to any anthropologist, to any humanist. I quote from this part, thus weaving the final strand of my configuration in Kroeber's own words and manner. The epilogue begins:

This has been a long undertaking, in time and in pages, and I want to consider in how far it may have been worth the expenditures.

Basically, it has been a "descriptive" job—the conveying to the intellectual world of an organized body of new information. That seems the main service which this volume renders; and I regard the service not deprecatingly but with satisfaction.

Intelligible description of course is not random itemization but an organized presentation with sufficient elucidation of background and context to make it meaningful in the culture to which it is presented. If the body of information conveyed has significance in the originating culture, it will have some significance in the receiving culture, though not an identical one. Some of the original values will be lost in the transfer; but new ones will be acquired within the incorporating culture, as it stores the information and values received—stores them mostly hidden away in its bone marrow, as it were. It is the task of the transmitter to keep the losses and malformations minimal, and to maximize the possible fidelity and value of what is transferred, by means of elucidation, comment, and initial comparisons. Full comparisons, in the sense of systematized ones, usually constitute a separate stage; but though often deferred, and sometimes long deferred, they can be provocatively suggested along with the original descriptive presentation. I have not done all that is possible in this respect, but I have done what time free of other claims permitted. . . .

I see my job in this volume as one of scholarship in the old-fashioned sense. It is work which one probably cannot do properly unless one likes the doing, and the doing can come close to becoming an obsessive addiction. It is work which one does in a sense humbly, yet with a pride of responsibility to certain standards, and to an elite to which one thereby belongs. As separate individuals, the larger world may treat scholars with some seeming negligence; but I have always found that in principle the world mostly respects and values scholarship, and passes a due measure of this respect on from our class to us as individuals. It may understand and want to understand only a small part of what we achieve; but it takes for granted that what we aim at is worth-while and commendable.

In return, I believe we owe a respect to our materials, to the knowledge we control and try to extend. Knowledge is the basis of understanding; and all increase of knowledge leads potentially to increase of understanding and a truer living, for each of us and for all. We should content ourselves with the pleasure and satisfactions which new insights bring to their discoverer. Control of knowledge is more than an opportunity to display virtuosity and earn plaudits. I do not deny originality nor genius; but without knowledge, even genius can do little. While the continuing goal of all science is deeper insight and ever more new understanding, much of this follows almost inevitably from increase of properly organized knowledge. Almost always it is when ideas and theories are forced on us by phenomena that they become sound and important. The scientist who sheds his load of knowledge to rise to greater heights by superior intellection alone, is trying to enhance himself, not his work; and he may end up by doing tours de force or uttering jargon.

I have long pondered to whom we owe the saving of human religious and aesthetic achievements such as are recorded here. It is probably not to the group that produced them. Why should we preserve Mohave values when they themselves cannot preserve them, and their descendants will likely be indifferent? It is the future of our own world culture that can be enriched by the preservation of these values, and our ultimate understandings grow wider as well as deeper thereby.

SUMMER 1960

HOME

A summer of children coming and going, seventeen of them, counting the six grandsons and three granddaughters; of happy, and shadowed times; of wildly different configurations of personalities and interreactions; of moods quiet as a pond or restlessly pulsating as the paramecia Kroeber showed the grandchildren under the microscope. On June 11, Kroeber's eighty-fourth birthday, after dinner, he told again the stories of the Yurok god Pulukukwerik and of Bear and Deer Woman. He told them with the straightforwardness and sense for meaningful detail that an old Yurok headman would bring to their telling, while his audience—old, young, and very young—listened by the fire in the redwood house even as Yuroks used to listen, uncounted generations of them, sitting by the fires in the pits of their redwood plank houses.

When we went to Kishamish that summer the children seemed in the grip of some nostalgic urge, reconstituting the Barntop Players Theatre and reviving the *Red Bull*, their old news sheet. They cleared the trails into the nearer hills, made when they were young by our friend Juan Dolores,

teaching their own young the old names they had given the trails, the large boulders, and other landmarks. They brought back the Kish Carnival, an earlier creation of Kroeber's—a day given over to races, games, to specially dreamed-up contests in which children and adults, including guests, participated; each event handicapped to adapt to whatever variety in ages, size, and competence was entered. There was a bazaar: pine cones, rocks, obsidian arrow points and spear heads picked up in the lower fields, wood carvings, original paintings, poems, and stories. There were lemonade, hot dog, and ice cream stands. There was the high moment of the giving of citations and awarding of prizes, the favorites with the new generation as with the older being medals made from the tops of tin cans, elaborately decorated and hammered and individualized by painting on them the names of the winner and the event. These were worn around the neck on a ribbon.

In July I was hospitalized for a routine operation. I could have saved myself my anticipatory worry about Kroeber while I was away: the children cooked his favorite dishes for him; someone was always at hand to bring him to the hospital for a visit with me; to fetch him home to a game of chess and a drink.

On July 29 word came from New Mexico that Clyde Kluckhohn, vacationing there, was dead of a heart attack, without warning, fifty-two years old. Clyde had stood in a particular and vital relation to each of our children who now had to come to living terms with his death, a task almost as difficult for them as for us. But there is no keeping in old age the elastic recovery of youth. For Kroeber, Clyde's death was a shadow, immanent, all but palpable, which lay across the way ahead. He entered into that shadow in grief for his friend, coming out into the sunshine again, but never wholly out. The sense did not leave him that his own shadow must lie soon, very soon, across another way—my way. And talking to me of Clyde's death, he talked to me of his own. Resistive then, I was to learn how compassionate and nurturing of me he had been to do this.

AUSTRIA

The summer over, the children gone, Kroeber and I were alone and in a mood of Indian-summer serenity. We went back to gardening, reading, writing, ending the day with talk which might go on past midnight. But not for long. In September Kroeber was to be in eastern Austria at Burg Wartenstein, European headquarters for the Wenner-Gren Foundation, in order to chair the symposium "Anthropological Horizons." Clyde was to have joined us in Vienna and to have been Kroeber's cochairman at the conference. Without Clyde my reluctance to the trip, already considerable, became larger: instinctive fears, sound enough no doubt but hard to name or to press, because Kroeber wanted to go. John Rowe has told me that Kroeber referred to the trip when talking to him as a "calculated risk" he chose to take, being professionally committed to the conference and personally and emotionally to our having a Paris holiday together. I knew how he felt: it was his desire which carried me along despite my fears. One can suffocate oneself or another in one's fears, remaining at home.

While packing and closing the house, even while putting the bags in the car, I had had no conviction of departure. Jean MacFarlane drove Kroeber and me to the airport;

midway across the San Francisco Bay Bridge I turned for a last look back. Fog, black in the overcast dusk, poured down over the hills, engulfing garden and house, cutting me off from them. Ahead were lights—bridge, city, airport; our direction was outward, away. Beyond my will, I found myself in this instant detached, floating, free. And I shivered within this freedom as I have done many times since.

A night's sleep at the airport hotel. Then aboard and aloft and ten hours and fifty minutes later at Orly airfield, 5:30 A.M. Paris time of a gusty, lightly raining, cold, grey morning. We stood at the top of the high ramp, dizzy from the champagne we had been drinking during the last hour in celebration of the pilot's having set a flying record between San Francisco and Paris.

Kroeber's Paris can be projected onto a map of the city as a somewhat askew ovoid circle, beginning on the Left Bank at the Pont de la Concorde, crossing to the Right Bank, keeping to the near side of the Place de la Concorde to the Rue de Rivoli, then east to include the Jardin des Tuileries and the Louvre. At about Pont Neuf, the perimeter moves away from the river to take in the district of the Mairie and the Place des Vosges and Place de la Bastille. Returning to the river on the Boulevard Henry IV, it crosses back to the Left Bank on Pont Sully, bends down the Quai St. Bernard to take in the Halle aux Vins and Jardin des Plantes, then continues just behind the Panthéon, thus bringing within the perimeters the Collége de France and Sorbonne complex and the Jardin du Luxembourg, returning to the Pont de la Concorde via Boulevards Raspail and Saint Germain, the latter contained within the ovoid shape for its entire length. From the Hotel du Quai Voltaire, where we were living, even the most

distant point within the circumference is comprehensibly at hand—an inner circle of Paris to be memorized on foot, to be seen and smelled and touched and savored from a café chair or a park bench. Within it were the streets, bookstores, restaurants and museums, except for the Musée de l'Homme, the art and the architecture Kroeber most wanted to experience.

From Paris we went to Vienna where Paul Fejos, then director of the Wenner-Gren Foundation, and his wife Lita met us. With them we drove to Burg Wartenstein, an eleventh-century castle which looks toward the Semmering pass, one of a line of hill castles which once guarded this route to Italy. Local tradition has it that wine on its way from the south to eastern Europe and, I suppose, beyond, was carried over this route. Some of it, to judge by the cellars at Wartenstein, did not make the entire journey.

Paul and Lita had asked us to come ahead of the Wartenstein symposium for a visit with them. The castle overlooks a forested land, the hills building up steeply to mountains, range beyond range. Yet it is a humane countryside, closely farmed with trails and even occasional benches between villages. Rural Austria is a land of good living and comfort, well-kept oxen and cows and horses, ample barns and tidy houses and truck gardens and fields; of dirndl-clad women and loden-clad men, sturdy old and sturdy young. As for the castle, it is a perfect copy in the large of the small castle with which one played knights and fair ladies as a child. Nothing is missing—crenellated walls, clock tower, the great keep. Even a crumbling tower which leans toward Italy. In this unrestored tower is a section of exposed Roman wall, each brick bearing the imprint of its maker; and a delicate terra cotta virgin and child, found buried in the rubble—of much later date, but old and unbroken. Appropriately, falcons nest high in the keep, some of them leaving at sunrise to return at sundown.

We walked through the woods to attend Sunday Mass in the hill-enfolded village whose life was most intimately associated with that of the castle, yesterday as today. Forester Haupt took Kroeber through the castle estate to acquaint him with its flora and fauna. Kroeber recognized a redwood tree growing there, alone but thriving, a *sequoia gigantea*. By what means and when it had come from California the forester could not say although he had lived most of his life at the castle. Mrs. Haupt, the cook, allowed Kroeber to pick wild strawberries from her carefully guarded plants: she had transplanted some of them to enlarge a natural small bed under a tree close to the kitchen.

With Paul and Lita we drove into the Semmering pass for a meal of pheasant and to Gloggnitz for haunch of deer. We went to some of the other castles, including the Esterhazy castle associated with Haydn. We picnicked in a wine vineyard where the vines grew to the flat western shore of the Neusiedler lake which forms part of the border between Austria and Hungary. (Many refugees who succeeded in eluding the Soviet patrols and reached this shore had been temporary guests of our host.)

Sun, castle, friends, days of pastoral peace. Kroeber looked rested, seemed vigorous, and was full of ideas for further travel and new work. Besides Fejos and Kroeber those who participated in the symposium were James Ackerman, Ignacio Bernal, Rushton Coulborn, John Dodds, C. von Fürer-

Haimendorf, Dell Hymes, Claude Lévi-Strauss, D. G. Macrae, Wilhelm Milke, Herbert Muller, Edward Shils, Milton Singer, and Eric Wolf. On the original roster were three others: Julian Huxley who was in Moscow that summer and fall, Carl Jung who at the last moment was too unwell to risk even the short trip from Basle, and, of course, Clyde Kluckhohn.

The symposium over, we went for some days to Vienna, days which except for visiting the Kunsthistorische Museum and the Cathedral we spent wandering the narrow streets, picking up dirndl dresses for the granddaughters, and sitting at sidewalk cafés. In the evening we walked from our hotel to the opera house where each night of our stay we heard an opera or saw a ballet. The early curtain left comfortable time for dinner after the performance.

PARIS

Back in Paris and on the Quai Voltaire once more. The Heizers—Nancy, Robert, and the children—were in the city, settled in a pension for the year. Together we drove, exploring in their Fiat. Memory brings me those days as a montage of painterly sky and river and streets, of a Dégas retrospective exhibit, of Monet's *Les Nymphéas;* of sitting on benches and curbs while Nancy read aloud from the Michelin Guide and Robert took pictures, at Sacré Coeur, along the Rue St. Louis, on the Point du Vert Galant, at the Bastille; of balen oysters, cool, fresh in their seaweed-filled baskets, eaten from the shell on a street corner; of cognac drunk at a sidewalk cafe; of an accumulating cache of roast chestnut shells on the floor of the Fiat.

We would go with the Heizers to Chartres the next day. Today, the fourth of October, Kroeber wanted a change from sightseeing, there were stirring in him some ideas he wanted to get on paper. It was raining, a good morning to stay in.

He wrote for an hour while I found a bookstore with a copy of Lévi-Strauss's *Tristes Tropiques*, which he wanted. We spent a half-hour or more reading, then, noticing that the sun was beginning to show, we went to the Louvre, only the distance of a bridge from our hotel. We chose a particular room or period for each visit. This morning—of all painters—Alfred chose Meissonier; we soon went to the nearby Watteaus and Corots.

Outside, the sun enlivened a sky of soft blue with softly piling clouds, and we wandered down the Rue de Seine, stopping at a workingmen's bar-lunch beside the Hotel de Seine for a bowl of soup before going on to the Luxembourg Gardens. On our way back to the river, in the square of St. Sulpice, we purchased some of the Aix-en-Provence plaster figurines on sale there.

Kroeber was tired, but there was mail from the children, and after reading it and resting he was ready to go to Le Vernouil, a restaurant whose chef had come to know us and to save a window bench for us toward nine o'clock. After dinner we walked back. It was no more than two or three blocks from Le Vernouil to the hotel, but the walk tired Kroeber, and for the first time he leaned a little on my arm as we walked.

EPILOGUE

While we undressed and drank a nightcap, Alfred, apparently refreshed, told me something of the monograph he had started in the morning; it was about the new Europe in which he sensed a single and growing pan-Western culture, whose similarities of outlook and values—to each other and to America—greatly outweighed the national differences.

Alfred said we would stay on in Paris, a good place for the writing he contemplated.

And then he could not get his breath.

I phoned our doctor; there was no answer and I remembered his saying he would be in the country for a few days.

I begged the night porter to get the fire department: but he did not understand it was oxygen that was needed. However, he did comprehend my panic and got a doctor.

Such unschooled artificial respiration as I could give brought Alfred some temporary relief. He tried to reassure me, saying that he felt no pain, just not enough breath. And then there was no breath at all.

The doctor, who came too late to do anything, was a kindly, weary-seeming man. He made out the papers which make dying legal. He said, you are alone, Madame?

Alone.

There is nothing to be done till morning?

Nothing.

You will be all right until then?

Yes. All right.

The doctor left. For the last time we were together, Alfred and I. Sitting beside him, I remembered sitting just this way, holding his hand then as now, when he was so very ill, in 1943, and when we both believed he would not recover. He could barely speak but he had said, "Tell about us—from the beginning." So I began our story, talking while he slept or roused and smiled briefly at something I said. Thus the flickering frightening moment passed for us.

I had to do something now. Not let this present moment go by only in terror and denial with nothing to gentle it, to relate it to the rest of our life.

I did what he had asked me to do that other time—and so it was, through those shadowed hours between life and death when, as the California Indians put it, the Spirit lingers, reluctant to depart, concerned for the living, I relived in memory our story, all of it this time, even to its ending. Paris was quiet for those hours. A soft persisting rain caused buildings and river to shimmer in a gray unreality. The world was contained in our single room. With daylight and morning sounds, Alfred was wholly gone from me into the abstractness of death. His Spirit had taken leave of the body, of the world of the living, to find its way to the Trail down which it must journey, to the Land of the Dead.

ACKNOWLEDGMENTS

The biography a wife writes of her husband is a personal statement for which she must take responsibility. There are few people to whom she may properly turn for criticism and advice. It has been an honor and a pleasure to have August Frugé, Director, and Max Knight, Editor, of the University of California Press, as my sponsors and advisors, as well as my critics. J. R. K. Kantor and John Barr Tomkins, Bancroft Library, University of California, Berkeley, have been most amiable and helpful in making materials and space for work available to me. Phyllis Dexter has added to her careful copying of the manuscript the graciousness of interest in its content. To check the accuracy of my reporting I have consulted four anthropologists: Robert Heizer on the Indian land claims; John Howland Rowe on archaeology; Harold Driver on the element survey; Robert Spencer on the Army Specialized Training Program. Whatever slanting these reports retain is wholly my own. Clifton Kroeber had earlier guided my understanding of Kroeber as historian when I undertook to edit the fourteen essays which compose *An Anthropologist Looks at History* (Kroeber 1963). Ted Kroeber convinced me that I should report Kroeber's psychoanalytic experience in more depth than I had done, and indicated how I should do it. Both Clifton and Ted have been available when questions arose. Karl Kroeber and Ursula Kroeber Le Guin were not at hand for repeated consultation, but they wrote to me particularly concerning Kroeber's interest in literature. In these several ways Kroeber's children have reacted to what I have written, and the book reflects aspects of their attitudes to their father, but I do not speak for them, nor presume to present any point of view but my own.

For the rest, there are three persons whom I wish to mention with reference to the preparation of the book. Hugo Rudinger who, as he has done before, gave most generously of his time and skill in bringing the faded and scratched photographs to such clarity that they could be used. Helen Farnsworth, who with Strunkian severity hunted out my misplaced commas and clauses. And John Quinn, who read the entire manuscript with critical attention particularly to any fatty or purple prose, and with whom David A. Comstock of the University of California Press collaborated in designing the book.

I remain in grateful debt to them all and I thank them all.

Theodora Kroeber

BIBLIOGRAPHY

Alfred Kroeber's complete bibliography is in print and available in libraries (see bibliography below). Listed here are only those books, articles, and monographs to which reference is made in the text, with the thought of making them more readily available to the reader.

BOOKS BY KROEBER

Peoples of the Philippines. American Museum of Natural History Handbook Series. No. 8. New York, 1919.

Anthropology. Harcourt Brace. New York, 1923 and 1948.

Handbook of the Indians of California. Smithsonian Institution. Bureau of American Ethnology. Bulletin 78. Government Printing Office. Washington, 1925.

Cultural and Natural Areas of Native North America. University of California Press. Berkeley, 1939.

Configurations of Culture Growth. University of California Press. Berkeley, and Los Angeles, 1944.

Culture (with Clyde Kluckhohn). Papers of the Peabody Museum of American Archaeology and Ethnology, Harvard University. Vol. 47, No. 1. Cambridge, 1952.

The Nature of Culture. University of Chicago Press. Chicago, 1952.

Style and Civilizations. Cornell University Press. Ithaca, N.Y., 1957.

A Roster of Civilizations and Culture. Aldine Publishing Company. Chicago, 1962.

An Anthropologist Looks at History. Edited by Theodora Kroeber. University of California Press. Berkeley and Los Angeles, 1963.

MONOGRAPHS AND ARTICLES BY KROEBER

"Animal Tales of the Eskimo." *Journal of American Folklore*. 1899. Vol. XII, No. xliv, pp. 17-23.

"Decorative Symbolism of the Arapaho." *American Anthropologist*. 1901. N.S. Vol. 3, No. 2, pp. 308-336.

"Shoshonean Dialects of California." *University of California Publications, in American Archaeology and Ethnology*. Berkeley, 1907. Vol. 4, No. 3, pp. 65-165.

"The Washo Language of East Central California and Nevada." *University of California Publications in American Archaeology and Ethnology*. Berkeley, 1907. Vol. 4, No. 5, pp. 251-317.

"The Yokuts Language of South Central California." *University of California. Publications in American Archaeology and Ethnology*. Berkeley, 1907. Vol. 2, No. 5, pp. 165-377.

"Eighteen Professions." *American Anthropologist*. 1915. N.S. Vol. 17, No. 3 pp. 283-288.

"The Speech of a Zuñi Child." *American Anthropologist*. 1916. N.S. Vol. 18, No. 4, pp. 529-534.

"The Superorganic." *American Anthropologist*. 1917. N.S. Vol. 19, No. 2, pp. 163-213.

"The Possibility of a Social Psychology." *The American Journal of Sociology*. 1918. Vol. XXIII, No. 5, pp. 633-650.

"On the Principle of Order in Civilization as Exemplified by Changes of Fashion." *American Anthropologist*. 1918. N.S. Vol. 21, No. 3, pp. 235-263.

"Totem and Taboo: An Ethnologic Psychoanalysis." *American Anthropologist*. 1920. N.S. Vol. 22, No. 1, pp. 48-55.

The Seri. Southwest Museum Papers, No. 6. Los Angeles, 1931.

"Quantitative Expression of Cultural Relationships. "*University of California Publications in American Archaeology and Ethnology*. Berkeley, 1932. Vol. 31, No. 4, pp. 211-256.

"Blood Group Classification." *American Journal of Physical Anthropology*. 1934. Vol. XVII, No. 3, pp. 377-393.

"Totem and Taboo in Retrospect." *The American Journal of Sociology*. 1939. Vol. XLV, No. 3, pp. 446-451.

"Los Metodos de la Arqueología Peruana," *Letras: Órgano de la Facultad de Letras y Petagógía*, No. 22, 205-226. Universidad Nacional Mayor de San Marcos, 1942.

"Yurok Narratives" (with Robert Spott). *University of California Publications in American Archaeology and Ethnology*. 1942. Vol. 35, No. 9, pp. i-viii, 143-256.

Peruvian Archaeology in 1942. Viking Fund Publications in Anthropology. No. 4, New York, 1944.

"The Ancient Oikoumenē as an Historic Culture Aggregate." Huxley Memorial Lecture for 1945. The Royal Anthropological Institute of Great Britian and Ireland. London, 1946.

Art Styles in Prehistoric Peru. University of Texas, Institute of Latin American Studies. 1948. Latin American Studies No. 5, pp. 56-79.

The Novel in Asia and Europe. Semitic and Oriental Studies; a volume presented to William Popper on the occasion of his seventy-fifth birthday, October 29, 1949, edited by Walter J. Fischel. University of California Publications in Semitic Phiololgy. Berkeley and Los Angeles, 1951. Vol. XI, pp. 233-241.

"Configurations, Causes and St. Augustine." *American Anthropologist.* 1951. No. 2, pp. 279-283.

"Sign and Symbol in Bee Communication." *Proceedings of the National Academy of Science.* 1952. Vol. 38, No. 9, pp. 753-757.

"Linguistic Time Depth Results So Far and Their Meaning." *International Journal of American Linguistics.* 1955. Vol. XXI, No. 2, pp. 91-104.

"On Human Nature." *Southwestern Journal of Anthropology.* 1955. Vol. 11, No. 3, pp. 195-204.

"An Anthropologist Looks at History." *Pacific Historical Review.* 1957. Vol. XXVI, No. 3, pp. 281-287.

"Parts of Speech in Periods of Poetry." *Publications of the Modern Language Association of America.* 1958. Vol. LXXIII, No. 4, part 1, pp. 309-314.

"The Personality of Anthropology." *The Kroeber Society Papers.* 1958. No. 19, pp. 1-5.

"Yurok Speech Usages." *Culture in History.* Essays in honor of Paul Radin, edited by Stanley Diamond. Published for Brandeis University by Columbia University Press, New York. 1960, pp. 993-999.

"Semantic Contribution of Lexicostatistics." *International Journal of American Linguistics.* 1961. Vol. XXVII, No. 1, pp. 1-8.

"Three Quantitative Classifications of Romance." *Romance Philology.* 1961. Vol. XIV, No. 3, pp. 189-195.

WORKS BY AUTHORS OTHER THAN KROEBER

Chardin, Père Teilhard de. *The Phenomenon of Man.* Harper. New York, 1959.

Clements, Forest E., Sara Schenck, and Theodora Brown. "A New Objective Method for Showing Special Relationships." *American Anthropologist.* 1926. Vol. 28, pp. 585-604.

Davis, Joseph S. *Carl Alsberg, Scientist at Large.* Stanford University Press. Stanford, 1959.

Driver, Harold E. "The Contribution of A. L. Kroeber to Culture Area Theory and Practice." Memoir 18. *International Journal of American Linguistics*. 1962. Vol. 28, No. 2.

Elmendorf, W. W. and A. L. Kroeber. "The Structure of Twana Culture" and "Comparative Notes on the Yurok Culture," Washington State University, Monographic Supplement No. 2. 1960.

Gannett, Lewis. *The Family Book of Verse*. Harper. New York, 1961.

Gibson, Ann Judith and John Howland Rowe. "A Bibliography of the Publications of Alfred Louis Kroeber 1876-1960." *American Anthropologist*. 1961. Vol. 63, No. 5, part 1.

Kroeber, Elsbeth (with Walter Wolff). *Adventures with Living Things*. D. C. Heath. New York, 1938.

Kroeber, Karl (with Alfred L. Kroeber and Theodora K. Kroeber). "Life against Death in English Poetry: A Method of Stylistic Definition." *Wisconsin Academy of Sciences, Arts and Letters*. 1969. Vol. 57.

Kroeber, Theodora. *The Inland Whale*. Indiana University Press. Bloomington, 1959.

———. *Ishi in Two Worlds*. University of California Press. Berkeley and Los Angeles, 1961.

——— and A. L. Kroeber. "Shropshire Revisited." *Kroeber Anthropological Society Papers* No. 25. Berkeley, 1961.

Lowie, Robert H., ed., *Essays in Anthropology*. In celebration of A. L. Kroeber's sixtieth birthday. University of California Press. Berkeley, 1936.

Pope, Saxton T. "A Study of Bows and Arrows." *University of California Publications in American Archaeology and Ethnology*. 1923. Vol. 13, No. 9.

Proskauer, Joseph M. *A Segment of My Times*. Farrar, Strauss. New York, 1950.

Rosenberg, James N. *A Painter's Self-Portrait*. Crown Publishing Co. New York, 1958.

Steward, Julian. "Alfred Louis Kroeber 1876-1960." *American Anthropologist*. 1961. Vol. 63, No. 5, part 1.

Stewart, Omer C. "Kroeber and the Indian Claims Commission Cases." Kroeber Anthropology Society Papers. No. 25. 1961.

Stocking, George W., Jr. *Race, Culture, and Evolution*. Macmillan. New York, 1968.